Vākyapadīya
Sphoṭa, Jāti and Dravya

Vākyapadīya
Sphoṭa, Jāti and Dravya

Sharda Narayanan

DK PRINTWORLD
Publishers of Indian Traditions

Cataloguing in Publication Data — DK
[Courtesy: D.K. Agencies (P) Ltd. <docinfo@dkagencies.com>]

Sharda Narayanan, 1968-
Vākyapadīya: sphoṭa, jāti and dravya
by Sharda Narayanan.
p. cm.
Includes verses in Sanskrit (Devanagari and roman).
Includes bibliographical references (p.) and index.
ISBN 13: 9788124606094

1. Bhartṛhari. Vākyapadīya. 2. Sanskrit language — Grammar. 3. Sanskrit language — Philosophy. I. Title.

DDC 491.25 23

ISBN 13: 978-81-246-0609-4 **ISBN 10: 81-246-0609-9**

First published in India, 2012

Published and printed by:
D.K. Printworld (P) Ltd.
Regd. office : *'Vedaśrī'*, F-395, Sudarshan Park
Ramesh Nagar Metro Station
New Delhi – 110 015
Phones : (011) 2545 3975; 2546 6019; *Fax* : (011) 2546 5926
E-mail: indology@dkprintworld.com
Web: www.dkprintworld.com

Acknowledgement

श्रीगुरवे नमः । (*śrī gurave namaḥ*)

I AM grateful for the blessings of my teacher, Late Vidvan Chakravarthy Anantacharya of Bangalore who taught me Sanskrit, Śāstra and high standards. Any shortcomings are entirely my own.

It has been a truly enriching experience to study some of our greatest masters for this research thesis and I owe reaching this milestone to the constant support and encouragement of my parents, Sri J. Sitapati Iyer and Smt J. Neela.

I am deeply indebted to my Supervisor, Dr Hariram Mishra, for his guidance, patience and encouragement throughout this study. I am also very happy to acknowledge my gratitude to Dr Shashiprabha Kumar, Former Chairperson and Dr Upender Rao Chaudhary, Chairman, Special Centre for Sanskrit Studies, JNU, and all the other staff members for their constant encouragement and assistance.

I am singularly fortunate that Prof. K.T. Pandurangi of Bangalore has taught me several sections of Kumārila Bhaṭṭa's *Ślokavārttika* and the Jāti Samuddeśa of *Vākyapadīya*. In New Delhi Dr A.S. Aravamudan, Lal Bahadur Shastri Rashtriya Sanskrit Vidyapeeth, has given me extensive assistance with Mīmāṁsā and *Nyāyamañjarī* texts, the classes being as timely and invaluable as they were thoroughly enjoyable. It has also been my great privilege to attend classes at JNU by Dr. George Cardona, and clarify several issues in the Jāti Samuddeśa with him, both at JNU and from overseas by e-mail.

I owe the neat formatting of this research entirely to my brother, Dr Kartik Sitapati. But for his devoting hours and days to a strange subject, I would still be struggling with pen on paper! It is also my pleasure to acknowledge my deep gratitude to my husband S.L. Narayanan for all his support in this venture.

यथाशक्ति यथामति किञ्चित् विधास्यते । क्षम्यन्तां स्खलितानि विद्वज्जनैः।
yathāśakti yathāmati kiñcit vidhāsyate । *kṣamyantāṁ skhalitāni vidvajjanaiḥ* ।

Sharda Narayanan

Contents

1

Introduction

THIS research study chiefly entails study of the Concept of *Jāti* and *Dravya* in the *Vākyapadīya* of Bhartṛhari followed by brief comparative study of relevant issues in other schools of Indian philosophy.

For chronology, please refer Appendix C.

The concept of *jāti* is crucial to the enunciation of *sphoṭa,* the single most outstanding contribution of *Vākyapadīya* to the field of language study. *Jāti* and *sphoṭa* are two sides of the same coin. It is only by extending the concept of *jāti* to the form of a word that the concept of *sphoṭa* can be established. The concept of *jāti,* already connected with the import of a word in Nyāya-Vaiśeṣika and Mīmāṁsā schools, was brought into the field of linguistics by Bhartṛhari, drawing from illustrious predecessors.

While the Vyākaraṇa and Mīmāṁsā schools are agreed to a good extent as regards the nature of *śabda* and *śābdabodha,* it is on the point of the temporal sequence of *śabda* leading to meaning that they part ways. All the syllables of a word can never be uttered at once; they have no simultaneous existence and are inevitably associated with a sequence in time. How then do they function together and have the potency to convey sense? What exactly is the meaning bearing aspect? As an answer to these questions, the Grammarian school has developed its own version of *jāti,* borrowing from other schools prevalent in its time, and has enunciated the *sphoṭa,* which is not accepted by Nyāya, Vyākaraṇa and Buddhist schools. The first accepts *jāti* in *śabda,* the second only in part while the third denies the very concept altogether.

Bhartṛhari's treatise is a monumental work that brought the status of *darśana* to Vyākaraṇa. The title, *Vākyapadīya* is usually explained as the work dealing with *vākya* (sentence) and *pada* (word). But it seems to me, rather, that it is written largely in the context of Mīmāṁsā being the science of interpreting sentence meaning and Vyākaraṇa being the science of explaining the word and its structure. The text abounds in references to issues discussed in Mīmāṁsā in the context of Vedic interpretation, especially in the second *kāṇḍa* and the Jāti Samuddeśa; nowhere is there any disparity in the conclusion drawn. Any differences of opinion are in the process of *śābdabodha* and the stand on *akhaṇḍa vākya sphoṭa.*

In my view, *vākya* refers to the field of Mīmāṁsā and *pada* to the field of Vyākaraṇa. The *Vākyapadīya* is the work dealing with issues relevant in Vākyaśāstra and Padaśāstra. Bhartṛhari has combined many issues from the two fields of Vedic interpretation and grammar as from a common background, without any spirit of challenge or conflict and presented his view, thoroughly substantiated with reasoning, in the voluminous *Vākyapadīya.* Clearly, he was not the only person who believed its tenets, as he reverently attributes its very authorship to his teacher.[1]

---

1. न्यायप्रस्थानमार्गांस्तानभ्यस्य स्वं च दर्शनम् ।
प्रणीतो गुरुणास्माकमयमागमसङ्ग्रहः ॥ — *VP* II.482

nyāya prasthānamānamārgāmstā nabhasya svaṁ ca darśanam ।
praṇīto guruṇāsmākamayamāgamasaṅgrahaḥ ॥

In the Mīmāṁsā doctrine there is duality in both *śabda* and *puruṣa* being eternal entities. While upholding the Veda as the only reliable means to understand *dharma* and the eternality of *śabda* along with the Pūrva-Mīmāṁsā, Bhartṛhari resolves this dichotomy by merging *śabda* and *puruṣa* into One, in *śabdatattva*.

This study requires extensive textual study with style of Sanskrit writing spanning many centuries. Before approaching the core text, Jāti Samuddeśa, the main issues in the philosophy of language have to be covered. The Brahmakāṇḍa, which is the mainstay of Vyākaraṇa *darśana*, expounds the philosophy of Bhartṛhari and is almost completely directed at establishing the doctrine of *sphoṭa*.

Chapter 1, being the Introduction, contains the Preface and Survey of Literature.

Chapter 2 traces the development of language study from the Vedic period to the *darśana*s. Part A discusses the various aspects of *vāk* and Part B is a comparative study of *śabda* as a *pramāṇa* the means of verbal cognition in the different schools of Indian philosophy.

Chapter 3 is a sketch of the main contribution of Bhartṛhari to the field of linguistic study and how it has impacted on philosophy in general. Many later writers were influenced by the concept of *sphoṭa*; some accepted it while others, like Kumārila Bhaṭṭa, argued vehemently against it.

Chapter 4 is a systematic, though brief study of the concept of *jāti* as introduced by Bhartṛhari in the first two *kāṇḍa*s of the *Vākyapadīya*. Although *sphoṭa* has been mentioned by some earlier writers, it is the *Vākyapadīya* that actually makes a major contribution to linguistic monism in the Sanskrit tradition.

Chapter 5 is a study of the Jāti, Dravya and Bhūyo Dravya Samuddeśas in the third *kāṇḍa* of the *Vākyapadīya*. All the *kārikā*s are explained and the development of the concept that Bhartṛhari builds up in the grammatical tradition is traced. This study makes use of the commentaries *Prakāśa* of Helārāja and *Ambākartrī* of Pt. Raghunatha Sarma and the translation of the *kārikā*s into English by K.A. Subramania Iyer.

Chapter 6 is a brief study of the concept of *jāti* in the philosophies of Nyāya and Mīmāṁsā. Its development over the centuries and the necessity of modifying tenets due to the sharp criticism from other schools, especially Buddhism, is traced.

Chapter 7 is a brief sketch of what conclusions may be drawn from such a research study. Part A is a summary of the topics covered and Part B is a sketch of Bhartṛhari's conception of *jāti* and *dravya*.

I have included relevant quotations from Sanskrit texts as part of the main essay. Quotations from eminent writers of modern times also frequently form a part of this dissertation as I have been deeply impressed by their insight and choice of words. In a way, this dissertation reflects the bilingual nature of study of Indian philosophy today. As my major subject was physics in postgraduate university, I have tried to focus on the scientific aspects of such topics as sound and space. This thesis also focuses on the linguistic philosophy of Bhartṛhari, a comprehensive study of his philosophy in general being beyond its scope.

Survey of Literature

PRIMARY TEXTS

The Brahmakāṇḍa is published with *Hariharaputrīyam* Commentary in Sanskrit by M.H. Sastry which has also been translated into English. This has been my gateway to the *VP* and is excellent in being rational, unorthodox and thorough, without rambling into technical details. The Brahmakāṇḍa has been critically studied by Vāmadeva Ācārya with *Pratibhā* Commentary in Hindi and Sanskrit. This edition is of great help in understanding the *kārikā*s as the author takes a very scientific and rational approach, explaining all his points of view to the modern reader. The *Paddhati* is an early Commentary in Sanskrit by Vṛṣabhadeva on the *Brahmakāṇḍa*. The *Vṛtti* is found with large parts missing on the *Vākyakāṇḍa*. Puṇyarāja has written a Sanskrit Commentary on the second *kāṇḍa*. The *Prakīrṇaka* or *Padakāṇḍa* has detailed Sanskrit Commentary by Helārāja from which *jāti* and *dravya samuddeśa*s have been studied in this research. The *Ambākartrī* Commentary in Sanskrit published in 1970 is Pt. Raghunatha Sarma's *magnum opus*. It not only explains all the *kārikā*s of the *VP* with *Vṛtti* and Helārāja's *Prakāśa* Commentary in the third *kāṇḍa* but also discusses the relevant issues in the full context of the grammatical tradition, making any difficult issue in the ancient text lucid and transparent.

The *Tarkapāda* of *Śābara-Bhāṣya* is the mainstay of linguistics in Mīmāṁsā school. The *Ślokavārttika* of the great writer Kumārila Bhaṭṭa has several sections on linguistics of which Sphoṭavāda, Ākṛtivāda and Apohavāda have been studied along with *Nyāyaratnākara* for this work. The *Śāstradīpikā* of Pārthasārathi Miśra is an excellent work that lucidly explains the Bhāṭṭa school of Pūrva-Mīmāṁsā philosophy. The *Prakaraṇapañcikā* of Śālikanātha explains the Prābhākara school of Pūrva-Mīmāṁsā and has a chapter on *jāti*.

The *Tarka Saṁgraha* combines the views of the early and later Naiyāyikas and presents the tenets in very simple language, organising the topics subjectwise. The *Nyāyamañjarī* of Jayanta Bhaṭṭa is a wonderful work wherein the writer expertly explains a wide range of topics from nearly every school's point of view, the style of writing combined with humour and poetry. The third *āhnika* discusses the nature of *śabda* as *varṇa* and *dhvani*. The fifth *āhnika* has a detailed discussion on the universal, *sāmānya* or *jāti* and the sixth *āhnika* discusses *sphoṭa* and *śabda* as language. Before establishing his own view according to Nyāya, he usually presents the Vyākaraṇa, Mīmāṁsā and Bauddha views with great thoroughness.

The *Sphoṭasiddhi* of Maṇḍana and the *Sphoṭa Nirṇaya* of Kauṇḍa Bhaṭṭa are important texts in the study of *sphoṭa*.

SECONDARY LITERATURE

G.N. Sastri, B.K. Matilal and K.K. Raja were pioneering writers of the twentieth century in English who discussed Sanskrit linguistics. Their works discuss the main issues in language or *śābdabodha* such as word and word-meaning, nature of *śabda* import of a word, word and sentence, *kāraka* theory, *sphoṭa, ākāṅkṣā, yogyatā, sannidhi, mukhya viśeṣa*, etc.

The Word and the World of B.K. Matilal traces the main issues in *śābdabodha* and also poetics. *Indian Theories of Meaning* by K. Kunjunni Raja early explained *abhidhā, lakṣaṇā, vyañjanā, sphoṭa* and *anvitābhidhāna-abhihitānvaya* theories of sentence-meaning.

The Philosophy of Word and Meaning by Gaurinath Sastri is a comprehensive work dealing with linguistic issues wherein the import of word being in *dravya* and *jāti* as discussed in the *Mahābhāṣya* is traced in detail. Two small books titled, *The Philosophy of Bhartṛhari* and *A Study in the Dialectics of Sphoṭa* by Gaurinath Sastri offer a world of insight into Bhartṛhari's views. The latter also traces the issue of *sphoṭa* in the arguments of Kumārila Bhaṭṭa, Jayanta Bhaṭṭa and Maṇḍana Miśra.

K.A.S. Iyer's prolific writing on *Vākyapadīya* forms a

complete foundation for any student on the subject. Bhartṛhari covers the philosophy of Bhartṛhari, both general and linguistic, giving details of commentaries and other specific issues. Iyer's translations of all the *kāṇḍa*s with notes form invaluable support for study on the subject leaving the student quite exhilarated at finding some small room for disagreement. Iyer's annotated, edited translation of Maṇḍana Miśra's *Sphoṭasiddhi* continues the discussion on *sphoṭa* and helps the student gain deeper insight on the subject.

K. Raghavan Pillai's critical text of Cantos I and II with English Translation, Notes and Summary on the *Vākyapadīya* presents the original text with excellent, insightful translation and notes, which are valuable aids for understanding the lengthy *Vākyakāṇḍa*.

Literature of this century on the *VP* is quite extensive. Tandra Patnaik's *Śabda* analyses the philosophy of language of Bhartṛhari. Gayatri Rath also makes a study of such issues as *sphoṭa, pratibhā, śabdatattva* sentence analysis, etc. in *Linguistic Philosophy in Vākyapadīya.*

Peri Sarvesvara Sarma makes a careful study of the Kāla Samuddeśa chapter and presents translation of the *kārikā*s along with Helārāja's *Prakāśa* Commentary. Mithilesh Chaturvedi makes a detailed study of the Vṛtti Samuddeśa in which technical points of compound formations abound. Jan Houben makes a detailed study of the Sambandha Samuddeśa. He gives a detailed introduction to the *VP* and also presents an overview of the topics arranged in the entire work. As Jāti and Dravya Samuddeśas are close in subject and arrangement to the Sambandha Samuddeśa, he presents a gist of these topics.

Ashok Aklujkar has given a summary of Bhartṛhari's philosophy in *VP* in the *Encyclopaedia of Indian Philosophy,* volume

V edited by Karl H. Potter. Aklujkar has published several research papers on *VP*; his Doctoral Dissertation on "The Philosophy of Bhartṛhari in the Trikandi", 1970, is remained unpublished.

The *Sphoṭa Nirṇaya* of Kauṇḍa Bhaṭṭa has been translated with critical notes by S.D. Joshi. In the introductory essay, Joshi puts the concept of *sphoṭa* in perspective, tracing its origins in early literature and clearly brings forth Patañjali's conception of *sphoṭa* in the *Mahābhāṣya*.

The Brahmakāṇḍa has been critically studied by Vamadeva Acharya with *Pratibhā* Commentary in Hindi and Sanskrit. This edition is of great help in understanding the *Kārikā*s as the author takes a very scientific and rational approach, explaining all his points of view to the modern reader.

Scholarly writing in Sanskrit and Hindi on Sanskrit Linguistics is vast. *Sphoṭamīmāṁsā* by Ram Narayan Mishra is a thorough study of *sphoṭa* from Vyākaraṇa, Āgama, Tantra points of view and also discusses the different levels of *Vāk*. Ramajna Pandeya's *Vyākaraṇadarśaṇapratimā* makes a systematic study of the main points in each *samuddeśa* of the *VP*. Kalika Prasad Shukla's *Vaiyākaraṇānām Anyeṣām ca Matena Śabdasvarūpatacchaktivicāraḥ*, and Yajnaveer Dahiya's *Saṁskṛta-bhāṣādarśaṇam* are modern treatises in Sanskrit on linguistics, covering the issues discussed over the past few centuries.

The *Śābdabodhamīmāṁsā* of N.S. Ramanuja Tatacarya is a comprehensive collection of the main arguments in linguistics from important writers of different schools of Indian philosophy down the ages.

Ramdev Tripathi gives a lucid and detailed account in Hindi with practical examples of main issues of linguistics in *Bhāṣāvijñāna kī Bhāratīya Paramparā aur Pāṇini*. Kanta Bhatia has made a systematic, topicwise study of the *Vākyakāṇḍa* in *Bhartṛhari kā Vākyapadīya Puṇyarāja kī Dṛṣṭi Meiṅ*. Ranganatha Sharma has written two small books in Kannada, one on the *Brahmakāṇḍa* and the other on the *Kālasamuddeśa*.

Ancillary texts of other schools such as Mīmāṁsā and Nyāya that aid the study of *Vākyapadīya* are many. The *Prakīrṇapañcikā* of Salikanatha with an Exposition in English by K.T. Pandurangi is more than a translation and explains each section to make the discussion clear to the reader. "Concept of Vāc in the Vedic Literature" by Pratibha Pingle compiles and explains references to Vāc in the Vedas, making it simple and gainful for the reader to consult. The *Śabdataraṅgiṇī* with Exposition in English by K.T. Pandurangi deals with linguistics and the Introduction in English clearly explains the Mīmāṁsā standpoint. The voluminous *Pūrvamīmāṁsā from an Interdisciplinary Point of View* edited by Prof. Pandurangi has many essays that discuss linguistics and other aspects. Peter Scharf in *The Denotation of Generic Terms in Ancient Indian Philosophy : Grammar, Nyāya and Mīmāṁsā* makes a detailed study of the import of the word being in the Universal. He mainly studies the *Mahābhāṣya, Nyāyabhāṣya* on *Gautamasūtra* 2.2.58-69 and Śabara on Ākṛtivāda.

Raja Ram Dravid's *The Problem of Universals in Indian Philosophy* is a comprehensive study of universal or class concept in all its aspects in the different schools of philosophy. It looks at both, universal as a class concept of real entities and as the import of a word. *The Buddhist Philosophy of Universal Flux* by Satkari Mookerjee explains the complex philosophy according to Diṅnāga's school.

John Vattanky has made a study of the detailed discussions on *Śābdabodha* in *Kārikāvalī, Muktāvalī* and *Dinakarī* in *The Nyaya Philosophy of Language*.

2

The Linguistic Tradition

The Need for a Holistic View

PHILOSOPHY represents the quest of the human spirit to understand the universe in which we live. It addresses man's curiosity on subjects such as structure of the universe, origin of the cosmos, the position and purpose of human life; basic questions that face every human being since time immemorial. Today the collective human wisdom and information is so vast that we need categorisation and classification into different subjects such as mathematics, chemistry, botany, history, etc., for convenience of study. But ancient philosophy was not restricted in this manner and we have discussions on varied topics finding place side by side in many texts that have come down to us. A good system of philosophy should smoothly transcend these ramifications and offer a holistic explanation of the various phenomena that come into experience.

The aim of every school of philosophy in ancient India was to provide a comprehensive model of the universe. As human knowledge is as yet imperfect, every system, however elegant and sophisticated, reaches certain limitations; there are always some issues where a conclusive solution is not possible. While modern sciences are restricted to meticulously describing phenomena around us and using the data for applied technology, philosophy ventures to encompass moral and spiritual issues where information is not always empirical and hence a consensus may not be achieved. Even in the model of the cosmos provided by modern science, there are points where the laws of physics as we understand break down; these are called singularities, e.g. the moment when time was yet to begin, or $t = 0$.

We can broadly divide our knowledge into two — one outward looking where the external world is grasped by the sense organs and the other inward looking, concerned with memory, feelings, intellect, reason, etc. Thus the phenomenal world outside is internalised by the process of cognition, *Pramāṇa*. The means of cognition are various. The most fundamental process by which all living things cognise the world is by means of sight, smell, sound, touch, texture, taste, etc. The next level in the order of complexity is inference. In the form of common sense, it is widely prevalent even among some animals. The next level is language wherein we are able to communicate and understand far more than we would with only direct perception and inference. It is language that enables us to share knowledge and elevates the mind to great heights.

There are many studies being conducted all over the world regarding language in the animal kingdom and it is an established fact that many animals have their own coded systems devised for communication amongst one another.

Since the dawn of civilisation in India, the significance of language as an intricate, vital means to knowledge was recognised and venerated. Since a teacher seated with his disciple in one corner of the earth could impart to him the secrets of the entire cosmos and open his eyes to the truth by the power of speech, *vāk* was venerated as the twin principle along with *Brahman* as the creator of the world. *Vāk* was described as springing from the Creator, Brahmā and also his consort, the twin Creative Principle. The sacred Vedas themselves are a manifestation of *vāk*.

The very word *veda* means knowledge. The Vedas teach that *Brahman* alone is real, which in the transactional level manifests as *sat, cit* and *ānanda.*[1] These correspond to (i) the external world, (ii) the realm of thought and language and (iii) consciousness or bliss. The external world enters the inner world through the realm of thought. The Vedas and Upaniṣads in particular, are replete with statements on the Oneness of *Brahman* which manifests in myriad forms creating the diversity we see before us.

एकं सत् विप्रा बहुधा वदन्ति । — *Ṛ̥V* 1.264.46

ekaṁ sad viprā bahudhā vadanti ।

सोऽकामयत बहक्तस्यां प्रजायेयेति ।। — *Taitt. Up.* 2.6.

so 'kāmayata bahaktasyāṁ prajāyeyeti ।।

Bhartṛhari has in the beginning of the *Vākyapadīya* pointed out the supremacy of this concept.

Parā Vidyā

तथैव लोके विद्यानाम् एषा विद्या परायणम् ।
पवित्रं सर्वविद्यानामधिविद्यं प्रकाशते ।।
tathaiva loke vidyānām eṣā vidyā parāyaṇam ।
pavitraṁ sarva vidyānāmadhividyaṁ prakāśate ।।

— *VP*, I.14

Vāk

Language study has early been considered vital in India to understand knowledge and consciousness, which is

1. Tripathi, 1977, p. 1.

considered one with the Supreme Being in many schools of Indian philosophy.

With its detailed theories on the origin, process and structure of language, India was remarkably advanced in the area of linguistics.

We can approach the language study in two ways — structure and semantics. While details of structure and syntax, *prakriyā*, would be on topics peculiar to the particular language under study, many issues pertaining to semantics have a universal nature relevant to all languages, as it is basically a study of the human thought process. Thus, linguistic philosophy is a theory of language, not languages. In the comprehensive or holistic approach that Indian thought adopts, the philosophical discussions are meant more to address these issues than to indulge in mysticism. The internal world of thought and speech which mirrors and recreates the external world, is itself a subject of intense study, as it takes us closer to understanding consciousness.

In almost every section of the Vedas, there is some important reference to *Śabda-Brahman*. Of the six Vedāṅgas, ancillary subjects that aid the study of the Veda, viz. Śikṣā, Vyākaraṇa, Nirukta, Chandas, Kalpa and Jyotiṣa, the first four deal with language.

एकः शब्दः सम्यक् ज्ञातः सुप्रयुक्तः स्वर्गे लोके च कामधुग्भवति ।

ekaḥ śabdaḥ samyak jñātaḥ suprayuktaḥ svarge loke ca kāmadhugbhavati ।

Language in India has come down in an oral tradition. Utmost importance was given to pronunciation, proper intonation and accent, more so in ritual chanting. Even in spoken language, the stress and tone variations in compound words conveyed different meanings. Most of the grammar rules of the sounds in Sanskrit language recorded by Pāṇini are lost forever. The Chinese language illustrates this phonetic aspect of how the same word, pronounced differently, can actually be two different words conveying totally different meanings.

The *Vyākaraṇa Mahābhāṣya* illustrates the importance of proper pronunciation with the anecdote of the *asura*s losing the battle with the *deva*s due to poor use of language, as the word is of such potency. Written language, or script, was only a means to aid the reader recall the utterance and had no significance on its own. The life of language is in the breath of utterance.[2]

वर्णानुमापकरेखोपरेखाविन्यासः लिपिः ।

varṇānumāpakarekhoparekhāvinyāsaḥ lipiḥ ।

In the earliest references in Ṛgvedic *mantra*s, sound from various sources such as thunderclap, birds, animals, winds, etc., are taken as significant, expressing the same creative power in Nature. Pratibha Pingle writes that after going through all the passages referring to *vāc*, it is possible to reduce the main shades of meaning to six:

1. *Vāc* as the goddess,
2. *Vāc* as a prayer,
3. *Vāc* as human, everyday speech,

---

2. Kapil Kapoor writes: Three words are used for language, *bhāṣā*, *vāk* and *vāṇī* and all three points to the sound substance of language. *Bhāṣā* is from the verb root *bhāṣ*., which means "to make sound/noise"; *vāk* is from verb root *vac* which means "to say something"; *vāṇī* is from the verb root *vañ* which means "to articulate musically". Speech involves a speaking voice and with language, *śabda*, as speech or sound, no truth claim is made or is possible about what is said, as the source of utterance is the individual consciousness. "Sanskrit Grammatical Tradition from Pāṇini to Nāgeśa", unpublished.

4. Sound of the non-human beings as of cattle, frogs, birds,
5. Sound of inanimate objects like *dundubhi, akṣa,* etc.,
6. Natural sound of water, thunder, etc.[3]

यावद् वै ब्रह्म विष्टितम् दतावती वाक् ।

yāvad vai brahma viṣṭitam tāvatī vāk ।

— *Ait. Brā.* 1.3.8

Vedic literature took all forms of life on earth as one organic system, recognising the same power of cognisance and interaction with the environment in all species.

यत्किञ्चेदम् प्राणिजङ्गमञ्च पतत्रि च वागेव आयतनम् आकाशः प्रतिष्ठा ।
देवीं वाचमजनयन्त देवास्ताम् विश्वरूपाः पशवो वदन्ति ।
सा नो मन्द्रेषाम् ऊर्जां दुहाना धेनुर्वागस्मान् उपसुष्ठुतैतु ।

yatkiñcedam prāṇijaṅgamañca patatri ca vāgeva āyatanam ākāśaḥ pratiṣṭhā ।
devīṁ vācamajanayanta devāstām viśvarūpāḥ paśavo vadanti ।
sā no mandreṣām ūrjāṁ duhānā dhenurvāgasmān upasuṣṭhutaitu ।

— *R̥V* 8.100.11

> The gods created the Goddess Speech; the animals in all forms speak this (speech). May that speech (when) well praised come to us (as) sweet-sounding milch-cow bestowing on us (lit. milking for us) refreshment and nourishment.

There are many quotations from the Vedic literature that amply illustrate the high regard that *vāk* was held in.[4]

The creative power of *vāk* along with *Brahman* is oft mentioned in Vedic literature. It is said that *oṁkāra* represents all speech; that alone is manifest in different forms as all the syllables.

---

3. Pingle, 2005, p. xx.

4. Tripathi, 1977, chapter 1.

ॐकार एव हि सर्वा वाक् ।
सैषा स्पर्शेष्वभिव्यज्यमाना बह्वी नानारूपा भवति ।

oṁkāra eva hi sarvā vāk ।
saiṣā sparśeṣvabhivyajyamānā bahvī nānārūpā bhavati ।

Oṁkāra is the source of all the Vedas, all knowledge. The word "Brahmā" also refers to knowledge. It is recorded in the Vedas that *vāk* has created this diverse Universe; there is nothing more primary than *vāk* itself.

वागेव विश्वा भुवनानि जज्ञे वाच् इत्सर्वम् यच्च मर्त्यम् ।
अथेद्वाग्भुजे वागुवाच् पुरुत्रा वाचो न परम् यच्च नाह ।

vāgeva viśvā bhuvanāni jajne vāc itsarvam yacca martyam ।
athedvāgbhuje vāguvāca purutrā vāco na param yacca nāha ।

— *Śata Brā* 6.3.4

In the grammatical tradition, Vyākaraṇa is considered to take man to the sublime levels of *mokṣa*, the highest goal of life. Patañjali says in his *Mahābhāṣya*:

महता देवेन नः साम्यम् स्यात् इत्यध्येयम् व्याकरणम् ।

mahatā devena naḥ sāmyam syāt ityadhyeyam vyākaraṇam ।

In Bhartṛhari's philosophy *Brahman* and *śabdatattva* are the same as Consciousness. Bhartṛhari extolls grammar as the finest means to the highest truth. By proper language study, we can understand the Vedas correctly; only then do we comprehend the truth and get close to *sākṣātkāra* or experiencing the truth, for which meditation on *śabdatattva*, *śabdapūrvayoga* or *vāgyoga* is the ultimate step. Even this moral and spiritual elevation is of two kinds, *abhyudaya* and *niḥśreyasa*. Different viewpoints on the concept of attaining *mokṣa* through Vyākaraṇa are explained in different texts. Bhartṛhari records ten under *Vṛtti* of *VP* I.5. It is not clear how much these correspond to each other or overlap, but going by the tone set by the *paspaśāhnika* it can be said that *sauṣṭhava* leads to *abhyudaya*. The higher form of *mokṣa, niḥśreyasa,* can be called Oneness with *Brahman,* attained by meditation. *Vāgyoga* or *śabdapūrvayoga* is explained under *Vṛtti* I.123 as a means of attaining *śabdatattva* or level of Undifferentiated Consciousness. The Vedas emphasise that there are several steps to reach the supreme level. Correct knowledge alone is not enough, but has to be followed by experience of the truth.

आत्मा वारे द्रष्टव्यः, श्रोतव्यः, मन्तव्यः निधिध्यासितव्यः ।

ātmā vāre dṛṣṭavyaḥ, śrotavyaḥ mantavyaḥ nidhidhyāsitavyaḥ ।

— *Bṛhad Up, Mai Brā*

The Fourfold Division

Vedic literature took all forms of life on earth as one organic system, recognising the same power of cognisance and interaction with the environment in all species. Some *mantra*s refer to a threefold division which in some places refer to the three Vedas or the three modes of recitation, slow, normal and fast. The *Ṛgveda* discusses three levels of speech.[5]

1. inarticulate speech,
2. primitive articulate speech, and
3. language proper.

In the *Śatapatha,* four steps in the development of human speech are mentioned:

1. the sound of crawling creatures,
2. that of birds,
3. that of higher animals like mammals,
4. human speech.

5. Attributed to Siddhesvar Varma by Tripathi, 1977, p. 20.

In the context of ritual, the Vedas describe everything in the world as connected to its divine origin, and focuses on its significance in that context. Different deities preside over different situations. The chanting of the hymn or formula is called *daivī vāc*. Language of ordinary transactions and worldly communication is called *mānuṣī vāc*. As opposed to this, we come across some other types of speech as *rākṣasī vāc*, *āsurī vāc*, etc. Whatever speech one speaks arrogantly, absent-mindedly or insanely is considered as *āsurī vāc*. Even the creaking sound of the axle is *āsurī vāc*.[6]

In Brāhmaṇa literature, the terms *nirukta* and *anirukta* appear frequently to describe the manner of utterance. The primary meaning of *nirukta vāc* is enunciated speech, i.e. said loudly and distinctly so as to be intelligible. The *nirukta* occurs side by side with *uccaiḥ*, in a loud voice, but is not a mere repetition of *uccaiḥ*, and implies something more than that. Again *nirukta* stands opposed to *upāṁśu* which means, in silence or more exactly, in a low voice (i.e. making the articulatory effort but without any audible phone). So inversely, *anirukta* can be equivalent to "in a low voice".[7] Thus *anirukta* includes all the notions that have an indefinite existence and *nirukta* is something definite, having definite shape.

तदेतत् तुरीयम् वाचो निरुक्तम् यत् मनुष्या वदन्ति ।
अथैतत् तुरीयम् वाचो निरुक्तम् यत् पशवो वदन्ति ।
अथैतत् तुरीयम् वाचो निरुक्तम् यत् वयाम्सि वदन्ति ।
अथैतत् तुरीयम् वाचो निरुक्तम् यदिदम् क्षुद्रसरीसृपाम् वदन्ति ।

tadetat turīyam vāco niruktam yat manuṣyā vadanti ।
athaitat turīyam vāco niruktam yat paśavo vadanti ।

6. Pingle, 2005, p. 267.

7. Ibid., p. xx.

athaitat turīyam vāco niruktam yat vayāmsi vadanti । ।
athaitat turīyam vāco niruktam yadidam
kṣudrasarīsṛpām vadanti ।
— *Śata* 4.1.3.16

Human beings are familiar with only a fourth of the whole range of *vāk*. In the *Nirukta*, Yāska quotes:

सा वै वाक् सृष्टा चतुर्धा, व्यभजत् एष्वेव लोकेषु त्रीणि पशुषु तुरीयम् । या पृथिव्यां साग्नौ सा रथन्तरे । यान्तरिक्षे सा वायौ सा वामदेव्ये । या दिवि सादित्ये सा बृहती सा स्तनयित्नौ । अथ पशुषु ।

sā vai vāk sṛṣṭā caturdhā, vyabhajat eṣveva lokeṣu trīṇi paśuṣu turīyam । *yā pṛthivyāṁ sāgnau sā rathantare* । *yāntarikṣe sā vāyau sā vāmadevye* । *yā divi sādity sa ebṛhatī sā stanyitnau* । *atha paśuṣu* । — *Mai Sa* 1.11.5; *Ni* 13.9

The fourfold division of *vāk* is referred to in different ways in different texts. It has its origin in the *Ṛgveda* and has been elaborated differently in various texts, particularly those of Vyākaraṇa and Tantra schools. The linguistic approach of Bhartṛhari has been elaborated by Nāgeśa under the influence of Tantra tenets.[8]

चत्वारि वाक् परिमिता पदानि तानि विदुर् ब्राह्मणा ये मनीषिणः ।
गुहा त्रीणि निहिता नेङ्गयन्ति तुरीयम् वाचो मनुष्या वदन्ति ।

catvāri vāk parimitā padāni tāni vidur brāhmaṇā ye maniṣiṇaḥ ।
guhā trīṇi nihitā neṅgayanti turīyam vāco manuṣyā vadanti ।
— *ṚV* 1.164.45

In the *Nirukta*, Yāska asks what these four divisions could mean. He says that in the tradition of the *ṛṣi*s these are *praṇava* (*oṁkāra*), *bhūḥ*, *bhuvaḥ* and *suvaḥ*.

In the grammarian tradition they are *nāma*, *ākhyāta*, *upasarga* and *nipāta*. In the Nairukta tradition they are *Ṛk*,

8. Tripathi, 1977, p. 20; also Raja, 1969, p. 147.

Sāman, Yajus and *Vyāvahārikī* or everyday language. The *yājñika*s consider them to be *mantra, kalpa, brāhmaṇa* and *laukikī* or everyday language. Yet others take these divisions to be that between sounds of different animals, flutes and people.

Sāyaṇācārya in his *Bhāṣya* to the *Ṛgveda* has listed seven ways[9] of interpreting the fourfold division mentioned in this verse by seven different systems, which correspond quite closely to Yāska's list. The notable difference is the inclusion in Sāyaṇa's list of the Mātṛkās, who hold the fourfold division to be *parā, paśyantī, madhyamā* and *vaikharī.*

We can clearly discern three levels of *śabda* in the *Mahābhāṣya*. When Patañjali says, *mahān devaḥ śabdaḥ*, it refers to the *śabdatattva*. While defining *śabda* at language level, he says,

> शब्दः स्फोटः ध्वनिः शब्दगुणः ।
> *sabdaḥ sphoṭaḥ dhvaniḥ śabdaguṇaḥ* ।

This refers to the mental level *madhyamā* and the audible level, *vaikharī*. In his other two well-known definitions of *śabda* in the *paspaśāhnika* also, both the levels are considered.[10]

Patañjali has enumerated four kinds of words, *nāma, ākhyāta, upasarga, nipāta,* i.e. noun, verb, prefix and particle, in the grammatical tradition. In the *Pradīpa*, Kaiyaṭa refers to the fact that of each of these divisions, only a fourth is available for those not well-versed in the science of linguistics or grammar. In the absence of a decisive criterion, Nāgeśa

---

9. Pingle, 1977, p. 285.

10. येनोच्चारितेन सास्नालङ्गलककुदखुरविषाणिनां सम्प्रत्ययो भवति सः शब्दः । अथवा प्रतीतपदार्थको लोके ध्वनिः शब्द इत्युच्यते ।

    yenoccāritena sāsnālaṅgalakakudakhuraviṣāṇināṁ sampratyayo bhavati saḥ śabdaḥ । *athavā pratītapadārthako loke dhvaniḥ śabda ityucyate* ।

explains this verse as referring to both groups of four — *nāma, ākhyāta, upasarga, nipāta* and also *parā, paśyantī, madhyamā, vaikharī*, in the *Udyota*. The second line, according to him, says that of each kind, three parts remain hidden to ordinary people, who use only the last quarter, *vaikharī*, at the level of spoken language.

An important chronicler of Śāstra, Jayanta Bhaṭṭa, while explaining lucidly the philosophy of the grammarians clearly equates *parā* level to *śabdatattva* and then explains the other three levels in accordance with Bhartṛhari's view.[11]

PARĀ VĀK

Bhartṛhari's explanation of the three different levels is linguistic and epistemological and quite different to what is elucidated in the Tantra and Pratyabhijñā schools. The first *kārikā* of the *Vākyapadīya* sums up the philosophy of Bhartṛhari.

अनादिनिधनम् ब्रह्म शब्दतत्त्वम् यदक्षरम् ।
विवर्ततेऽर्थभावेन प्रक्रिया जगतो यतः ।

anādinidhanam brahma śabdatattvam yadakṣaram ।
vivartate'rthabhāvena prakriyā jagato yataḥ ।

— *VP* I.1

The *śabdatattva* is the root cause of everything — the world and its understanding. The world in its infinite variety is only myriad manifestations of the One Undifferentiated Principle. The *Vṛtti* quotes —

सूक्ष्माम् अर्थेनाप्रविभक्ततत्त्वाम् एकाम् वाचम् अनभिष्यन्दमानाम् । उतान्ये विदुरन्यामपि च एनाम् नानारूपाम् आत्मनि सन्निविष्टाम् इति ।
sūkṣmām arthenāpravibhaktatattvām ekām vācam anabhiṣyandamānām । *utānye viduranyāmapi ca enām nānārūpām ātmani sanniviṣṭām iti* ।

---

11. *Nyāyamañjarī*, Āhnika 6.

Ambākartrī quotes from the *Chāndogya Upaniṣad*:

वाचारम्भणम् विकारो नामधेयम् मृत्तिकेत्येव सत्यम् ।

vācārambhaṇam vikāro nāmadheyam mr̥ttiketyeva satyam ।

That this supreme principle undergoes or appears to possess differentiation to create the whole cosmos, and that the study of language or thought process is a means to realise the *śabdatattva* is explicit in *kārikā* 12.

प्राप्तरूपविभागाया यो वाचः परमो रसः ।
यत्तत्पुण्यतमम् ज्योतिस्तस्य मार्गोऽयमाञ्जसः ।

prāptarūpavibhāgāyā yo vācaḥ paramo rasaḥ ।
yattatpuṇyatamam jyotistasya mārgo 'yamāñjasaḥ ।

— *VP* I.12

The sole principle is *parā vāk*. It undergoes or adopts a seeming variety brought about by differentiation in *varṇa*, *pada* and *vākya*. The word, *gauḥ* for instance is specifically composed of the syllables *ga*, *au* and *ḥ* and it recalls the animal to one's mind. Consciousness takes this path from a latent, undifferentiated level to a specific, manifest level in the form of *gauḥ*. The *Vr̥tti* quotes —

गवादयश्च बाह्यार्थरूपा इव विभागः पुनः श्रुतिरूपत्वेन परिणमन्ते ।

gavādayaśca bāhyārtharūpā iva vibhāgaḥ punaḥ śrutirūpatvena pariṇamante ।

Ambākartrī —

बाह्यः शब्दः कार्यम् वाग्रूपेणान्तर्निलीना गवादयः कारणम् । अन्तःस्थितिः प्रागुक्तः कारणम् बाह्या गवादयः कार्यमिति ।

bāhyaḥ śabdaḥ kāryam vāgrūpeṇāntarnilīnā gavādayaḥ kāraṇam । *antaḥsthitiḥ prāguktaḥ kāraṇam bāhyā gavādayaḥ kāryamiti* ।

The different levels of *vāk* are enumerated by name only once in the entire *Vākyapadīya* and are clearly explained in the *Vṛtti* under the following *kārikā*.

> वैखर्या मध्यमायाश्च पश्यन्त्याश्चैतदद्भुतम् ।
> अनेकतीर्थभेदायास्त्रय्या वाचः परम् पदम् । — *VP* I.142
>
> *vaikharyā madhyamāyāśca paśyantyāścaitadadbhutam* ।
> *anekatīrthabhedāyāstrayyā vācaḥ param padam* ।

While extolling the importance of linguistics, Bhartṛhari says in *VP* I.142 that the science of Vyākaraṇa is the ultimate step for *vāk* with its three divisions of *vaikharī, madhyamā* and *paśyantī; parā* is not mentioned as it is not within the purview of grammar, which analyses by divisions, *apoddhāra*. *Parā* is the source of all the three, on par with *Brahman*, but cannot encompass the ultimate truth, which is on par with *śabdatattva*.

PAŚYANTĪ VĀK

Vṛtti

> प्रतिसंहृतक्रमा सत्यप्यभेदे समाविष्टक्रमशक्तिः पश्यन्ती ।
>
> *pratisaṁhṛtakramā satyapyabhede samāviṣṭakramaśaktiḥ paśyantī* ।

The third level is beyond sequence, *samhṛtakramā*, where thought is in the form of an idea, yet to reach the differentiation of word and meaning, without change or variation. This stage has potential or potency for temporal differentiation that comes when the word takes on full form and structure. We can feel this stage as equivalent to the point where a thought strikes us, as an intuition or *pratibhā*, from where the idea takes on definite form which can be communicated to others.

MADHYAMĀ VĀK

Vṛtti

मध्यमा त्वन्तःसन्निवेशिनी परिगृहीतक्रमेव बुद्धिमात्रोपादाना । सा तु सूक्ष्मप्राण वृत्त्यनुगता क्रमसंहारभावेऽपि व्यक्तक्रमपरिग्रहैव केषाञ्चित् ।
madhyamā tvantaḥ sanniveśinī parigṛhīta krameva buddhimātropādānā । *sā tu sūkṣmaprāṇa vṛttyanugatā krama saṁhārabhave 'pi vyaktakramaparigrahaiva keṣāñcit* ।

That which is in the *buddhi*, intellect alone, without associating with *prāṇa* or articulatory apparatus, but has sequence or form, is called *madhyamā*, the intermediary stage. Since it is accompanied by the subtle breath, it appears to have sequence imposed on it, but being one with the mind which is devoid of temporal sequence, it is also without structure in time. This is the level we operate while reading silently with our eyes, or in silent recalling of a verse. It also corresponds to the *upāṁśu* chanting. The *Vṛtti* refers to both these levels.

VAIKHARĪ VĀK

Vṛtti quotes —

परैः संवेद्यं यस्याः श्रोत्रविषयत्वेन प्रतिनियतम् श्रुतिरूपं सा वैखरी ।

paraiḥ saṁvedyaṁ yasyāḥ śrotraviṣayatvena pratiniyatam śrutirūpaṁ sā vaikharī ।

When air that becomes *prāṇa* (life breath) strikes at the different places of articulation such as throat, palate, etc. and takes on the form of syllables or sounds such as *ka*, *kha*, it is not just air having *vāyutva*, but becomes *śabda*, taking on audibility. It exists along with the life breath that is inhaled and exhaled. The latent consciousness imparts *śabdatva* and *varṇatva* to the *prāṇa* which starts as inhaled air. This manifest level of speech is *vaikharī*, audible to the speaker and the hearer. It has definite sequence and form. It could be highly mixed up or uttered in distinct phonemes. Even the sound of a drum, cart wheel or flute is *vaikharī*.[12] That is *vaikharī* which has the form of audible sound waves.

Madhyamā and *vaikharī* can be viewed as two sides of the same coin, which goes back to Patañjali's concept of *śabda*.

As R.N. Mishra explains:

इत्थं मध्यमावैखरीभ्यां युगपदेव नाद उत्पद्यते, तत्र मध्यमानादोऽर्थवाचक स्फोटात्मकशब्दव्यञ्जकः। वैखरीनादो ध्वनिः सकलजनश्रोत्रग्राह्यो भेर्यादिनादवन्निरर्थकः

ittham madhyamāvaikharībhyām yugapadeva nāda utpadyate, tatra madhyamā nādo 'rthavācaka sphoṭātmakaśabdavyañjakaḥ । *vaikharīnādo dhvanīḥ sakalajanaśrotragrāhyo bheryādinādavannirarthakaḥ* ।

> In this way speech, *nāda*, is caused by *madhyamā* and *vaikharī* simultaneously. The *madhyamā nāda* conveys import while the *vaikharī* manifests *śabda*. The *vaikharī nāda* is sound waves, *dhvani*, which can be perceived by the ear by everyone; like the sound of a drum, it conveys no meaning.[13]

THE FOUR LEVELS IN MEDITATION

In the mystical traditions of Tantra and Śaiva Siddhānta, speech is described as arising in four stages, from subtle to gross form.

परा वाक् मूलचक्रस्था पश्यन्ती नाभिसंस्थिता ।
हृदयस्था मध्यमा ज्ञेया वैखरी कण्ठदेशगा ।[14]

parā vāk mūlacakrasthā paśyantī nābhisaṁsthitā ।
hṛdayasthā madhyamā jñeyā vaikharī kaṇṭhadeśagā ।

The subtle levels are cognised only by *yogī*s and *ṛṣi*s whereas

---

12. Iyer, 1983, p. 67.

13. *Sphoṭamīmāṁsā*, p. 7.

14. Nāgeśa in *Parama Laghu Mañjūṣā*.

ordinary people can cognise the gross, manifest form of language in spoken form. The subtlest level arises in the *mūlacakra*, then comes near the navel or diaphragm, *nābhi* where it is half manifest. From there it rises upward to the *hṛdayadeśa* (chest). There, along with the life breath, it becomes ready to manifest. It then proceeds to the throat region where it receives articulation and beomes fully manifest. It is the fourth level that we can hear and use for communication.

While meditating on Vāg-Brahmā, the aim is to hear *oṁkāra* and meditate upon it. The descriptions of Tantra are relevant in the context of meditation or *dhyāna*. Yogic meditation calls for the mind to focus on *oṁkara* that is generated deep in the recesses of the mind. Before producing the manifest, audible chant, the breath has to be drawn deep, beyond the chest, right from the region of the diaphragm. From as deep into the abdomen as possible, the breath is slowly exhaled, the *yoga* practitioner aware of the region where the breath is entering, filling the chest, then the throat from where it manifests the *oṁ* sound. Thus Vāg-Brahmā is understood in one aspect in creation and in another in the practice of *yoga*. Thus the apparent differences in Bhartṛhari and Nāgeśa's views do not put them in opposition. One describes the psychological process and the other the physiological, considering that these texts date back five to ten centuries.

BHARTṚHARI'S DIVISION OF VĀK

We have no mention of *paśyantī, madhyamā* and *vaikharī* in any text on Śāstra prior to Bhartṛhari. The verses quoted in the *Vṛtti* are in all probability from the *Mahābhārata*. That Bhartṛhari's evolution of speech up to *vaikharī* level is totally psychological is beyond doubt. In the context of discussing production of audible speech between *kārikā*s 100 to 110, he records the different views current in his time, which correspond to the Śikṣākāra-Mīmāṁsaka view of sound being transformations of air, the Nyāya view of sound being vibrations in space and the Jaina view of sound particles or *pudgala*. His own view is that consciousness combines with *prāṇa* to articulate sound.[15]

Modern writers such as K.A.S. Iyer, Gaurinath Sastri and Raghunath Sarma follow the text closely and do not list *śabdatattva* and the three levels together. Iyer writes that *paśyantī* is "near" to *śabdatattva*.[16] Other writers such as Ram Narayan Mishra, Ramdev Tripathi and Vamadeva Acharya state explicitly that *vāk* has four divisions to it. Vamadeva Acharya takes *cit* as of two kinds — *parātmā* or *parā vāk* and *jñānātmā* or *aparā vāk* which is then of three kinds, *parā, paśyantī* and *vaikharī*.[17] Ashok Aklujkar accounts the division as fourfold,[18] taking the first two as *parā-paśyantī* and *paśyantī*.

The issue of *paśyantī, madhyamā* and *vaikharī* seeks clarity in the centuries between Patañjali and Bhartṛhari, from which Vyākaraṇa texts have not survived to our time.

K.A. Subramania Iyer asks if it is only coincidence that the three *kāṇḍas* of the *VP* seem to correspond with this

---

15. वितर्कितः पुरा बुद्ध्या क्वचिदर्थे निवेशितः ।
करणेभ्यो विवृत्तेन ध्वनिना सो नुगृह्यते । — *VP*, I.47
vitarkitaḥ purā buddhyā kvacidarthe niveśitaḥ ।
karaṇebhyo vivṛttena dhvaninā so nugṛhyate ॥

अथायमान्तरो ज्ञाता सूक्ष्मे वागात्मनि स्थितः ।
व्यक्तये स्वस्य रूपस्य शब्दत्वेन विवर्तते । — *VP*, I.112

athāyamāntaro jñātā sūkṣme vāgātmani sthitaḥ ।
vyaktaye svasya rūpasya śabdatvena vivartate ॥

16. *Bhartṛhari*, p. 67.

17. Ibid., p. 15.

18. *Encyclopaedia of Indian Philosophy*, vol V, ed. Karl H. Potter.

threefold division of that aspect of language that comes within the ken of grammar, or is it any deliberate intent with which the author organised the *Trikāṇḍī* to correspond to *paśyantī, madhyamā* and *vaikharī* respectively.[19] Although the different topics do frequently overlap in all three books, the main subject of the Brahmakāṇḍa is *śabdatattva* and *Brahman;* that of the Vākyakāṇḍa is sentence meaning wherein division is only apparent but not real and that of the Padakāṇḍa is related with the *padārtha,* concerning the real, differentiated sequence in words.[20]

Śābdabodha

The word *śabda* broadly has three different meanings:

(i) Sound (*dhvani*), the audible aspect

(ii) Word, the linguistic aspect

(iii) *Śabda pramāṇa,* the process of cognition using language.

The study done in recent times in the field of linguistics is extensive and the literature available on cognition through word, i.e., *śābdabodha,* is very vast. Gaurinath Sastri, B.K. Matilal and K. Kunjunni Raja are foremost among writers in English who have given vital assistance to modern students. The *Śābdabodha Mīmāṁsā* gives a comprehensive account of the major issues in the important Sanskrit texts. In addition, there are many books on the subjects of Nyāya, Mīmāṁsā and Vyākaraṇa that deal with the topic of *śābdabodha* in detail. This section in this work gives a brief account comparing Mīmāṁsā, Nyāya and Vyākaraṇa schools on the following points:

19. *Bhartṛhari,* p. 68.

20. This section was presented at the 13th World Sanskrit Conference at Edinburgh in July 2006 titled, "Vāk in Bhartṛhari Threefold or Fourfold?"

(i) Place of *śabda* among *pramāṇa*s

(ii) Place of Vedas as *pramāṇa*

(iii) Place of grammar or Śāstra

(iv) Nature of *śabda*, eternity, meaning, relationship of Word,

(v) Process of production, transmission and reception of sound.

THE PŪRVA-MĪMĀṀSĀ

Śabda is of paramount importance in *Pūrva-Mīmāṁsā*, as Veda is Word. The very purpose of this science is to understand *dharma*, for which Veda is the only means. While admitting six *pramāṇa*s as in total, only *śabda* is reliable in explaining *dharma*, as all other means of cognition are either defective or totally fail. Vedas are eternal and *apauruṣeya*, that is, not composed by any personal being. So *śabda* has a supreme place in Pūrva-Mīmāṁsā as a pure, perfect, eternal entity, on par with *Puruṣa*. The Tarkapāda in *Śābara-Bhāṣya* quite completely explains the philosophical standpoint on this issue and later writers of Mīmāṁsā have expanded on this:

> The area of semantics is deeply probed by philosophy, psychology, anthropology and other human sciences that deal with the mind. It is the behaviour of the mind that is reflected in the behaviour of language. Mīmāṁsā philosophy that gives utmost importance to *śabda-pramāṇa* is deeply concerned with language. It studies all aspects concerning the import of language. Its studies belong to a period of our intellectual history when psychology, sociology, human sciences, etc. were not bifurcated from philosophy. Therefore its handling of the problems of language involves the approach of these disciplines also. Mīmāṁsā reveals remarkable insight on these aspects.[21]

21. K.T. Pandurangi, 2006, p. xx.

Dharma is what is for the larger good; it is of paramount importance, both in worldly transactions and in Vedic context.[22] Mīmāṁsā hails *śabda* as an independent authority on *dharma* and as the only reliable means of cognition on such matters as *yajña* and *yajñaphala*. To the objection that we do not see immediate results being obtained by the sacrificer after completion of *citra yāga*, the answer is that this is no ground for doubt; the result will definitely be obtained in due course. Since there is no immediate cause-effect relation seen, *apūrva*, a kind of religious merit, is posited as being formed as a result of *yāgānuṣṭhāna*, which in turn causes the result to fructify. Ordinary words of a person in daily life may by unreliable, such as for example: "There are five fruit trees on the river bank there" which upon verification may turn out false. But such a thing never happens in the case of Vedas. Vedas are not composed by any person, *apauruṣeya* and also, they are never found to be proven wrong. There is nothing to hinder (*bādhaka*) their being taken to be true.

> Purva-Mīmāṁsā considers language to be autonomous at three levels: (i) the relation between word and meaning, (ii) sentence meaning, (iii) the purport of a passage or discourse. The relation between word and meaning is natural. It is not fixed by any agency or God. When a meaningful expression is expressed its meaning is also expressed. It is comprehended through elder's conversation from generation to generation. No generation fixes it.[23]

The word and its meaning are connected in a natural eternal relation which has no beginning, no author. Knowing the

---

22. Definition of Veda: प्रत्यक्षेणानुमित्या वा यस्तूपायो न बुध्यते । एतम् विदन्ति वेदेन तस्माद्वेदस्य वेदता ।।

    pratyakṣeṇānūmityā vā yastūpāyo na budhyate ।
    etam vidanti vedena tasmādvedasya vedatā ।।

23. K.T. Pandurangi, p. 132.

relation from an elder is *upadeśa*. As it is impossible to trace the origin of this relation to any author, or to even bring about the relation between a word and its meaning without using some other words, there is no point looking for its origin. It is best to take the given situation as always existing, with the words and their associated meaning as eternal pairs, which we make use of as and when required. Thus in Pūrva-Mīmāṁsā philosophy, *śabda* is not only a vital *pramāṇa*, but also has independent ontological status. Considering only articulate language, it is of *varṇa* or phoneme form. It is because the *varṇa*s (phonemes) are eternal, immutable, all-pervading, timeless entities, that the Vedas are supreme and reliable.

औत्पत्तिकस्तु शब्दस्यार्थेन संबन्धस्तस्य ज्ञानमुपदेशोऽव्यतिरेकश्चार्तेऽनुपलब्धे तत्प्रमाणं बादरायणस्य अनपेक्षत्वात् ।।५।।[24]

autpattikastu śabdasyārthena saṁbandhastasya, jñānamupadeśo 'vyatirekaścārte 'nupalabdhe tatpramāṇaṁ bādarāyaṇasya anapekṣatvāt ।।5।।

What is a Word

Śabda is meant to convey sense or an idea. Both Jaimini and Śabara say that the main purpose of words is to yield sense. In the *Śābara-Bhāṣya*, the question is raised as to what is a word. The answer is that the very phonemes constitute the word, there is no separate entity over and above the phonemes that has a separate existence in totality. The audibility of *śabda* is a crucial requirement for its definition; so anything other than the syllables, literally, is an unnecessary fiction. Śabara quotes the grammarians' position in mentioning *saṅghāta* and denounces it. Due to the transitory sequence of utterance, how can the sounds directly convey

24. *Jaimini-Sūtra.*

sense? Is it the *smṛti* (memory) of these sounds that aid meaning? But the memory impressions would have the same defect of sequence. So the *saṁskāra* (mental impression) caused by each *varṇa*, together with the final syllable, convey meaning. Thus the cause-effect relation between word and meaning remains intact and it is more economical than postulating *sphoṭa*, which requires the *saṁskāra* anyway.

The grammarians quote the example of Yāska stating that even *kriyā* (action) occurring with temporal and spatial sequence is still considered as one single entity, viz. action; but it is shot down as an unsuitable example for unity of word. Only the *varṇa*s are experienced, no other word such as unified word *sphoṭa* is perceived by the sense organs, so there is none other.

अथ गौरित्यत्र कः शब्दः । गकारौकारविसर्जनीया इति भगवान् उपवर्षः । श्रोत्रग्रहणे ह्यर्थे लोके शब्दशब्दः प्रसिद्धः । ते च श्रोत्रग्रहणाः ।

न च अक्षरव्यतिरिक्तोऽन्यः कश्चिदस्ति समुदायो नाम यतोऽर्थप्रतिपत्तिः स्यात् ।[25]

atha gaurityatra kaḥ śabdaḥ । *gakāraukāravisarjanīyā iti bhagavān upavarṣaḥ* । *śrotragrahaṇe hyarthe loke śabdaśabdaḥ prasiddhaḥ* । *te ca śrotragrahaṇāḥ* ।

na ca akṣaravyatirikto 'nyaḥ kaścidasti samudāyo nāma yato 'rthapratiprattiḥ syāt ।

Word Meaning is Ākṛti

Śabara clearly states that the import of the word is in *ākṛti.*

अथ गौरित्यस्य शब्दस्य कोऽर्थः । सास्नादिविशिष्टाकृतिरिति ब्रूमः ।[26]

atha gaurityasya śabdasya ko 'rthaḥ । *sāsnādiviśiṣṭākṛtiriti brūmaḥ* ।

25. *Śābara-Bhāṣya*, 1981, p. 36.

26. *Śābara-Bhāṣya*, p. 39.

Jaimini raises the question whether *ākṛti* or *vyakti* is the meaning of the word, in *Ākṛtyadhikaraṇa*.

Ordinarily the word *ākṛti* is understood in the sense of configuration or *avayava saṁsthāna*; i.e. arrangement of its parts in an object, but here it means the class concept or universal, *sāmānya* or *jāti*. Śabara makes it clear by explaining

द्रव्यगुणकर्मणाम् सामान्यमात्रमाकृतिः ।

dravyaguṇakarmaṇām sāmānyamātramākṛtiḥ ।

Kumārila states in the beginning of the Ākṛtivāda that *ākṛti* and *jāti*, *sāmānya* are synonymous in Mīmāṁsā.

जातिमेवाकृतिं प्राहुर्व्यक्तिराक्रियते यया ।
सामान्यं तच्च पिण्डानामेकबुद्धिनिबन्धनम् ॥३॥

jātimevākṛtiṁ prāhurvyaktirākriyate yayā ।
sāmānyaṁ tacca piṇḍānāmekabuddhinibandhanam ॥3॥

K.T. Pandurangi discusses[27] the main objections to *ākṛti* being the import of a word as presented by *pūrvapakṣin* in following three points:

1. Vedic injunctions enjoin offering a *paśu*, sprinkling water on rice, etc. acts. These cannot be performed on the universal, *paśutva*, *vrīhitva*, etc. These can be acted upon the *vyakti*, i.e. the object. Therefore, *vyakti* has to be taken as the meaning.

2. There are certain injunctions such as six cows be given, twelve cows be given, twenty-four cows be given. These numbers cannot be of *ākṛti*, nor so many *ākṛti*s of cows can be given. *Ākṛti* is one in all.

3. It is stated that if a *paśu* duly taken for the sacrifice

27. Pandurangi, 2006, p. 135.

escapes another has to be taken. Now, if *ākṛti* is the meaning, there is no another *ākṛti* to replace the first.

These arguments hold good under the assumption that a word conveys *ākṛti* or *vyakti* exclusively. However, *ākṛti* and *vyakti* are invariably associated. When two items are invariably associated with each other, the cognition of one provides the cognition of the other. In experience, we find that *vyakti* is also comprehended when we hear a word. The issue to settle is whether the word conveys one or the other or both, whether the *vyakti* is comprehended directly from the word or through *ākṛti* conveyed by the word. We can apply the test by *anvaya vyatireka*, that is, positive and negative verification.

A person who cognises *ākṛti* even without words, cognises *vyakti* also. On the other hand, a person who hears the word but is unable to recall the *ākṛti* conveyed by it will not be able to cognise *vyakti*. This clearly reveals that the word does not convey *vyakti* but it is *ākṛti* conveyed by the word that helps to cognise the *vyakti* as per the maxim that when an item related with another is cognised it provides the cognition of the other. It cannot be urged that we take *vyakti viśiṣṭa ākṛti* as the meaning. This will prevent using the same word with reference to another individual, since that is not conveyed by this word. The driving point of this discussion is that *ākṛti* is the meaning of the word. Since *vyakti* is also conveyed the objections raised by *pūrvapakṣin* do not apply. Taking universal as the meaning of a word does not come in the way of implementing the Vedic injunctions, as also instructions such as "close the door".

G.V. Devasthali discusses the significance of taking *ākṛti* as meaning of a word under *pravṛttinimitta*s of a word of which *jāti* or *ākṛti* is foremost.

> . . . since when there is nothing in particular to be conveyed by a word it conveys *jāti* or *ākṛti*. Such words are called *jātinimitta śabda* or *jātiśabda*. However, we have to bear in mind one important rule, viz. words which are found to denote *jāti* in one place must be accepted as such in all places! The word *barhiḥ* for example, in ordinary parlance is used as a *jāti śabda*, without any reference to any *saṁskāra* at all. In Vedic texts it appears to denote consecrated grass. Are we then to take the word *barhiḥ*. in the Vedas as *jāti śabda* or as a *saṁskāra śabda*? This question is to be answered by observing the above-mentioned rule, and hence the conclusion is that the word is to be understood as a *jāti śabda* and not as a *saṁskāra śabda*. Thus it may be stated that whenever *jāti* is found to be the *pravṛttinimitta* of a word, as a rule in the language, it must be accepted as a *jāti śabda*, though in some special cases the word might appear to denote something else, *saṁskāra*, for example, *MS* 1.4.10

The other *pravṛttinimitta*s of a word are *saṁskāra*, refinement, e.g. *yūpa*, *yoga*, connection, e.g. *prokṣaṇī*, *sambandha*, e.g. *putra*, *rūḍhi*, custom, e.g. *kuśala*, etc.

The *Pratinidhiśāstra* that explains how the Ākṛtivāda affects the substitution or replacement procedure in Vedic ritual is the crucial grounds on which the *vyaktivādin*s put forth their view. Bhartṛhari addresses the issue in the Jāti Samuddeśa and his views on substitution of items in the context of Vedic ritual form an important part of the discussions. Again the acceptance of Ākṛtivāda would lead to the futility of the *Pratinidhiśāstra*; for the substitution would be an impossibility if *Ākṛti* is accepted as the real import of words like *paśu*. For the work *anya* will have no sense, since any *paśu* will be the same.

But this Vyaktivāda of the *pūrvapakṣin* can't be said to be wholly satisfactory. Take, for example, texts like *Śyenacitam Cinvīta*. If the word *śyena* is not *ākṛtivācaka*, how can you obey the above injunction? For what is needed for making a *śyena* is the *sādṛśya* of the figure prepared with the bricks, with an actual *śyena*. This similarity must naturally be with the form which is common to all *śyena*s, or, *śyenatva jāti*.

Thus it will be seen that if some texts seem to favour the Vyaktivāda, there are others which seem to favour the Ākṛtivāda. Thus, so far as the scriptural texts are concerned both views are equally supported by them. . . . It is therefore, necessary to seek some more decisive grounds on which to solve this problem.

Such a definite ground we get in the fact, that the same word is used with reference to several individuals, which decides the issue in favour of the Ākṛtivāda.[28]

The Relation of Word and Meaning

This is stated to be *pratyāyya pratyāyaka,* i.e. that which is made known and that which makes known. The natural relation is not between word and object, but between word and meaning, or import. It is not as if upon uttering "knife" or "candy", the mouth is cut or tastes sweet![29]

स्याच्चेदर्थेन संबन्धः क्षुरमोदकशब्दोच्चारेण मुखस्य पाटनपूरणे स्यातां यदि संस्लेशलक्षणं संबन्धम् अभिप्रेत्योच्यते ।

syāccedarthena saṁbandhaḥ kṣuramodakaśabdoccāreṇa

28. Devasthali, p. 29.

29. Also:

न तावत् संयोगोऽस्ति तद्भावे हि क्षुरादिशब्दोच्चारणे मुखस्य पातनादि स्यात् । न कार्यकारण द्वयोरपि नित्यत्वात् । — *SD*, p. 182.

na tāvat saṁyogo 'sti tadbhāve hi kṣurādiśabdoccāraṇe mukhasya pātanādi syat ।
na kāryakāraṇa dvayorapi nityatvāt ।

mukhasya pāṭanapūraṇe syātāṃ yadi saṁsleśalakṣaṇaṁ saṁbandham abhipretyocyate । — *SB* p. 34

The point is also raised that were the relation natural, the meaning should be comprehended the first time a word is heard — but this does not happen in experience. It is only after one is taught that the meaning of a particular word is such and such that that word sparks meaning to flash in the mind. The Mīmāṁsaka agrees to this process of learning language from elders — those already knowing the language, *vṛddha vyavahāra*. We observe one-to-one relation in the world between hearing a word and cognising the meaning and understand the nature of *śabda*.

The fact that one does not understand a word the first time one hears it does not detract from its nature of conveying meaning.

यो ह्यत्र व्यपदेश्यः संबन्धस्तमेकं न व्यपदिशति भवान् प्रत्याय्यस्य प्रत्यायकस्य च यः संज्ञासंज्ञिलक्षण इति ।

प्रत्यायक इति हि प्रत्ययं दृष्ट्वा अवगच्छामः न प्रथमश्रुत इति प्रथमश्रवणे प्रत्ययमदृष्ट्वा ।[30]

yo hyatra vyapadeśyaḥ saṁbandhastamekaṁ na vyapadiśati bhavān pratyāyyasya pratyāyakasya ca yaḥ saṁjñāsaṁjñilakṣaṇa iti ।

pratyāyaka iti hi pratyayaṁ dṛṣṭvā avagacchāmaḥ na prathamaśruta iti prathamaśravaṇe pratyayamadṛṣṭvā ।

The Nature of Śabda

According to Mīmāṁsā, articulate sound is *varṇa rūpa*, eternal, immutable, all-pervading and each one is identical to itself. On being perceived by the auditory sense organ, i.e. ear cavity, it causes cognition of meaning. But this definition

30. *ŚB*, p. 35.

seems to have many shortcomings, as the opponent points out, from *Jaimini-Sūtra* 6 to 11, in the 6th *adhikaraṇa*, wherein eternity of *śabda* is discussed.[31]

Since *śabda* is heard only when it is uttered or produced, it is *kārya*. If it is eternal and omnipresent, how is it that it is heard only occasionally? It cannot be manifested occasionally, as it never even existed earlier. It is transitory and ephemeral, certainly not *nitya*. Sound is said to be produced in the world, and to die out. In different places, we hear distinct sounds at the same time and the syllables undergo mutation, as in the case of *sandhi*. Sometimes a sound heard is loud, sometimes low. All this goes to prove that *śabda* is produced, ceases to exist after a while, has parts that lend it high or low volume collectively, is many, produced in great variety in different places.

The opponents' objections are all resolved by the Mīmāṁsā Siddhānta from *Jaimini-Sūtra* 12 to 23 that says[32] that

---

31. कर्मैके तत्र दर्शनात् ॥६॥ अस्थानात् ॥७॥ करोतिशब्दात् ॥८॥ सत्त्वान्तरे च यौगपद्यात् ॥९॥ प्रकृतिविकृत्योश्च ॥१०॥ वृद्धिश्च कर्तृभूम्नात् ॥११॥

    karmaike tatra darśanāt ॥6॥ *asthānāt* ॥7॥ *karotiśobdāt* ॥8॥ *sattvāntare ca yoga padyāt* ॥9॥ *prakṛtivikṛtyośca* ॥10॥ *vṛddhiśca kartṛbhūmnāt* ॥11॥

32. समं तु तत्र दर्शनम् ॥१२॥ सतः परमदर्शनं विषयानागमात् ॥१३॥ प्रयोगस्य परम् ॥१४॥ आदित्यवद्यौगपद्यम् ॥१५॥ वर्णान्तरमविकारः ॥१६॥ नादवृद्धिपरा ॥१७॥ नित्यस्तु स्याद् दर्शनस्य परार्थत्वात् ॥१८॥ सर्वत्र यौगपद्यात् ॥१९॥ संख्याभावात् ॥२०॥ अनपेक्षत्वात् ॥२१॥ प्रख्याभावाच्च योगस्य ॥२२॥ लिङ्गदर्शनाच्च ॥२६॥

    samaṁ tu tatra darśanam ॥12॥ *sataḥ paramadarśanaṁ viṣayā-nāgamāt* ॥13॥ *prayogasya param* ॥14॥ *ādityavadyaugapadyam* ॥15॥ *varṇāntaramavikāraḥ* ॥16॥ *nādavṛddhiparā* ॥17॥ *nityastu syād darśanasya parārthatvāt* ॥18॥ *sarvatra yaugapadyāt* ॥19॥ *saṁkhyābhāvāt* ॥20॥ *anapekṣatvāt* ॥21॥ *prakhyābhāvācca yogasya* ॥22॥ *liṅgadarśanācca* ॥26॥

there is nothing to contradict the fact that *śabda* is one, eternal, all-pervasive and immutable, with independent authority as far as *pramāṇa* goes; all the objections can be explained away by considering that acoustic wave, or *dhvani* is instrumental in manifesting the eternal *śabda*. All the transitory attributes belong to *dhvani*, not *śabda*. *Dhvani* is *kārya, anitya*. It is *dhvani* that upon reaching the ear produces the *saṁskāra*, refinement that enables the person to cognise *śabda*. It is cognised to different extents and differently in different places, because it has limited extent in space and differs in different places. Detailed discussions on the nature of sound are found in Mīmāṁsā texts in the debate on the eternal nature of *śabda*. For the Nyāya-Vaiśeṣikas, sound is a transient quality, *anitya, kārya* that is produced and later perishes. But the Mīmāṁsā school upholds the eternity of the Vedas, hence in their philosophy, *śabda* is *apauruṣeya, nityavarṇarūpa*. Inarticulate sound such as clapping of hands is not relevant in the linguistic approach of the Mīmāṁsā and hence not analysed. While each *varṇa* is held to be one and eternal, it is an undeniable fact that its utterance and audibility is ephemeral. To explain this, it is pointed out that *dhvani* is responsible for the manifestation of the *varṇa* and it is *dhvani* that is *kārya* and *anitya*.

The phoneticians who discuss Vedic chanting in the Śikṣā texts describe the process and apparatus of articulation. They hold that the physical basis of sound is a series of air with movements. The *ātmā* joins the *buddhi*, which combines its activity with the *manas*. This impells the breath to manifest the voice which moves upward and upon hitting the roof of the mouth, the *mūrdhā*, it articulates the *varṇa*s which are of five types. This process teaches that speech is a conscious act in a living being, achieved by the concentration of the mind and is manifested by air.

Pāṇinīya Śikṣā

आत्मा बुद्ध्या समेत्यार्थान्मनो युङ्क्ते विवक्षया ।
मनः कायाग्निमाहन्ति स प्रेरयति मारुतम् ।।६।।
मारुतस्तूरसि चरन् मन्द्रं जनयति स्वरम् ।
प्रातः सवनयोगं तच्छन्दो गायत्रमाश्रितम् ।।७।।
सोदीर्णो मूर्धन्यभिहतो वक्त्रमापद्य मारुतः ।
वर्णान् जनयते तेषाम् विभागः पञ्चधा स्मृतः ।।९।।

ātmā buddhyā sametyārthānmano yuṅkte vivakṣayā ।
manaḥ kāyāgnimāhanti sa prerayati mārutam ।।6।।
mārutastūrasti caran mandraṁ janayati svaram ।
prātaḥ savanayogaṁ tacchando gāyatramāśritam ।।7।।
sodīrṇo mūrdhanyabhihato vaktramāpadya mārutaḥ ।
varṇān janayate teṣām vibhāgaḥ pañcadhā smṛtaḥ ।।9।।

Ślokavārttika

नादो वायुगुणः वायुर्वा यदि कल्प्येत ।

nādo vayuguṇaḥ vayurvā yadi kalpyeta ।

Nyāyaratnākara

वायुरेव ताल्वादिस्थानसंयोगात् शब्दगुणको निष्पद्यते । शब्दस्यापि वायुगुणत्वम् वेदितव्यम् ।
vāyureva talvādisthānasaṁyogāt śabdaguṇako niṣpadyate śabdasyāpi vāyuguṇatvam vedītavyam ।

The air particles themselves flow in all directions, taking the sound with them, and on impact with tangible bodies, they get obstructed and the movement ceases, as in the arrow, when the moving force is exhausted.

Nyāyamañjarī (3rd *Āhnika):*

स गच्छन् सर्वतो दिक्षु उद्दमवेगाहितक्रियः शरवत् वेगशान्त्येव न दूरम् गन्तुर्महति । शिक्षाविदस्तु पवनात्मकमेव शब्दमाचक्षते ।
sa gacchan sarvato dikṣu uddamavegāhitakriyaḥ śaravat

vegaśāntyeva na dūram ganturmahati śikṣāvidastu pavanātmakeva śabdamācakṣate ।

The *Śābara-Bhāṣya* explains that *nāda*, the physical basis of sound is a wave motion of air, being the transmission of conjunctions and disjunctions in the minute particles of air, the wave originating in the first impact, and being continued by the successive impacts of the minute particles.

सम्योगविभागनैरन्तर्येण क्रियमाणः शब्दमभिव्यन्जन्तो नादशब्दवाच्यः अभिघातेन हि प्रेरितवायवः स्तिमितानि वाय्वान्तराणि प्रतिधावमानाः सर्वतो दिक्कान् सम्योगविभागान् उत्पादयन्ति यावद्वेगम् अभिप्रतिष्ठन्ते । ते च वायोरप्रत्यक्षत्वात् सम्योगविभागेनोपलभ्यन्ते । अनुपरतेष्वेव तेषु शब्द उपलभ्यते । नोपरतेषु अत एव च अनुवातम् दूरात् उपलभ्यते शब्दः ।

sumyogavibhāganairantaryeṇa kriyamāṇaḥ śabdamabhivyanjanto nādaśabdavācyaḥ abhighātena hi preritavāyavaḥ stimitāni vāyvāntarāṇi pratidhāvamānaḥ sarvato dikkān samyogavibhāgān utpādayanti yāvadvegam abhipratiṣṭhante । *te ca vāyorapratyakṣatvāt samyogavibhāgenopalabhyante* । *anuparateṣveva teṣu śabda upalabhyate*। *no parateṣu ata eve ca anuvātam dūrāt upalabhyate śabdaḥ* ।

While presenting the Mīmāṁsā view on *śabdasvarūpa*, Jayanta Bhaṭṭa explains that sound is produced in air when the molecules or particles are compressed or impressed upon.

प्रयत्नप्रेरितकौष्ट्यमारुतसंयोगविभागानन्तरम् उपलभ्यमानः शब्दस्तत्कार्य एवेति गम्यते । उच्चारणात् ऊर्ध्वमनुपलब्धेरनित्यः शब्दः । तदेवम् व्यङ्ग्येऽपि प्रयत्नानन्तरमुपलम्भसम्भवाद् अनैकान्तिकत्वम् अभिव्यञ्जकानाञ्च पवनसंयोगविभागानाम् अचिरस्थायित्वात् न चिरम् उच्चारणाद् ऊर्ध्वम् उपलभ्यते शब्दः ।[33]

prayatnapreritakauṣṭyamārutasaṁyogavibhāgānantaram upalabhyamānaḥ śabdastatkārya eveti gamyate । *uccāraṇāt*

33. *NM*, vol. I, p. 288.

ūrdhvamanupalabdheranityaḥ śabdaḥ । *tadevam vyaṇgye 'pi prayatnānamtaramupalambhasambhavād anaikāntikatvam abhivyāñjakānāñca pavanasaṁyogavibhāgānām acirasthāyitvāt na ciram uccāraṇād ūrdhvam upalabhyate śabdaḥ* ।

In the above quote, *saṃyoga-vibhāga* are taken as compression and rarefactions in air. Again,

ध्वनयो हि नाम संयोगविभागविशेषितवायवः वायुवृत्तयो वा संयोगविभागास्ते हि शब्दस्य व्यञ्जका इष्यन्ते ।[34]

dhvanayo hi nāma saṁyogavibhāgaviśeṣitavāyavaḥ vāyuvr̥ttayo vā saṁyogavibhāgāste hi śabdasya vyañjakā iṣyante ।

In the philosophy of Mīmāṁsā, the eternality of *śabda* and *apauruṣeyatva* of Vedas have to be maintained. If *varṇa* is eternal and omnipresent, how is it that we do not hear all the phonemes all the time, everywhere? There has to be some criterion, some alteration in the environment whereby the sound is heard only at certain points in time. This is the *saṁskāra*, refinement, that is responsible for a sound to be audible at a particular instant and not at others. The answer is that *dhvani*, audible sound, manifests *śabda*. This is produced by the apparatus of articulation at the time of utterance, is borne by air molecules and reaches the ear, which perceives it. Since sound trains have specific location, sound is heard in a limited region.

न च शब्दसंस्कारे सर्वपुंसाम् उपलब्धिप्रसङ्गः ध्वनीनाम् प्रादेशिकत्वात् तद्देशे शब्दः संस्क्रियते न सर्वत्र । अतः संस्कृतेन शब्देन यस्येन्द्रियं सन्निकृष्टं स एव शृणोति नान्यत्रेत्युपपन्नं ।

na ca śabdasaṁskāre sarvapuṁsām upalabdhiprasaṁgaḥ dhvanīnām prādeśikatvāt taddeśe śabdaḥ saṁskriyate na sarvatra । *ataḥ saṁskr̥tena śabdena yasyendriyaṁ sannikr̥ṣṭaṁ sa eva śr̥ṇoti nānyatretyupapannaṁ* ।

---

34. *NM*, vol. I, p. 195.

The auditory sense organ does not travel to the sound, but the sound waves themselves reach the ear cavity. Further, the ear can also sense the direction from which the sound is coming, — so in an indirect way, the direction, quarter or *dik* can also be inferred.

> किन्तु श्रोत्रं हि स्वदेशस्थितं शब्दं बोधयदपि न देशविशिष्टं बोधयति ।
>
> *kintu śrotraṁ hi svadeśasthitaṁ śabdaṁ bodhayadapi na deśaviśiṣṭaṁ bodhayati ।*

By whatever body the sound is produced, it has to pass through the intervening medium, air, to reach the ear. Thus it is proven that sound is a quality of air and not space, as held by the Nyāya-Vaiśeṣikas.

Śāstradīpikā:

> वायुगुणत्वं तु युक्तम् । वीणामुखशङ्खादिसंयोगात् भेरीदण्डसंयोगाद् अन्यतो वा निष्पाद्यमाना वायवः तच्छब्दविशेषगुणका निष्पन्नाः सर्वासु दिक्षु प्रविशमाणाः श्रोत्रेण संयुज्यन्ते ततश्च संयुक्तसमवायात्तद्गतः शब्दः श्रोत्रेण गृह्यते । यस्मादेव वायुगुणः शब्दस्तस्माद् यत्कैश्चिदुच्यते शब्दलिङ्गमाकाशमिति तन्निरस्तम् ।
>
> *vāyuguṇatvaṁ tu yuktam । vīṇāmukhaśaṅkhādisaṁyogāt bherīdaṇḍasaṁyogād anyato vā niṣpādyamānā vāyavaḥ tacchabdaviśeṣaguṇakā niṣpannāḥ sarvāsu dikṣu praviśamāṇāḥ śrotreṇa saṁyujyante tataśca saṁyukta samavāyāttadgataḥ śabdaḥ śrotreṇa gr̥hyate । yasmādeva vāyuguṇaḥ śabdastasmād yatkaiściducyate śabdaliṅgamākāśamiti tannirastam ।*

Padārtha and Vākyārtha

The primary meaning of a word with which it is invariably associated is called the *abhidhā vr̥tti* or *śakti*. *Vr̥tti* or the function of a word is its relation to its sense.[35] There are many ways in which we can learn the meaning of words. Eight are well

35. Raja, 1969, p. 24.

known in Śāstra and are listed. In the case of words with multiple meanings, we take the help of associated factors to understand the purport intended so that the meaning can be ascertained without doubt.[36]

The word may convey an extended meaning also, called *lakṣaṇā* or secondary meaning, that is in some way connected with the *abhidhā*. Yet another extended sense, *vyañjanā* or hinted meaning, is admitted in normal language. It is prized in poetry but is not suited for Śāstra, where precision is required and is therefore not accepted as reliable by Nyāya.

The sentence is constituted of words, but what actually is sentence meaning? Just as a word is a string of phonemes, so is a full utterance, a string of phonemes, a sentence that conveys sense. The sentence as a whole, in totality, is not admitted by the Mīmāṁsaka, in the same way that *sphoṭa* is rejected. There are two schools in Mīmāṁsā that explain the process of sentence meaning in two different ways (i) *abhihitānvaya* theory followed by Kumārila Bhaṭṭa and (ii) *anvitābhidhāna* theory followed by Prabhākara Miśra's camp. The *abhihitānvaya* theory seems to follow the *Śābara-Bhāṣya* more closely in saying that words convey their independent meanings and retire; the word-meanings then connect semantically to convey the meaning of the whole sentence as a unit. The *anvitābhidhāna* view, on the other hand, says that the words directly convey their import in the context of the sentence that is the word-meanings in a sentence are already related to one another and are not isolated or independent. Kumārila's followers reject this view as it carries the defect of *anyonya āśraya* or mutual dependence of word-meaning and sentence-meaning. Jaimini's *sūtra*s are not partial to either view and seem to lend support to both views.

36. Raja, 1969, p. 50.

The purpose of the utterance is one. Mīmāṁsā is celebrated as the Vākyaśāstra and there is rich debate in Indian tradition on the form and meaning of a sentence, its *mukhya viśeṣya*, the *ākāṅkṣā*, *yogyatā*, *sannidhi* and other issues.[37]

THE NYĀYA VIEW

Śabda, or Verbal Testimony, is an important *pramāṇa* in the Nyāya system, along with *pratyakṣa*, *anumāna*, and *upamāna*. Some schools of thought, notably Vaiśeṣika, Cārvāka and Buddhists, do not consider *śabda* as a reliable means of cognition, and some include it under *Anumāna* or Inference. The Nyāya Śāstras of Gautama show clearly how *śabda* is an independent *pramāṇa* which cannot be brought under inference.

It can be argued that just as in inference, the knowledge of *liṅga* gives rise to the cognition of *hetu* which cannot be directly perceived, the hearing of the word gives rise to its meaning, which may not be directly visible. Thus it can be shown that the process of verbal cognition is on the same lines as inference. Thinking on these lines, the *Nyāya-Sūtra* goes:

> शब्दोऽनुमानमर्थस्यानुपलब्धेरनुमेयत्वात् । — 2.1.49
> *śabdo'numānamarthasyānupalabdheranumeyatvāt* ।

There do not seem to be enough grounds to distinguish between *anumāna* and *śabda*, as there is enough difference to show disparity between *pratyakṣa* and *anumāna*, or *anumāna* and *upamāna*. Just as the *liṅga*, when understood, points to the *hetu*, the word, *śabda*, when understood, points to the meaning, *artha*.

> उपलब्धेरद्विप्रवृत्तित्वात् । — 2.1.50
> *upalabdheradvipravṛttitvāt* ।

---

37. K.K. Raja, p. 191.

Just as *vyāpti jñāna* helps in the case of Inference, the *sambandha jñāna* helps in the case of verbal cogniton. Upon hearing the word, the meaning is inferred.

सम्बन्धाच्च । — 2.1.51

sambandhācca ।

Then, the objection is resolved with the next *sūtra*.

आप्तोपदेशसामर्थ्याच्छब्दादर्थसंप्रत्ययः ।

āptopadeśasāmarthyācchabdādarthasaṁpratyayaḥ । — 2.1.52

What nobody has seen, that is, in the case of meaning that cannot be understood by direct perception, such as "heaven", "Apsaras", "Kuru country is in the north", "(there are) seven continents, oceans surround the earth", etc. it is not just from words that we obtain meaning. What then? The fact that such information is from a reliable speaker is what makes the words convey proper meaning, which is not a factor in the case of Inference. Therefore, verbal testimony is distinct from Inference. But the Vaiśeṣikas hold that verbal cognition is through *anumāna*[38] (p. 5).

The Vedas are held sacred and as Ultimate Authority in spiritual matters in the Nyāya system. From very early texts, the authority of the Vedas is what has led to detailed analysis of *śabda* as a means of cognition.

From the *Tarkasaṁgraha* the definition as a means to cognition is as follows:

> Word is a sentence spoken by an authority. Authority is a person who speaks truth.[39]

Sentence is a group of words, e.g. "bring a cow". Word is a

38. *Śābdabodhamīmāṁsā*, 2005, p. 8.

39. Athalye-Bodas, p. 329.

thing having power (of conveying meaning). Power is a convention made by God that a certain sense be understood from a certain word.

From its fundamental definition, *śabda* is associated with Consciousness. It is not an independent, impersonal entity, as in Mīmāṁsā. The *samaya* or *saṅketa,* the relation between word and meaning, is brought about by a conscious being. Thus, the relation between word and its meaning is conventional. In the case of the Vedas, the convention is made by God. In the case of words that have sprung up in later usage, e.g. *pāribhāṣika* words or technical jargon, it is brought about by human agency. This division is not very rigid, as there is no difference in their process or power of denoting particular objects. An "authoritative person", *āpta* again is "he who speaks truth". Truth is an object as it really exists in reality. The verbal knowledge *śābdabodha* of truth is the representation of a thing just it exists. These definitions of *āpta* and *yathārtha* are very characteristic because they clearly show that according to Naiyāyikas the ultimate test of the truth of verbal knowledge was not the authority attaching to the speaker himself, but the fact of his words being in harmony with the reality of things. Word is that which has the power to convey meaning. The primary relation between word and meaning is *śakti.*

शक्तम् पदम् ।

śaktam padam ।

Sentence is a group of words that convey sense if it has *ākāṅkṣā, sannidhi* and *yogyatā.* The Naiyāyikas take the *mukhya viśeṣya* as the subject (*karttā*), around which all other words revolve in a sentence. Sentences have valid meaning in worldly language according to whether spoken by *āpta* or otherwise. But Vedic utterances are all valid, without need to verify by any other means. All orthodox systems of philosophy take the validity of Vedas as supreme. The extended meaning of a word or sentence, *lakṣaṇā*, or implication is also accepted as the secondary *vṛtti*. But *vyañjanā* is shown to be only inference, not a third type of *śābdabodha*.

Analysing *saṅketarūpa śakti* further, we ask what does the word, e.g. *ghaṭa*, actually denote? Is it the object jar, the common property of being a jar that resides in it, or both together? This is an important question as it lies at the basis of several antagonistic theories of *śābdabodha* proposed by different schools. The opinions on this point are as various and numerous as opinions can possibly be on any single topic. Of these views four are the most important, namely *kevala jāti, kevala vyakti, jātiviśiṣṭa vyakti* and *apoha*. The first is adopted by the Mīmāṁsakas, the second by modern Naiyāyikas, the third by ancient Naiyāyikas and the last belongs to the Bauddhas.[40]

When we say *gām ānaya* the action can be performed only on the object, the *vyakti*: Modern Naiyāyikas rely on this simple fact and take the word to denote *vyakti*: The capacity of being the subject of any act *artha kriyā kāritva* resides in the concrete object *vyakti* alone, and hence it is the *vyakti* on which *saṅketa* is made. But there are objections to this view. If the word *ghaṭa* refers to one individual jar, we would require as many words are jars in the world, and the *saṅketa* of each would have to be learnt separately, as they have no connection with each other. Then there are the problems of *ānantya* and *gaurava*. And this would defeat the very purpose of concept of *sāmānya*, or cognition by categorisation. However, there is only one word *ghaṭa* and when we know its significance as expressing *kambu grīvādimat vastu*, we apply it to all objects

40. Athalye-Bodas, p. 334.

having that shape. When we say *go* we at once denote the *go vyakti*, the class notion *gotva* and the peculiarity *sāsnādimatva* which distinguishes a cow from other animals. In other words, *go* signifies *vyakti*, *jāti* and *ākṛti* at the same time.

In Nyāya philosophy, *ākṛti* is *avayava saṁsthāna* or configuration, which is not the same as universal or *jāti*. A clay cow, for instance, has the same shape as a real one, but nobody mistakes it to manifest the same universal as a living animal. The *ākṛti* inheres in the *vyakti* and helps cognise the *jāti*. The denotation of a word can never be in the configuration, according to Nyāya. Configuration is as particular as the individual itself. There may be similarity in *ākṛti* of several objects, but it cannot be taken as a common feature. In the case of objects such as clay, gold, silver, etc. the words cannot refer to the *ākṛti* as they may not even possess any specific shape. *Jāti* or *sāmānya* is an ontological real in Nyāya philosophy. Therefore, any common feature that chiefly serves to identify different individuals of a class as the same, such as *upādhi*, or *sādṛśya* or *ākṛti*, cannot qualify as a *jāti*. The definitions of these issues in *Nyāyakośa* put their similarities and differences in perspective.[41]

---

41. *Ākṛti* — आकृतिः जातिलिङ्गाख्या । जातेर्गोत्वादेर्हि सास्नादिसंस्थानविशेषो लिङ्गम् । अवयवसंस्थानविशेषः ।

ākṛtiḥ jātiliṅgākhyā । jātergotvāderhi । sāsnādisaṁsthānaviśeṣo liṅgam ।

Jāti — समानप्रसवात्मिका जातिः ।

samānaprasavātmikā jātiḥ ।

Upādhi — निमित्तम्। तदर्थश्च प्रयोजकम् । धर्ममात्रं स च क्वचिद् जात्यादिः । क्वचिद्भिन्नोऽपि भवति ।

nimittam । tadarthaśca prayojakam ।
dharmamātraṁ sa ca kvacid jātyādiḥ ।
kvacidbhinno 'pi bhavati ।

→

In the *Nyāyasiddhāntamuktāvalī*, this issue is discussed in detail in the Śabdakhaṇḍa chapter. The *Dinakarī* states that for the sake of simplicity only one denotative function is only in the individual, universal and form because one cannot have a knowledge of the one without the other. That is why in *Nyāya-sūtra jātyākṛtivyaktayaḥ padārthaḥ*, the word *padārthaḥ* is put in the singular number.

The modern Naiyāyikas, however, point out that the denotative function is only in the individual qualified by the universal, because, even without the recollection of form, there is verbal knowledge of cows and so on qualified by cowness and so on.

Dinakarī[42]

अवयवसंस्थानविशेषरूपाया आकृतेः शक्यत्वेऽपि न जातिवत्तदवच्छेदकत्वम् । सामानाधिकरण्यसंबन्धस्य शक्यतावच्छेदकतावच्छेदकत्वकल्पने गौरवात् । अत्र च परस्परपरित्यागेन परस्परस्य बोधाभावात् त्रिष्वैकैव शक्तिः । एतद्बोधनायैव सूत्रे जात्याकृतिव्यक्तयः पदार्थ इत्येकवचनमिति संप्रदायः । नव्यास्तु संस्थानानुपस्थितावपि गोत्वादिना गवाद्यन्वयबोधाज्जातिविशिष्टव्यक्तावेव शक्तिः ।
avayavasaṁsthānaviśeṣarūpāyā ākṛteḥ śakyatve 'pi na jativattadavacchedakatvam । sāmānādhikaraṇyasaṁbandhasya

---

→ *Sāmānya* — नित्यत्वे सति अनेकसमवेतत्वम् । सामान्यं स्याद् अनेकसमवायि च । तच्च द्रव्यगुणकर्मवृत्ति नित्यं चेति बोध्यम् ।
nityatve sati anekasamavetatvam । sāmānyaṁ syād anekasamavāyi ca । tacca dravyaguṇakarmavṛtti nityaṁ ceti bodhyam ।

Vyakti — पदार्थमात्रम्। यथा जात्यादिरपि व्यक्तिः। तल्लक्षणञ्च व्यक्तित्वम्। तच्च प्रमेयत्वम्। व्यक्तिः गुणविशेषाश्रयो मूर्तिः।
padārthamātram । yathā jātyādirapi vyaktiḥ । tallakṣaṇañcavyaktitvam । tacca prameyatvam । vyaktiḥ guṇaviśeṣāśrayo murtiḥ ।

42. Vattanky, pp. 66, 208-9.

śakyatāvacchedakatā vacchedakatvakalpane gauravāt । *atra ca parasparaparityāgena parasparasya bodhābhāvāt triṣvaikaiva śaktiḥ* । *etadbodhanāyaiva sūtre jātyākṛtivyaktayaḥ padārtha ityekavacanamiti saṁpradāyaḥ* । *navyāstu saṁsthānānupasthitāvapi gotvādina gavādyanvayabodhājjātiviśiṣṭavyaktāveva śaktiḥ* ।

This was the view of the Naiyāyikas, who adopted a middle course and took *śakti* to be in *jātiviśiṣṭa vyakti*. *Śabda* being *kārya* and *anitya*, *śabda* has *jāti* of several kinds. That is, a word *ghaṭa* has the following *jāti*s in it *śabdatva*, *ghaṭa śabdatva* and the alphabets also have *gakāra jāti* and *ṭakārajāti.*

The Nature of Sound as per Nyāya-Vaiśeṣika

The Nyāya theory of sound is remarkably advanced and accepted in Śāstra. Coming to the nature of sound, *ākāśa* is defined in terms of *śabda*, which is considered a quality that is peculiar to *ākāśa* alone.

शब्दगुणकम् आकाशम् ।

śabdaguṇakam ākāśam ।

Although *ākāśa* is static, all-pervasive and eternal, sound is non-pervasive and transient — it is produced, is audible for a short duration and then perishes. Sound differs largely in its nature and behaviour from odour, taste, colour and touch, the four recognised specific qualities of the first four *dravya*s — viz., earth, water, fire and air. Again, the specific quality of a tangible reference is found to last as long as the substance exists, e.g. the white colour of a conch or shell. But sonority is only an occasional or accidental characteristic of a sound-producing body, say, when the conch is blown or dropped on a hard floor. Other substances have the properties within themselves, e.g. coolness of water, or sweetness of sugar.

Odour is also detected only when the particles of earthly

matters waft in the breeze and enter the olfactory sense. But sound is heard even in a place where the sound-producing body is absent; one can hear a canon fired miles away. Sound thus shows peculiarities which cannot be seen in the qualities of the tangible substances, and therefore belongs to an intangible substance.

श्रोत्रग्रहणो योऽर्थः स शब्दः ।
सम्योगविभागाच्च शब्दाच्च शब्दनिष्पत्तिः ।

śrotragrahaṇo yo 'rthaḥ sa śabdaḥ ।
samyogavibhāgācca śabdācca śabdaniṣpattiḥ ।

Every sound has a beginning and an end. It is produced by three means, *saṁyoga, vibhāga* and *śabda* itself. When we clap our hands, sound a drum or drop a metal plate, it is *saṁyoga*, impact brought about, that produces sound. When we snap or break a stick, or tear paper, it is *vibhāga*, dissociation, that brings about sound. Since the sound is heard even at a distance away from where it is produced, it follows that it has to reach the ear. This is achieved by the sound produced generating another, which in turn generates another *śabda*, so that a series is produced which propagates like a wave train, *śabda-santāna*, till it reaches the ear and becomes audible. It is this last sound that is actually heard, not those that precede it.

शब्दप्रकरणम् । शब्दोऽम्बरगुणः श्रोत्रग्राह्यः क्षणिकः कार्यकारणोभयविरोधो सम्योगविभागशब्दजः प्रदेशवृत्तिः समानासमानजातीयकारणः । स द्विविधो वर्णलक्षणो ध्वनिलक्षणश्च ।

śabdaprakaraṇam । *śabdo 'mbaraguṇaḥ śrotragrāhyaḥ kṣaṇikaḥ kāryakāraṇobhayavirodho samyogavibhāga śabdajaḥ pradeśavṛttiḥ samānāsamānajātīyakāranaḥ* । *sa dvividho varṇalakṣaṇo dhvanilakṣaṇāśca* ।

THE PROPAGATION OF SOUND

Many passages in works like *Nyāyamañjarī* describe the

production and propagation of sound with remarkable scientific accuracy. Sound is basically of two kinds, produced by *saṁyoga* and *vibhāga*, impact and breaking asunder. To explain how sound can be heard at a distance, it is shown that sound vibrations travel in a series, like the waves or ripples caused by dropping a pebble in a pond. From one point, another sound that travels uniformly outwards in all directions is produced. From every point on the new wave, another is produced so that the whole series travels outward. This is in fact the very definition of a wavefront arrived at by sixteenth-century physicists in Europe to explain motion of sound and light waves.

In the two-dimensional plane, the analogy of ripples in a pond is given. When the same phenomenon is in three-dimensonal space, each point sound gives rise to a spherical waveform moving outward in all directions. The analogy of sound propagation in three-dimensional space is the *kadamba* flower, which has globular inflorescence and appears like concentric spheres expanding outward as it grows.

Taṛkasaṅgraha (p 33):

> श्रोत्रग्राह्यो गुणः शब्दः । आकाशमात्रवृत्तिः । स द्विविधः । ध्वन्यात्मको वर्णात्मकश्च । ध्वन्यात्मको भेर्यादौ । वर्णात्मकः संस्कृतभाषादिरूपः ।
>
> *śrotragrāhyo guṇaḥ śabdaḥ । ākāśamātravṛttiḥ । sa dvividhaḥ । dhvanyātmako varṇātmakaśca । dhvanyātmako bheryādau । varṇātmakaḥ saṁskṛtabhāṣādirūpaḥ ।*

Nyāyabodhinī

> शब्दं लक्षयति श्रोत्रेति । शब्दत्वे अतिव्याप्तिवारणाय गुणेति । रूपादौ अतिव्याप्तिवारणाय श्रोत्रेति । स त्रिविधः संयोगजो विभागजः शब्दजश्चेति । यथा भेरीदण्डसंयोगजो झन्कारादिशब्दः हस्ताभिघातसंयोगजन्यो मृदङ्गादिशब्दः । वंशे पाट्यमाने दलद्वयविभागजः चट चट शब्दः । शब्दोत्पत्तिदेशमारभ्य श्रोत्रदेश पर्यन्तम् वीचीतरङ्गन्यायेन कदम्बमुकुलन्यायेन

वा निमित्तपवनेन शब्दधारा जायन्ते । तत्र उत्तरोत्तरशब्दे पूर्वपूर्वशब्दा: कारणम् ।

śabdaṁ lakṣayati śrotreti । śabdatve ativyāptivāraṇāya guṇeti । rūpādau ativyāptivāraṇāya śrotreti । sa trividhaḥ saṁyogajo vibhāgajaḥ śabdajaśceti । yathā bherīdaṇḍasaṁyogajo jhaṅkārādiśabdaḥ hastābhighātasaṁyogajanyo mṛdaṅgādiśabdaḥ । vaṁśe pāṭyamāne daladvayvibhāgajaḥ caṭa caṭa śabdaḥ । śabdotpattideśamārabhya śrotradeśa paryantam vīcītaraṅganyāyena kadambamukulanyāyena vā nimittapavanena śabdadhārā jāyante। tatra uttarottaraśabde pūrvapūrvaśabdāḥ kāraṇam ।

On the first of these two hypotheses, the airwaves implied in the transmission of sound is the nature of what we call transverse waves; on the second, of the nature apparently of longitudinal waves.

सन्तानसिद्धिः । तत्राद्यः शब्दः सम्योगविभागहेतुकः । तस्मात् शब्दान्तराणि कदम्बगोलन्यायेन परिशेषात्तु सर्वदिक्कानि ।

santānasiddhiḥ । tatrādyaḥ śabdaḥ samyogavibhāga hetukaḥ । tasmāt śabdāntarāṇi kadambagolanyāyena pariśeṣāttu sarvadikkāni ।

As the momentum of the impact series (which constitutes the efficient cause of the sound waves) grows feebler and feebler in the course of transmission through the air particles, the sound at last dies away. Gaṇgeśa, in the *Cintāmaṇi* holds that the propagation is not from molecule to molecule, but travels in ever-expanding circles as in water waves, perhaps in spherical layers by compression of masses of air; and these airwaves, the vehicle of sound, are exceedingly swift. This explains the velocity of sound.

THE APOHA THEORY

The Buddhists held the view that the primary import of a

word is only *apoha* or *atadvyāvṛtti*, distinction from all others different from it. In their view, there is no such thing as *jāti*, or universal, but only a mental construct, a fiction. The individual particular is unique and momentary, having no relation to anything but itself, and so cannot form the content of verbal convention or cognition. But what do we understand by a word, say, *ghaṭa*? It is an undeniable fact that the word does correspond to an objective external reference. What *ghaṭa* then really signifies is that a certain thing possessing some peculiarities which distinguish it from all other things. *Ghaṭa* itself does not convey any real idea, but only that it is not anything else. The speaker thinks that he is presenting an objective fact to the hearer, while the hearer is deluded into thinking that the import is an objective reality. The import of a word is actually a negative implication which is believed to be an objective universal. The word, a positive reality, which is at bottom negation of negation and a concept without an objective basis. The Realists have severely criticised this doctrine and the controversy seems endless.[43]

THE GRAMMARIANS' VIEW

Vyākaraṇa initially meant Padaśāstra, which explained form, structure and meaning of words, while Vākyaśāstra or Mīmāṁsā analyses the semantics of sentence. Both these schools study language; hence *śabda* is taken to mean only articulate sound. The *Mahābhāṣya* presents many issues in the philosophy of language and with the *Vākyapadīya*, Vyākaraṇa *darśana* became an extensive field in its own right, showing that rich debate was current in Indian philosophy.

Śabda-pramāṇa is considered vital in Vyākaraṇa, the only reliable means of knowing *dharma* and to understand Vedas.

43. Sastri, 1959, p. 143.

Patañjali gives the fivefold purpose of studying Vyākaraṇa as *rakṣā, ūha, āgama, laghu, asandeha.* True knowledge of Vedas and understanding the correct Word can lead to *niḥśreyasa.* This is the *sāyujya* that Patañjali mentions.

Vyākaraṇa takes word in the latest form, *śabdatattva,* as equated to *Brahman* or Consciousness.

अनादिनिधनं ब्रह्म शब्दतत्त्वं यदक्षरम् ।
विवर्ततेऽर्थभावेन प्रक्रिया जगतो यतः ॥१॥

anādinidhanaṁ brahma śabdatattvaṁ yadakṣaram । *vivartate 'rthabhāven prakriyā jagato yataḥ* ॥1॥

Bhartṛhari examines the efficiency of other *pramāṇa*s in understanding *dharma,* and pronounces them all as inadequate. It is Chandas, Veda alone, that can teach *dharma* and offer an explanation acceptable to all. Logic may seem very effective and convincing, but what one clever man can show to be reasonable can always be coloured by another man's cunningness.[44] Even the intuitive, spiritual knowledge of *yogī*s and *ṛṣi*s has its source in the Vedas,[45] says Bhartṛhari.

What is a word?, asks Patañjali. In reply he gives two alternative definitions:

येनोच्चारितेन सास्नालाङ्गूलककुदखुरविषाणिनां संप्रत्ययो भवति स शब्दः ।
अथवा प्रतीतपदार्थको लोके ध्वनिः शब्द इत्युच्यते ।

---

44. *VP,* I.34 : यत्नेनानुमितोऽप्यर्थः कुशलैरनुमातृभिः।
अभियुक्ततरैरन्यैरन्यथैवोपपाद्यते॥

yatnenānumito'pyarthaḥ kuśalairanumātṛbhiḥ ।
abhiyuktatarairanyairanyathaivopapādyate ॥

45. *VP,* I.30 : न चागमादृते धर्मस्तर्केण व्यवतिष्ठते।
ऋषीणामपि यज्ज्ञानं तदप्यागमपूर्वकम्॥

na cāgamādṛte dharmastarkeṇa vyavatiṣṭhate ।
ṛṣīṇāmapī yajjñānaṁ tadapyāgamapūrvakam ॥

yenoccāritena sāsnālāṅgūlakakudakhuraviṣāṇinām saṁpratyayo bhavati sa śabdaḥ । *athavā pratītapadārthako loke dhvaniḥ śabda ityucyate* ।

Like the Mīmāṁsā definition, word is that which, upon utterance, conveys the meaning.

THE ETERNAL NATURE OF ŚABDA

Is the word eternal or not? Kātyāyana's *Vārttika* begins with *siddhe śabdārthasambandhe*. This shows that in Vyākaraṇa, *śabda*, *artha* and *sambandha* between them are all *nitya*. What is *nityatva*? The grammarian's broad outlook and ability to accommodate a variety of views is evident right from the first chapter of the *Mahābhāṣya*.

In the very definition of *nityatva*, Patañjali displays deep acumen and tolerance. The grammarians do not have a rigid ontological standpoint on most issues and only see how the words can convey the concept, no matter what the viewpoint.

Patañjali says that the tenets of Vyākaraṇa are built on the premise that *śabda* is *nitya*, going by *siddhe śabdārthasambandhe*. *Siddha* in normal usage of language refers to both eternal *nitya* and produced entities, *kārya*. According to *Saṁgrahagrantha*, we must consider it as *nitya*.

यद्येव नित्य: अथापि कार्य: उभयथापि लक्षणं प्रवर्त्यमिति । नित्यपर्यायवाची सिद्धशब्द: । अयं खलु नित्यशब्दो नावश्यं कूटस्थेष्वविचालिषु भावेषु वर्तते। किं तर्हि। आभीक्ष्ण्ये वर्तते ।[46]

yadyeva nityaḥ athāpi kāryaḥ ubhayathāpi lakṣaṇaṁ pravartyamiti । *nityaparyāyavācī siddhaśabdaḥ* । *ayaṁ khalu nityaśabdo nāvaśyaṁ kutastheṣvavicāliṣu bhāveṣu vartate* । *kiṁ tahir* । *ābhīkṣṇye vartate* ।

46. *MBh*, pp. 22-27.

Is this eternal nature of the word based on its meaning being the form (class) or the individual? Is the import of the word *jāti* or *vyakti*? The answer is, class or universal. Why is that? Because the universal is permanent, while the individual is transitory. So the word, its import and their relation are eternal.

आकृतिर्हि नित्या द्रव्यमनित्यम् ।
नित्याकृतिः । कथम् । न क्वचिदुपरतेति कृत्वा सर्वत्रोपरता भवति ।
द्रव्यान्तरस्था तूपलभ्यते ।

ākr̥tirhi nityā dravyamanityam ।
nityākr̥tiḥ । katham । na kvaciduparateti kr̥tvā sarvatroparatā bhavati। dravyāntarasthā tūpalabhyate ।

Or, alternatively, we could take the form or structure, *ākr̥ti*, transitory and the substance (*dravya*) as real (*nitya*). How is this known? This is what happens when a lump of clay takes the shape of a jar, cauldron, etc. Or when the same piece of gold may first have the shape of earrings and later take on form of a bangle. Here, the class, earring or necklace, etc. is transitory while the substance, *dravya* remains the same.

द्रव्यं हि नित्यमाकृतिरनित्या ।
आकृतिरन्या चान्या भवति द्रव्यं पुनस्तदेव । आकृत्युपमर्दनेन द्रव्यमेवावशिष्यते ।

dravyaṁ hi nityamākr̥tiranityā ।
ākr̥tiranyā cānyā bhavati dravyaṁ punastadeva। ākr̥tyupamardanena dravyamevāvaśiṣyate ।

Further, we see a different, more flexible view on the concept of universal or class. The words *ākr̥ti* referring to structure/shape/form and *jāti* referring to class/universal are not used in a technical sense. In the *Mahābhāṣya*, we first came across two very important concepts, viz. the *jāti* and *pravāhanityatā* of *śabda*. These two issues are path-breaking and define the points where Vyākaraṇa differs from Mīmāṁsā.

How is the word *nitya*? After all, sound is ephemeral; it is produced, lasts a short while and then perishes. The same in the case of an active thought in the mind. But the same word can be repeatedly pronounced; even if one is destroyed, its form exists in another individual. Patañjali explicitly states that not only permanent, immutable, motionless entities are *nitya*. Whatever endures[47] is also *nitya*. This is the subject of study in the Jāti Samuddeśa and Dravya Samuddeśa in the third *kāṇḍa* of the *Vakyapadīya*.

The concept of *pravāha nityatā* is beautifully summed up by Bhartṛhari in the following *kārikā* that whether *nitya* or *kārya*, we cannot trace the origin of a word; like the case of the chicken and the egg, it is not possible to say which came first and it is better to accept them as given and as existing all the time.

नित्यत्वे कृतकत्वे वा तेषामादिर्न विद्यते ।
प्राणिनामिव सा चैषा व्यवस्था नित्यतोच्यते ।
nityatve kṛtakatve vā teṣāmādirna vidyate ।
prāṇināmiva sā caiṣā vyavasthā nityatocyate ।

— *VP*, I.28

IMPORT OF A WORD

In the *Mahābhāṣya* the word *ākṛti* is used in both senses, as the configuration or shape of a particular thing and also the class property or universal which aids in identifying the object.

Peter M. Scharf makes a careful analysis of the different instances where the word is used in the two different senses and observes,

---

47. तदपि नित्यं यस्मिंस्तत्त्वं न विहन्यते।
tadapi nityaṁ yasmiṁstattvaṁ na vihanyate ।

> In the second sense, it is synonymous with the term *jāti,* both of which terms are used by Patañjali to refer to both the class and class property. However, this does not imply that an author who uses the term *ākṛti* in both senses is limited to conceive of a class property as an entity with concrete structure perceptible by the senses.[48]

Gaurinath Sastri presents the discussion in the *Mahābhāṣya* on whether the import of a word is in *jāti* as endorsed by Vājapyāyana or in *vyakti* as advocated by Vyāḍi.[49]

When we say "cow" we do not mean an individual cow of a specific colour or size, but any cow. The fact that the same word is used to denote innumerable individual animals shows that the import of the word is in the class concept, *sāmānya* or *jāti.* It is not as if the individual is not denoted at all — in fact the case ending with gender and number does correspond to the individuals, but the *vyakti* cannot be the denotation of the word. Firstly, the number of individuals being infinite, the word cannot denote all of them — if it does, a person will not be able to even comprehend the word. Secondly, if the word denotes a particular individual of that class, another word will have to be found to denote another word of the same class! Thirdly, a word can never truly grasp all peculiarities of an individual — these can only be known by direct apprehension or intuition,[50] so it is only the class concept that the word denotes. When a boy is shown one cow, he has no trouble recognising another one at a different place having different features. This simple practical fact is the basis of the whole theory.

---

48. Scharf, 1996, p. 17.

49. *The Philosophy of Word and Meaning*, 1959, Import of Words.

50. Ibid., p. 144.

गौरस्य कदाचिद् उपदिष्टो भवति । स तं अन्यस्मिन् देशेऽन्यस्मिन् कालेऽन्यस्मिन् च वयोवस्थायां दृष्ट्वा जानाति अयं गौरिति ।[51]

gaurasya kadācid upadiṣṭo bhavati । *sa taṁ anyasmin deśe 'nyasmin kāle 'nyasmin ca vayovasthāyāṁ dr̥ṣṭvā jānāti ayaṁ gauriti* ।

The strongest argument in favour of the Individualist theory is that actions cannot be performed on the universal, and so in practice, word denotes the individual. We cannot explain usage such as "A horse is born" or "A dog is dead" if the word denoted the universal.

The *Mahābhāṣya* asks how we can know what is indicated as the import of a word? Is it the *ākrti*, class, or is it the individual object, *dravya*? Is there any criterion to choose between the two? Patañjali answers that both are to be considered as the import of a word; sometimes it is *ākr̥ti* or *jāti*, at other times *dravya* or *vyakti*.

He quotes Pāṇini as authority and shows that Pāṇini has formulated *sūtra*s incorporating both senses of a word.

किं पुनराकृतिः पदार्थः आहोस्विद् द्रव्यं । उभयमित्याह । कथं ज्ञायते । उभयथा ह्याचार्येण सूत्राणि पठितानि । आकृतिं पदार्थं मत्वा जात्याख्यायामेकस्मिन् बहुवचनमन्यतरस्यां इत्युच्यते । द्रव्यं पदार्थं मत्वा सरूपाणाम् इत्येकशेष आरभ्यते ।

kiṁ punarākr̥tiḥ padārthaḥ āhosvid dravyaṁ । *ubhayamityāha* । *kathaṁ jñāyate* । *ubhayathā hyācāryeṇa sūtrāṇi paṭhitāni* । *ākr̥tiṁ Padārthaṁ matvā jātyākhyāyāmekasmin bahuvacanamanyatarasyāṁ ityucyate* । *dravyaṁ padārthaṁ matvā sarūpāṇām ityekaśeṣa ārabhyate* । — p. 21

When a general statement is made, say, that cows should be venerated, we can say *gauḥ pūjyaḥ* or *gāvaḥ pūjyaḥ* In *jātyākhyāyām*

51. *MBh*, vol. II, p. 91.

anyatarasyām, Pāṇini accepts *jāti* as the referent of the word. When *jāti* is the referent, the word can be used either in singular or plural.

In *sarūpāṇām ekaśeṣa ekavibhaktau*, Pāṇini accepts *dravya* as both, the form of the word, and the import of the word, i.e. *śabda jāti* and the *artha jāti*. When a number of particulars are indicated, only one word is taken as representative and the others are elided to avoid repetition.

Later in the *paspaśāhnika*, *jāti* in *varṇa*s or phonemes is also clearly stated, as opposed to the Mīmāṁsā position.

Bhartr̥hari puts this issue in a nutshell by stating that the triad of Pāṇini, Kātyāyana and Patañjali have taken *śabda*, *artha* and their *sambandha* to be eternal in *VP* I.23, discussed in Chapter 4

The word has a form, formed in totality by the *varṇa*s comprising it. That is, it has a whole structure formed by the phonemes. What Patañjali refers to as *saṁghāta* or *sphoṭa* is over and above the phonemes that are uttered in sequence. The *sphoṭa* gives identity to the word, and also is responsible for the fact that the word endures in the mind. Thus, as the phonological structure of the word, *sphoṭa* and *jāti* are two sides of the same coin.

This point is emphasised in the first *kāṇḍa, Vākyapadīya*, wherein most of the *kārikā*s are devoted to the doctrine of *sphoṭa*. The *Vr̥tti* on this *kārikā* stresses that *śabda* is *nitya* because its form is *nitya*. The word is known by its structure, its acoustic pattern.

This form is different to the *śabdatvasāmānya*. *Śabdatva* is the largest set, the universal set, in mathematical parlance, while the smaller classes such as *vr̥kṣa-śabdatva*, etc. are subsets. Just as several universals exist in a pot, *ghaṭa*, viz.

dravyatva, pṛthivītva and *ghaṭatva,* each being a subset of the previous, in the same way, a particular word, e.g. *vṛkṣa* has the following series of universals in it: *guṇatva, śabdatva, vṛkṣaśabdatva.* This is in agreement with the Nyāya view on nature of *śabda,* which the Vyākaraṇa school takes as applicable to *dhvani,* sound waves.

Only when there is some transformation confined to certain space lasting a certain duration, of the nature of compressions and rarefactions in air molecules, is a sound perceived; thereby it derives its nature of being *kārya,* by action. Therefore, we talk of both universal and specific utterances. When even the same phoneme, e.g. *va* is uttered, the articulatory effort is slightly different depending on whether the *va* is part of the word *vṛkṣa* or *vṛka.* But we call both by the same label *va.* This illustrates the existence of both the *jāti* in *va* and the two *vyaktis,* in *vṛka* and *vṛkṣa.* The grammarians do not have to implicitly adopt the definition of *jāti* as stated in other schools. It is not as if only entities with parts that vividly manifest the class concept can possess universal. Although uttered in sequence, words also manifest the universal. Specific actions are also considered to have universal such as walking, cooking, etc., for the entire duration in which each occurs, as the entire class can never be manifest all at once.

The *Vṛtti* under *VP* I.23[52] says:

यदा तु दिग्विशेषावधिपरिच्छिन्नसंयोगविभागकार्य्याणां कर्मणां प्रबन्धः क्रमेणोपलब्धो भवति, अथ जातिविशेषोपाधियुक्ता व्यवहाराः प्रकल्पन्ते । यदा त्वन्वयप्रबन्धः क्रमेणोपलब्धो भवति, अथ जातिविशेषोपाधियुक्ता व्यवहारा अवतिष्ठन्ते ।

yadā tu digviśeṣāvadhiparicchinnasaṁyogavibhāgakāryyāṇāṁ karmaṇāṁ prabandhaḥ krameṇopalabdho bhavati, atha

52. *Brahmakāṇḍa,* p. 44.

jātiviśeṣopādhiyuktā vyavahārāḥ prakalpante । *yadā tvanvayaprabandhaḥ krameṇopalabdho bhavati, atha jātiviśeṣopādhiyuktā vyavahārā avatiṣṭhante* ।

Further,

न चावश्यं शास्त्रान्तरे परिदृष्टा जात्यभिव्यक्तिप्रक्रिया वैयाकरणैः परिगृह्यते । न ह्यभिव्यक्तिमताम् अभिव्यञ्जकैराश्रितानामेवाभिव्यक्तिर्नियमेन क्रियते । तत्रासत्यपि शब्दव्यक्तिसमवाये शब्दाकृतेः वर्णावयवावग्रहप्राप्तसंस्काराभिः क्रमोत्पन्नाभिर्बुद्धिभिः पूर्वमगृहीता, अव्यक्तं गृहीता वा संस्कृतेऽन्तःकरणे चरमविज्ञानेन आकृतिः परिच्छिद्यते ।

na cāvaśyaṁ śāstrāntare paridṛṣṭa jātyabhivyaktiprakriyā vaiyākaraṇeḥ parigṛhyate । *na hyabhivyaktimatām, abhivyañjakairāśritānāmevābhivyaktirniyamena kriyate* । *tatrāsatyapi śabdavyaktisamavāye śabdākṛteḥ varṇāvayavāvagrahaprāptasaṁskārābhiḥ kramotpannābhir-buddhibhiḥ pūrvamagṛhītā, avyaktaṁgṛhītā vā saṁskṛte 'antaḥkaraṇe caramavijñānena ākṛtiḥ paricchidyate* ।

— p. 45

PRĀKṚTA DHVANI AND VAIKṚTA DHVANI

Even within the audible sound, *dhvani*, that manifests the true *śabda*, Bhartṛhari makes an inner distinction as *prākṛta* and *vaikṛta dhvani*.[53] At the first moment of articulation, when the *sphoṭa* impells the organs of articulation such as tongue, throat, etc., at the time of manifestation, they are called *prākṛta dhvani*s, which are essential for the purpose of recreating *sphoṭa*. Fresh from the mould, as it were, it is the *prākṛta dhvani* thaṭ reveals the phonological structure that is inherent in *sphoṭa*. The *prākṛta dhvani* does possess *hrasva*, *dīrgha*, *pluta* of the *varṇa*, which is necessary for conveying the difference in, for example, *nada* and *nāda*. The *prākṛta dhvani* reveals the

53. Subramania Iyer, *Bhartṛhari*, Poona: Deccan College, p. 119.

sphoṭa in a flash. The reason for the *sphoṭa* to remain in the mind for a while, or to continue to flash for the duration of utterance are the *vaikṛta dhvani*s which are produced subsequent to the *prākṛta dhvanis*, *vaikrṭa dhvani*s possess variation of utterance in speed, tone, volume, etc.

Harking back to the popular Nyāya explanation of propagation of sound, *prākṛta dhvani* is what is produced by the *saṁyoga vibhāga* of the *karaṇa*, instruments of articulation, the first sound. *Vaikṛta dhvani*s are the secondary sounds produced later on by the *prākṛta dhvani*s.

These undergo distortion which may change the quality of the sound we hear. *Prākṛta dhvani*s have no distortion and represent the *sphoṭa* in manifest form.

As Yajnaveer Dahiya explains:

> इदमत्र प्रतिपत्तव्यम् – यं प्राकृतध्वनिरिति मन्यन्ते तमेव तार्किका वाचक शब्दरूपेण व्यवहरन्ति यं च ते वैकृतध्वनिरिति स्वीकुर्वन्ति तं च तार्किका ध्वनिरिति पदेनावगृण्हन्ति ।[54]
>
> *idamatra pratipattavyam — yaṁ prākṛtadhvaniriti manyate tameva tārkikā vācaka śabdarūpeṇa vyavaharanti, yaṁ ca te vaikṛtadhvaniriti svīkurvanti taṁ ca tārkikā dhvaniriti padenāvagṛṇhanti* ।

Thus *prākṛta dhvani* and *vaikṛta dhvani* pair have slightly different significance which are also akin.

1. The *prākṛta dhvani* is the true prototype of the *sphoṭa*, the manifestation of the phonological structure, while the *vaikṛta dhvani*s are those which bear possible variation in speed, timbre, volume, etc.

2. The organs of articulation directly produce *prākṛta*

54. *Bhartṛhari*, p. 161.

dhvani while these then produce the *vaikṛta dhvanis*. Upon reaching the ear, the latter are responsible for the continued perception of *śabda* for the entire duration of utterance.

The *sphoṭa* has no kind of division, sequence in time, or speed of utterance. In common usage, the attributes of the sounds which manifest the *sphoṭa* are imputed to the *sphoṭa* itself. The *sphoṭa* is wrongly imagined as short or long, following the nature of the word uttered which conveys it. Even the nature of a *varṇa* as being *hrasva, dīrgha* or *pluta,* i.e. the duration of utterance, actually belong to the primary sounds, *prākṛta dhvani* and is only in name attributed as belonging to the *śabda*. The *prākṛta dhvani* reveals the identity of that word; but the attribute of speed, such as slow, fast or medium-paced, *vṛtti*, actually belong to the *vaikṛta dhvani* or secondary sounds which enable us to hear the word.

स्वभावभेदान्नित्यत्वे ह्रस्वदीर्घप्लुतादिषु ।
प्राकृतस्य ध्वनेः कालः शब्दस्येत्युपचर्यते ।।
शब्दस्योर्ध्वमभिव्यक्तेर्वृत्तिभेदम् तु वैकृताः ।
ध्वनयः समुपोहन्ते स्फोटात्मा तैर्न भिद्यते ।।

svabhāvabhedānnityatve hrasvadīghaplutādisu ।
prākṛtasya dhvaneḥ kālaḥ śabdasyetyupacaryate ।। — *VP*, I.76
śabdasyordhvamabhivyaktervṛttibhedam tu vaikṛtāḥ ।
dhvanyaḥ samupohante sphoṭātmā tairna bhidyate ।। — *VP*, I.77

Conclusion

Vyākaraṇa and Mīmāṁsā are agreed on the nature of sound. Word is manifest by the audible *dhvani*, or acoustic waves, which are transformation in air molecules. These travel in series, as in waves. When they reach the ear cavity, they are perceived by the hearing organ. From *kārikā* 100, 110, Bhartṛhari records the different views current in his time on the production of sound, which has been discussed in chapter 3.

The Nyāya-Vaiśeṣikas were realists with an interest in examining the nature of all the different entities in the world. The thrust of the Mīmāṁsā philosophy on the other hand, is interpretation of the Vedas and language study — only articulate sound was of relevance. The perspective of Śikṣā and Vyākaraṇa are also naturally language-oriented. The *Vākyapadīya* records several views current in its time (fifth century CE) on the nature of *śabda* but the two views presented in this paper sum up those of physical relevance. It is remarkable that over 20 centuries ago, the nature of sound was examined in such detail. Conspicuous is the failure to combine the two ideas of waves in space and undulations in air, which would have brought the theory closer to the truth. Each school had its own compelling reasons not to accept the other's view; *pāriśeṣanyāya* leads them to two differing views. While the propagation of *dhvani* by *śabdaja* series is generally accepted by all, the *saṁyoga-vibhāga* pair has different significance in different Śāstras.

In the Vaiśeṣika School, it is the impact and tearing asunder of sound-producing bodies. In the Mīmāṁsā School it refers to the conjunction and disjunction or compressions and rarefactions of air particles.

In Śikṣā and Vyākaraṇa they refer to the contact and separation of various parts of the mouth used for articulation such as throat, tongue, lips, palate, etc.

Although *vega saṁskāra*, momentum is recognised and tabulated as a *guṇa*, the effects of force as such are not studied probably because over the centuries Indian philosophy was directed more and more at the spiritual goal of life, and was not deeply experimental in nature.

As summed up rather strongly by Athalye-Bodas: The whole of the above theory of sound is faulty owing to the inveterate habit of the Indian philosophers to indulge in speculations in matters that can be known only by actual observation or experiments. Instead of investigating the nature of sound in such practical directions, the Naiyāyikas exhausted their energies in discussing whether sound was eternal or non-eternal.

Sphoṭa explains how language, or the thought process comprising the activity of speaking a language, has four different levels. In the undifferentiated state called *śabdatattva* it is consciousness, the enlivening spark in all living creatures and is denoted as *parā*, which is also equated with *brahmajñāna* or *Brahman*. In the *paśyantī* stage the idea is formed in the mind, though not with explicit form with *prakṛti pratyaya*, etc. This leads the mind to focus on the actual words that will effectively convey this idea. The string of words with semantic relation, with clear structure of *prakṛti pratyaya*, etc. is still in the *madhyamā* stage, but without sequence in time, as it is not yet uttered or joined with the *prāṇa* (the vital breath). This is *sphoṭa* having the form of word in the mind. When it is actually uttered by the speaker, the hearer recognises the *sphoṭa* which conveys the meaning. Thus *sphoṭa* is the cause of utterance and the cause of understanding, *artha pratīti*. This is the complete process of *śābdabodha*, in a nutshell. The grammarians' view offers the most satisfactory explanation of language covering homonyms, *śleṣa* or pun, silent reading or whispering, *upāṁśu kathana* and covers *śabda* in all its aspects.

3

Linguistic Philosophy of Bhartṛhari

The Word and the World

AFTER the triad of Pāṇini's *Aṣṭādhyāyī*, Kātyāyana's *Vārttika* and Patañjali's *Mahābhāṣya*, the next major work of the Vyākaraṇa tradition that has survived to our time is Bhartṛhari's *Vākyapadīya*. The *Saṁgraha* of Vyāḍi, composed in the centuries before Patañjali, is now lost. The *Vākyapadīya* represents the richness of debate that flourished in linguistics and other related philosophical subjects in the early centuries of the Christian era, amply illustrated by works in Nyāya-Vaiśeṣika and Mīmāṁsā of that period.

A treatise in grammar of any language is expected to deal with the technical details of that particular language. But the *Vākyapadīya* is a mixture of philosophy, general linguistics and Sanskrit grammar. There are, in all the *kāṇḍas*, especially the third one, many *kārikās* which discuss points bearing on the technical side of Sanskrit grammar, points already raised in the *Mahābhāṣya*. Philosophical speculations abound in the *Mahābhāṣya* and in the *Vākyapadīya* they reach a systematic finish. The aim of philosophy in India has never been academic study alone; the purpose of all knowledge was to help in achieving the goals of life.[1]

Both Patañjali and following him Bhartṛhari have found

1. Iyer, *Bhartṛhari*, p. 55.

an Eternal Word which runs through each and every ephemeral verbal identity.[2] There are many issues discussed in the *VP* that relate to the views of different schools of philosophy on word and meaning. Though discussions give examples from the Sanskrit language they have relevance to language in general. These may be taken as Bhartṛhari's contribution to general linguistics including semantics. Vyākaraṇa, a Vedāṅga, has also come to be counted as a *darśana*. When Madhvācārya lists Vyākaraṇa as a philosophical system in the *Sarvadarśanasaṁgraha* calling it Pāṇini *darśana*, it is from Bhartṛhari's tenets that he quotes. Pāṇinīya is used to mean Vyākaraṇa, but it is always Bhartṛhari's philosophy that is addressed in the discussions of writers such as Kumārila Bhaṭṭa, Jayanta Bhaṭṭa, Pārthasārathi Miśra, Abhinavagupta and Śāntarakṣita.

While presenting the views of other schools, Bhartṛhari displays great temperance and spirit of accommodation. Very rarely does he adopt a polemical style, unlike most other writers in Nyāya, Mīmāṁsā or Buddhist schools. It is only in the Vākyakāṇḍa, when the *padavādin* argues in favour of the reality of the word as against the unity of the sentence as a whole, does he adopt a decisive, unrelenting tone. The grammarian's standpoint is that since they are studying the language common to all schools, it should be able to accommodate the divergent views.

Patañjali sets this tone in the *Mahābhāṣya* itself, while discussing the eternality of words,

किं न एतेन इदं नित्यमिदमनित्यमिति ।

kiṁ na etena idaṁ nityamidamanityamiti ।

What does it matter to us know what is eternal and what is

2. G.N. Sastri, 1991, Preface.

not? Bhartṛhari in his *Mahābhāṣya Dīpikā* points out that Vyākaraṇa is not meant to be of help to anyone in particular but is common to all.

नेदं कस्यचिदेकस्य सहायभूतम् । सर्वसाधारणम् ।

nedaṁ kasyacidekasya sahāyabhūtam । *sarvasādhāraṇam* ।

The language has to accommodate to all the Vedas, to all branches of learning. This view adds richness to the study; more the ways in which the details of the Sanskrit language can be explained, the better.[3] Continuing Patañjali's viewpoint, Bhartṛhari thus takes the view that (i) Vyākaraṇa is common to all systems of philosophy and has to accommodate itself to them and (ii) that grammar is not concerned with defining the nature of external reality and that for it, the object is what the word presents.[4] Patañjali says in the *Mahābhāṣya*:

शब्दप्रमाणका वयं यच्छब्द आह तदस्माकं प्रमाणम् ।

śabdapramāṇakā vayaṁ yacchabda āha tadasmākaṁ pramāṇam ।

Bhartṛhari echoes this as

किमस्माकं वस्तुगतेन विचारेण । अर्थस्त्वस्माकं यः शब्देनाभिधीयते ।

kimasmākaṁ vastugatena vicāreṇa । *arthastvasmākaṁ yaḥ śabdenābhidhīyate* ।

Helārāja puts these points as follows:

सर्वपार्षदं हीदं शास्त्रम्।

---

3. प्रज्ञा विवेकं लभते भिन्नैरागमदर्शनैः ।
किय‌द्दूरं वा शक्यमुन्नेतुं स्वतर्कमनुधावता ॥

Prajñā vivekaṁ labhate bhinnairāgemadarśanaiḥ ।
Kiyaddūraṁ vā śakyamunnetuṁ svatarkamanudhāvatā ॥

— *VP*, II, 495

4. Iyer, *Bhartṛhari*, p. 75.

वैयाकरणानां शब्दार्थोऽर्थः न वस्त्वर्थोऽर्थः ।

sarvapārṣadaṁ hīdaṁ śāstram ।
vaiyākaraṇānāṁ śabdārtho 'rthaḥ na vastvartho 'rthaḥ ।

For him (Bh) the limit of language is the limit of reality.[5] While accommodating the views of other *darśanas*, Bhartṛhari is clear where his own view differs. The eye of grammar is not directed outward towards the nature of external reality, but inward, towards the method of thinking, reasoning and grasping the world, towards linguistic forms. It is upon understanding the notions of language that we can comprehend what these notions embody. That is why Bhartṛhari gives his own definitions of *jāti, dravya, kāla, guṇa, liṅga,* etc. in the context of the definitions of other schools. But he never lets us forget that the same *śabda-tattva, Brahman,* pervades all aspects of the diverse cosmos and gives it unity. All discussions on *jāti, dravya, guṇa, liṅga,* etc., are connected with the *śabda-tattva* in Bhartṛhari's monistic philosophy.

All cognition, Bhartṛhari says, is connected with the Word. If this linguistic potency is withdrawn, there will be no consciousness, no cognition nor sensation of objects. The language in its manifested form is our only way of grasping anything and expressing our understanding of any object or activity in the world. The fact that direct perception is not verbalised is an objection to this theory. But even perception has the potency for linguistic expressibility.[6]

न सोऽस्ति प्रत्ययो लोके यद् शब्दानुगमादृते ।
अनुविद्धमिव ज्ञानं सर्वं शब्देन भासते ।

na so 'sti pratyayo loke yad śabdānugamādṛte ।
anuviddhamiva jñānaṁ sarvaṁ śabdena bhāsate । — *VP*, I.123

5. Tandra Patnaik, 1994, p. 12.

6. Ibid., p. 26.

Kapil Kapoor quotes from the Jāti Samuddeśa and writes:

> Bhartṛhari's theory of reality being a linguistic (mental) construct is in harmony with his philosophical foundations in the theistic philosophies in Sāṁkhya, Vaiśeṣika and Advaita thought.

For example, it is granted that the core denotation of the word is the expression of Being, *sattā* and that with reference to objects, words express both (a) universals (*ghaṭatva*) and (b) substances (a *ghaṭa*), *dravya*, as it is through particular forms as the limiting factors that the ultimate reality (*sattā*) is expressed.

सम्बन्धिभेदात् सत्तैव भिद्यमाना गवादिषु ।
जातिरित्युच्यते तस्यां सर्वे शब्दा व्यवस्थिताः ॥

sambandhibhedāt sattaiva bhidyamānā gavādiṣu ।
jātirityucyate tasyāṁ sarve śabdā vyavasthitāḥ ॥

— *VP*, III.i.33

This is no mystic conception — it actually expresses both the physical and linguistic reality.[7]

The whole cognisable world is in the form of *dharma-dharmī* and *nāma-rūpa*, which correspond to word and meaning ultimately. Bhaṭṭojidīkṣita observes in *Śabdakaustubha* that the grammarian in the course of his quest of an insignificant coin, has been rewarded with the discovery of a priceless gem when he chances to adumbrate a unique system of thought while engaged in speculations on the physical structures of linguistic forms.[8]

वराटिकाण्वेशणाय प्रवृत्तस्चिन्तामणिं लब्धवान् ।

varāṭikāṇveśaṇāya pravṛttiscintāmaṇiṁ labdhavān ।

7. "Sanskrit Grammatical Tradition from Pāṇini to Nagesa", JNU, unpublished, p. 26.

8. Sastri, *Dialectics of Sphoṭa*, p. x.

The gem is the undying and sequenceless *śabda-tattva.*

Śabda is word, both the perishable sound and the imperishable Word. But Bhartr̥hari is mainly concerned with that which is articulated and bears meaning.[9]

The first four *kārikās* in Brahmakāṇḍa summarise Bhartr̥hari's philosophy of *Śabda-Brahman*. Behind all verbal expressions through which we communicate our thoughts to others and which exhibit sequence among their constituent members there is an indivisible principle which the grammarian urges us to discover. All plurality of sound, speed of utterance, even grammatical abstractions or *apoddhāra* are only artificial devices that have pragmatic, provisional validity.

This concept has its origins in Vedic literature.

यावद् ब्रह्म विष्ठितं तावती वाक् ।

yāvad brahma viṣṭitaṁ tāvatī vāk ।

— *R̥V*, X.114.8

The Absolute and *vāk, śabda,* form a couple inseparable and existing for all time.

The *VP* starts with a statement on the immanence of Ultimate Reality, which also serves as the *maṅgala śloka.*

अनादिनिधनं ब्रह्म शब्दतत्त्वं यदक्षरम् ।
विवर्ततेऽर्थभावेन प्रक्रिया जगतो यत: ॥

anādinidhanaṁ brahma śabdatattvaṁ yadakṣaram ।
vivartate 'rthabhāvena prakriyā jagato yataḥ । — *VP*, I.1

The first line gives four epithets for the Ultimate Reality while the second line says that from it is the genesis of the cosmic world.

---

9. द्वावुपादानशब्देषु शब्दौ शब्दविदो विदु:।
एको निमित्तं शब्दानामपरोऽर्थे प्रयुज्यते। — *VP*, I.44

Brahman is without beginning or end; *Brahman* is *śabda-tattva* which is eternal and the cause of all the phonemes. It is Bhartṛhari's premise, *pratijñā*, that the essence of *śabda* and *Brahman* are One. *Brahman* is described as One whose essence is *śabda*. We cannot comprehend anything having existed before creation or after dissolution, except for *Brahman* alone. Hence it is right to describe it as *anādinidhanam*.

Ambākartrī, p. 3:

न हि ब्रह्मण: सर्गप्रवृत्ते: प्राक् किञ्चिन्नासीत् सर्गनिवृत्तेश्च पश्चान्नास्ति किमपीति कल्पयितुं शक्यते अनादित्वात् प्रवृत्तिनिवृत्तयो: कालपरिच्छेदासंभवात् ।

na hi brahmaṇaḥ sargapravṛtteḥ prāk kiñcinnāsīt sarganivṛtteśca paścānnāsti kimpīti kalpayituṁ śakyate anāditvāt pravṛttinivṛttinvṛttayoḥ kālaparicchedāsaṁbhavāt ।

Brahman is beyond all description, but can be understood in two aspects, of unity and diversity, by the power of *vidyā* and *avidyā* respectively. When understood as one by *vidyā*, it is said to be the *saṁvartta* state; when apprehended in all the variety of the universe by *avidyā*, it is called the *vivartta* state. *Vivartta* is the condition when the sole truth is cognised as many different entities as in the cognition of several items in the dream state. *Brahman* is called *akṣara* as it is the source of phonemes.

Ambākartrī on *VP*, I.1:

एकस्य तत्त्वाद् अप्रच्युतस्य भेदानुकारेण असत्यरूपोपग्राहिता विवर्त: स्वप्नविषयप्रतिभासवत् ।
इत्येवं ब्रह्मोपादानिका वर्णव्यक्तिर्घटव्यक्तिरिव मृदुपादानिका ।

ekasya tattvād apracyutasya bhedānukāreṇa asatyarūpopagrāhitā vivartaḥ svapnaviṣayapratibhāsavat ।

ityevaṁ brahmopādānikā varṇavyaktirghaṭavyaktiriva mṛdupādānikā ।

This *kārikā* which contains the whole of Bhartṛhari's philosophy of *Śabda-Brahman* in a nutshell has an immaculate choice of words that are relevant in the narrow sphere of linguistics also. *Akṣara* also means phoneme, *artha* also means meaning and *prakriyā* means technical operations in grammar!

The *Vṛtti* quotes an ancient text that mentions *vivartta* of two kinds, *mūrtivivartta* connected with place and *kriyāvivartta* connected with time.

Vṛtti:

उक्तञ्च मूर्तिक्रियाविवर्तौ अविद्याशक्तिप्रवृत्तिमात्रम् तौ विद्यात्मनि तत्त्वान्यत्वाभ्याम् अनाख्येयौ । एतधि अविद्याया अविद्यात्वम् इति ।

uktañca mūrtikriyāvivartau avidyāśaktipravṛttimātram tau vidyātmani tattvānyatvābhyām anākhyeyau । *etadhi avidyāyā avidyātam iti* ।

Ambākartrī:

गेहे घटः क्षेत्रे गौरित्यादिना देशभेदावग्रहरूपेण यत् गोघटादिरूपाणाम् अर्थानाम् अवस्थानम् स मूर्तरूपो विवर्तः । यत्तु तेषामेव जायते नश्यति वा घट इत्यादिना उत्पादविनाशादि क्रियोपहितरूपेणावस्थानम् स क्रियारूपो विवर्तः ।

gehe ghaṭaḥ kṣetre gaurityādinā deśabhedāvagraharūpeṇa yat goghaṭādirūpāṇām arthānām avasthānam sa mūrtarūpo vivartaḥ । *yattu teṣāmeva jāyate naśyati vā ghaṭa ityādinā utpādavināśādi kriyopahitarūpeṇāvasthānam sa kriyārūpo vivartaḥ* ।

Mūrtivivartta is the appearance of diverse objects in different locations, i.e. they are differentiated by difference in shape, size, location, i.e. place or dimension in space. *Kriyāvivartta* refers to the fact that all action is defined by time — the perceptibility of anything that is happening is only with the passage of time. So it is *mūrtivivartta* and *kriyāvivartta*, place and time, that describe and define all that we cognise. Without this sequence we would not be able to distinguish between cognitions.

The Ultimate Reality is eternal and immutable, free from the attributes wrought by place and time that define our ordinary cognition. In today's scientific context, it can be said that all phenomena are described by coordinates of space and time, which are necessarily relative concepts, fixed to any particular frame of reference. The three Cartesian coordinates of location correspond to three dimensions of length, breadth and depth while the fourth is time. That space and time define the myriad diversity of the cosmos is quite clear from the explanation of the two kinds of *vivarttas*.

This idea is further dwelt upon in the following *kārikās*:

एकमेव यदाम्नातं भिन्नं शक्तिव्यपाश्रयात् ।
अपृथक्त्वेऽपि शक्तिभ्यः पृथक्त्वेनेव वर्तते ।

ekameva yadāmnātaṁ bhinnaṁ śaktivyapāśrayāt ।
apṛthaktve 'pi śaktibhyaḥ pṛthaktveneva vartate ।

— *VP*, I.2

As the long tradition teaches us, *Brahman* is one but by the different powers or capacities, it appears divided into the variety we see around us. Although not really different, by the multiplicity of the powers, it appears to be different in different cases. Here the word *eka* is used to denote identity or sameness, not number. The purpose is to show that everything in the world, although appearing to be of great multiplicity, is actually non-different to *Brahman*. Numerical unity is not intended here, but identity of nature.

Vṛtti:

यावद् विकारविकारिविषयमेकत्वरूपं पृथक्त्वरूपं वा सर्वं तत्प्रत्येकत्वानति-
क्रमेणेत्येतदाम्नातम् ।

yāvad vikāravikāriviṣayamekatvarūpaṁ pr̥thaktvarūpaṁ vā sarvaṁ tatpratyekatvānatikrameṇetyetadāmnātam ।

The world is *vikāra*, while *Brahman* is *vikāri*, but they are not different from each other. Just as jars and pots are *vikāra* of clay *vikārī* which is undergoing change, or ornaments which are transformations of gold, in the same way, the ultimate common material, so to speak, is *Brahman*.

Ambākartrī, p. 11:

लोके ये घटरुचकादयो विकाराः ये च मृत्सुवर्णादयो विकारिणस्तत्र विकारिणामेकत्वे विकाराऽञ्च परस्परं नानात्वेऽपि तत्सर्वं सर्वप्रकृतेर्ब्रह्मण एकत्वादेकमित्याम्नातं ब्रह्मणि एकत्वञ्च भेदव्यवच्छेदमात्रम् न त्वेकत्वसंख्यायोगरूपम् ।

loke ye ghaṭarucakādayo vikārāḥ ye ca mr̥tsuvarṇādayo vikāriṇastatra vikāriṇāmekatve vikārā 'ñca parasparaṁ nānātve 'pi tatsarvaṁ sarvaprakr̥terbrahmaṇa ekatvādekamityāmnātaṁ brahmaṇi ekatvañca bhedavyavacchedamātram na tvekatvasaṁkyāyogarūpam।

Vr̥ṣabhadeva explains in the *Paddhati* here that unlike in several other schools like Sāṁkhya, Bauddha, Nyāya, Vaiśeṣika, etc., which are dualistic or pluralistic philosophies, Bhartr̥hari has here used *eka* to deny divisions of any kind in his Monistic view. For authority to take this stand, he quotes the Veda, *āmnāya*.

Paddhati, p. 14:

एकशब्दो भेदप्रतिषेधवचनः । ततोऽन्यद्भिनत्तीति । किं पुनरत्र प्रमाणमित्याह आम्नातमिति । आम्नायो वेदः । तत्र पठितमाम्नातम् । शक्तयोऽत्र घटादयः पदार्थाः योग्यता वा। ते च भिन्नरूपाः । ते च तस्यात्मभूता एवेति शक्तिव्यपाश्रयेणापि न तस्य भेदः ।

ekaśabdo bhedapratiṣedhavacanaḥ । *tato 'nyadbhinattīti* । *kiṁ punaratra pramāṇamityāha āmnātamiti* । *āmnāyo vedaḥ* । *tatra paṭhitamāmnātam* । *śaktayo 'tra ghaṭādayaḥ padārthāḥ yogyatā vā*। *te ca bhinnarūpāḥ* । *te ca tasyātmabhūtā eveti śaktivypāśrayeṇāpi na tasya bhedaḥ* ।

It is the one ultimate reality that is diversified and considered many, due to diverse potencies; although not different, they appear different. All six states of being referred to in *Nirukta*,[10] which are causes for difference in being, are due to the power of time, which though one and undifferentiated, seems to have divisions imposed on it by external, relative factors. It is time that brings about sequence in uttering, without which the *sphoṭa* cannot be manifested. This makes *kālaśakti* very important in Bhartṛhari's philosophy. He names it the only independent power of *Brahman*. *Śabda-tattva* is the one root cause, from which springs forth the entire cosmos.

अध्याहितकलां यस्य कालशक्तिमुपाश्रिताः ।
जन्मादयो विकाराः षड् भावभेदस्य योनयः ॥

adhyāhitakalāṁ yasya kālaśaktimupāśritāḥ ।
janmādayo vikārāḥ ṣaḍ bhāvabhedasya yonayaḥ ॥
— *VP*, I.3

The *Vṛtti* here refers to the elucidation in the Jāti Samuddeśa:

जातिसमुद्देशे तु न्यक्षेण भावविकारा वक्ष्यन्ते ।

एकस्य सर्वबीजस्य यस्य चेयमनेकधा ।
भोक्तृ भोक्तव्य रूपेण भोगरूपेण च स्थितिः ।

jātisamuddeśe tu nyakṣeṇa bhāvavikārā vakṣyante ।

ekasya sarvabījasya yasya ceyamenakadhā ।
bhoktṛ bhoktavya rūpeṇa bhogarūpeṇa ca sthitiḥ ।
— *VP*, I.4

This harks back to Vedic utterances quoted in the *Ambākartrī*

10. *janma, sthiti, vṛddhi, vipariṇāma, kṣaya, nāśa.*

वाचारंभणं विकारो नामधेयं मृत्तिकेत्येव सत्यम् ।

vācārambhaṇaṁ vikāro nāmadheyaṁ mṛttiketyeva satyam ।

Although the source of all activity and variety is One, it appears as if there is great multiplicity and mutually exclusive entities such as the enjoyer, the enjoyed and the enjoyment. For example, in a simple sentence consisting of subject, verb and object, we cannot comprehend how all three can be the same thing. Such is the power of *avidyā* in all *vyāvahārika* levels. But the truth is beyond that and there is nothing actually different from *Brahman* and all appearance of differentiation is also due to its own powers.

Vivartta and Pariṇāma

There is much debate in the philosophical tradition of the last 14 centuries and among modern scholars on the position of *vivartta* and *pariṇāma* in Bhartṛhari's metaphysics. Is the manifestation of the world that springs from *Brahman* an unreal appearance, illusion caused by *avidyā, vivartta* as expounded in Ādi Śaṅkara's Advaita Vedānta? Or is it real, formal transformation, *pariṇāma*? Sāntarakṣita and his commentator Kamalaśīla explain the first *kārikā* of Brahmakāṇḍa in both views one after the other, without referring to Advaita Vedānta.[11] Vācaspati Miśra refers to both interpretations in *Nyāyakārikā*. M. Biardeau points out that nowhere in the *kārikā*s does Bhartṛhari explicitly call the manifestations as unreal, so it is *pariṇāma* that he means. K.A. Subramania Iyer is of opinion that Bhartṛhari's views are in close corroboration with those of Śaṅkara. Gaurinath Sastri prefers the *pariṇāma* view.[12]

Pt. Vamadeva Acharya writes that since both words are

11. Iyer, *Bhartṛhari*, p. 130.

12. *Philosophy of Bhartṛhari*, pp. 40-41.

used in a synonymous sense, the difference in connotation was not relevant in Bhartṛhari's time. The definition of *pariṇāma* is

उपादान सम सत्ताक कार्यापत्तिः परिणामः ।

upādāna sama sattāka kāryāpattiḥ pariṇāmaḥ ।

The definition of *vivartta* is

उपादान विषम सत्ताक कार्यापत्तिः विवर्तः ।

upādāna viṣama sattāka kāryāpattiḥ vivartaḥ ।

Two contrary terms cannot be applied in the same sentence. Therefore it is apparent that the difference in connotation was a later development. There is evidence that the words were understood synonymously by earlier writers. The Buddhist philosopher Śāntarakṣita and his commentator Kamalaśīla both use the word *pariṇāma* to explain *vivartate* in *VP* I.1 while quoting Bhartṛhari in order to refute him. Later in the *Tattvasaṅgraha* itself, Bhartṛhari's philosophy is presented from the Advaita viewpoint as the eternal *brahma-tattva* which actually has no divisions, appearing as the world in all its diversity due to *avidyā*. Kamalaśīla elaborates on this verse saying that *Brahman* is not really changing; but due to the ignorance or darkness caused by *avidyā* covering the mind, the eye imagines that it is seeing variety in the different forms and colours.[13]

The words *vivartta* and *pariṇāma* are used in the same sense

13. *Tattvasaṁgraha*:
नाशोत्पादसमालीढं ब्रह्म शब्दमयं परम् ।
यत्तस्य परिणामोऽयं भावग्रामः प्रतीयते ।।१२८।।
अथाविभागमेवेदं ब्रह्मतत्त्वं सदा स्थितम् ।
अविद्योपप्ल वाल्लोको विचित्रं त्वभिमन्यते ।।१४४।।

Pañjikā:

न च तस्य परमार्तेन परिणामः ।
किन्तु अविद्यातिमिरोपहतबुद्धिलोचना नीलादिभेदेन विचित्रमिव मन्यते ।

together by Bhartṛhari in *kārikā* 120 of the Brahmakāṇḍa. He says that it has long been known in tradition that everything is a transformation of world and the entire universe has sprung from Chandas, which is Veda, *oṁkāra*, standing for *śabda-tattva*.[14] This is an important issue that is again and again discussed and reaches clarity in the *jāti* and *dravya samuddeśa*s where a cosmological view is taken.

Vivartta means "extension", "circular movement" and "reversion" or "backward movement".

The word seems to be used in *VP* in the sense of *viśeṣeṇa vartate,* meaning the numerous activities of the world. It appears to be, in my view, that this division in the sense of the transformation being real or unreal is not necessary for clarity in Bhartṛhari's philosophy; it could mean both kinds. After all, everything originates in *Brahman*, both, illusory *vivartta* and formal *pariṇāma*. Bhartṛhari endorses relative status of reality and even grammatical devices in different levels of understanding.

To understand the transformation in one or the exclusive sense would necessarily restrict the definitions while Bhartṛhari tries so hard to show the expedience of such devices. In the realm of *śābdabodha* also, the question is of no relevance; *padārtha* could be *vivartta* and *pariṇāma* of *śabda*. The concept of *upādāna kāraṇa* or *samavāyī kāraṇa*s in material objects does not apply in the case of *śabda* being *kāraṇa* for *artha* or *buddhi* being *kāraṇa* for uttering *śabda*. In this case, *śabda* is *kāraṇa* by *jñānatva,* just as it is *kāraṇa* for *pravṛtti* and *nivṛtti.*

In Bhartṛhari's view of origin of sound, the process is described as totally psychological.

---

14. शब्दस्य परिणामोऽयमित्याम्नायविदो विदुः ।
छन्दोभ्य एव प्रथममेतद् विश्वं व्यवर्तत ॥१२०॥ — *VP*, I

अथायमान्तरो ज्ञाता सूक्ष्मे वागात्मनि स्थितः ।
व्यक्तये स्वस्य रूपस्य शब्दत्वेन विवर्तते ।

athāyamāntaro jñātā sūkṣme vāgātmani sthitaḥ ।
vyaktaye svasya rūpasya śabdatvena vivartate ।

— *VP*, I.112

Sphoṭa

The term *sphoṭa* is derived from the root *sphuṭ* which means "to burst" and is defined in two ways: in its linguistic sense, it is normally defined as "that from which the meaning bursts forth", i.e. "the word denoting a meaning — *sphuṭati artho yasmāt*. Secondly it means "an entity manifested by sounds", *sphuṭyate varṇaiḥyaḥ*, i.e. *varṇābhivyaṅgyaḥ*. Although the sounds are produced serially, the *sphoṭa* manifested by different sounds is bereft of the time-series pattern.[15]

While examining process of cognition by language, i.e. *śabda-pramāṇa*, we arrive at the indivisible meaning-bearing unit (*sphoṭa*). The Mīmāṁsā and Vyākaraṇa schools are agreed to a good extent as regards the process of *śābdabodha*. The difference is that while the Mīmāṁsā philosophy adheres to the *nityatva* of individual *varṇa*s to maintain *apauruṣeyatva* of *śabda*, the problem of temporal sequence in language remains unresolved. How can a word or sentence, which is pronounced in succession, never simultaneous and also evanescent, function together to convey meaning? Cognition by *śabda* is neither through memory nor inference, as the meaning is perceived immediately upon hearing a word. The word is what triggers the flash of understanding and when an idea flashes in the mind, it can be verbalised as word. Bhartṛhari's brilliant answer to the issue is the indivisible *sphoṭa*. It is not something technically constructed or posited

15. S.D. Joshi, 1967, p. 57.

in Śāstra, but something that even the common man can perceive.

According to Mīmāṁsā, each *varṇa* is unique and eternal, manifested by the *dhvani* each time it is uttered. As a group albeit with sequence, they by their very nature, automatically, convey meaning. Every time a word is uttered, e.g. the word, *gauḥ*, said by eight different speakers, the same syllables, *g*, *au*, and *visargaḥ*, manifest by the eight different speakers, convey the meaning of cow. But in Bhartṛhari's view, the very fact that the word *gauḥ* has been uttered by eight different speakers means that a word with the same archetype, *gauḥ* has been uttered eight times. That is, all eight utterances are of the same type. This is the essence of the relation between *jāti* and *vyakti*, or class and individual. It is by recognising the identity brought about by the class-concept that the particular utterance, e.g. by a child or man or parrot is understood. This in a nutshell, is the *sphoṭa*, very closely associated with the concept of universal or *jāti*. Thus the word first reveals itself before revealing the meaning. Each word has two powers: that of revealing its object or its import, *grāhakatva*, and the other, of revealing its very form *grāhyatva*. These two aspects are also called name, *saṁjñā* and named, *saṁjñin*. The *grāhya* aspect comes into use in grammar, as operations are done on the words themselves and not on what they mean. Some looked upon the universal aspect, *jāti* as the *saṁjñā* and the particular aspect *vyakti* as the *saṁjñā*.

स्वं रूपमिति कैस्तु व्यक्तिः संज्ञोपदिश्यते ।
जातेः संसृष्टा जातिस्तु प्रतिपद्यते ।।
संज्ञिनीम् व्यक्तिमिच्छन्ति सूत्रे ग्राह्यमथापरे ।
जातिप्रत्यायिता व्यक्तिः प्रदेशेषूपदिश्यते ।।

svaṁ rūpamiti kaistu vyaktiḥ saṁñyopadiśyate ।
jāteḥ saṁsṛṣṭā jātistu pratipadyate ।।

saṁñinīm vyaktimicchanti sūtre grāhyamathāpare ।
jātipratyāyitā vyaktiḥ pradeśeṣūpadiśyate ॥ — *VP*. I.68-69

The enunciation of *jāti* or *sāmānya* has very early beginnings in Indian philosophy and has evolved over time as the debate between the different schools developed. The grammarians' view of *jāti* need not coincide with that of other schools exactly, as explained in the *Ambākartrī*. This is the main focus of this study. Much of the dialogue in linguistics is between Mīmāṁsā and Vyākaraṇa. In Mīmāṁsā the eternal relation between word and the thing meant is not direct contact, *saṁyoga* or *saṁśleṣa* but in the form of purport. In Vyākaraṇa also, the connection is mental.

बुद्ध्यारूढ एव शब्दस्यार्थो न बाह्यः ।

buddhyārūḍha eva śabdasyārtho na bāhyaḥ ।

There are many words such as *kinnara, apsaras, rākṣasa, gandharva, svarga, naraka*, etc., which are current in popular usage, but not accurately understood by anybody.[16] Just as the relation of a word is not with the external object, but with its import, the latter is also not associated with the audible sound waves. *Sphoṭa* is the paradigm in the mind which has an identity as a whole. It can be understood in totality in a flash. The *sphoṭa* of a word or sentence has no size — the words "elephant" and "ant" have equivalent size in our understanding. The disparity in their actual sizes has no bearing. In practice, the syllables are uttered in sequence. From grasping or hearing parts, we understand the totality in totality. As an intermediate step, we understand parts as parts which are provisional means to reach the whole. Although cognition proceeds in parts, it is holistic. It is this mental process which Bhartṛhari refers to as the unreal

16. Ramdev Tripathi, 1977, p. 573.

means to reach the truth. *Sphoṭa* as enunciated in *VP,* I.44 is discussed in detail in Chapter 4.

In the case of articulated words, *upādāna śabda,* the import of a word is in the meaning bearing unit, not in the syllables alone. The sounds are required to reveal the word, but when the word is grasped as a unit, it immediately causes the meaning to flash in the mind. Since the process is so quick, we do not realise it or the fact that the sounds we hear are not exactly what we are grasping and that the purport of what we hear is actually a result of this. While we can discern between a cognition and its object, we tend to perceive the *dhvani* and *śabda* as one. Bhartṛhari devotes many *kārikā*s to pointing out this simple fact in the Brahmakāṇḍa and gives many illustrations from daily life. The enunciation of *sphoṭa* is done in a very positive, convincing manner without adopting a polemical tone.

The Akhaṇḍa Vākya

Though individual words in a sentence do have their individual meaning, they are only steps in comprehending the meaning of an utterance in totality. Bhartṛhari's *sphoṭa* corresponds to the whole sentence-meaning, which strikes the hearer at one shot. Grammarians have some to be known as the upholders of the doctrine of *sphoṭa,* the doctrine that the real expressive word is an indivisible entity called *sphoṭa* which is over and above the sounds (*dhvani*s) which are many in number and are uttered by the speaker in temporal sequence in order to manifest the *sphoṭa,* the real expressive word which has usually the form of the sentence and which is an indivisible unity.

Though Bhartṛhari talks of the three different kinds of *sphoṭa*s associated with phonemes, words and sentences, only the whole sentence is the true meaning-bearing unit, the *akhaṇḍa vākya*. The entire second *kaṇḍa* is devoted to explaining and illustrating this point in different contexts. While all intermediate steps of breaking up the sounds or meanings into parts only have pragmatic, transactional importance, it is the indivisible, unified meaning as a whole that flashes in the mind that is of value. Bhartṛhari does not talk of *varṇa-sphoṭa, pada-sphoṭa* in a technical sense. These came much later, put forth by Kauṇḍa Bhaṭṭa, as the concept of *sphoṭa* developed in greater detail.

It is the sentence alone that is fit for communication. In the natural manner that language is used, we make sense of the uttered sentence as a whole, as *saṁhitā*. The common man is not aware of the technical grammatical analysis of an utterance when he hears it the meaning just flashes in his mind in one shot. This is *pratibhā*, flash of understanding.

Even though a great grammarian himself, Bhartṛhari gives priority to the natural process of cognition over the technical requirements of grammar. We cannot question what is already current in the world, what is in the nature of things, but only try to understand and explain it in conformity to universal experience. Even Kumārila Bhaṭṭa says in the Ākṛtiyāda that there is no point in *paryanuyoga*, trying to find a logical reason for natural phenomena such as fire being hot, etc.

From the *akhaṇḍa-avākya* point of view, it is very easy to explain how elliptic sentences, *apabhraṁśa* words and compound words convey a unified meaning. It is clear in these cases that the meaning in totality is significant while the words used are only secondary, only a means towards it. It does not even matter which particular language, say, French or Hindi, a person may be using; the urge to communicate the idea in the mind, as sentence-meaning, has no form.

The criteria by which *apoddhāra* is brought about in a particular language will conform to the rules of *prakriyā* of that language. But their significance is only provisional and artificial. This is what Bhartṛhari means by their being unreal and the meaning alone being real.[17]

पदप्रकृतिः संहिता ।

padaprakṛtiḥ saṁhitā ।

This can be explained in two ways: *tatpuruṣa samāsa* explains it as *padānām prakṛtiḥ saṁhitā,* which follows Bhartṛhari's view. *Bahuvrīhi* explains it as *padāni prakṛtiḥ yasyāḥ sā saṁhitā* which gives greater precedence to words.

The completeness of sense in a sentence structure cannot be fixed by any conventional definitions such as *padasamūho vākyam, ekatiṅ vākyam* or *vākye mukhyaviśeṣaḥ*. A sentence can even have a structure outside these definitions and still convey complete sense. For instance, *dvāram* when what is meant is *dvāram 'pidhehi*. In such cases the circumstances and context help bring about the intended meaning. Language is not something we always use in a precisely defined manner. In practical situations, the point is, words are vital to communicate sense, but only incidental and secondary to the purport.

Bhartṛhari on the Concept of Pratibhā

Bhartṛhari is the first linguistic philosopher to connect the linguistic potency in the mind with *pratibhā*, flash of understanding or genius. In his holistic approach, the *śabda-tattva* from which the ability to communicate springs forth is fundamental and deep-rooted; it is the very consciousness that empowers all living creatures. Thus he compares the latent *śabda* in an infant, whence the ability to learn a particular

---

17. उपायाः शिष्यमाणानां बालानामुपलापनाः ।
असत्ये वर्त्मनि स्थित्वा ततः सत्यं समीहते ॥ — *VP*, II.238.

language springs, to the instinct of birds building their nests and the newborn calf-suckling from its mother. *Pratibhā* means flash of immediate, intuitive illumination. *Prati* + *bhā*, to shine, illuminate. With the grasp of a situation, there is a flash of intuition or instinct that comes from within that takes a decision in the mind. It is the creative function of the mind. The logical structure that it may have is beyond description.

As far as human beings are concerned, it is indivisible. Gayatri Rath writes:

> Bhartṛhari's concept of *pratibhā* has many faces. Its linguistic features are discussed psychologically. It is similar as basic instinct which is the guiding principle of all sorts of activities on this earth. This instinctive type of *pratibhā* has further been utilised, adjusted, extended by rhetoricians mainly as an extension of poetic expression.[18]

The knowledge obtained by the contact of the senses with the outside world, from the words of others and even from the application of logic or human rationale, is variable and unreliable. According to Bhartṛhari, there is another kind of knowledge which is reliable. It is rooted within ourself and taking place all the time, when we see something or hear words. It is a flash of understanding, not only of the data presented to us by the senses but also of what to do in a certain situation. It is a capacity to take in a situation and act accordingly. All living beings, from the highest to lowest have it, including animals and birds. When we hear and comprehend a sentence, its meaning is understood in a flash. Bhartṛhari declares this flash of understanding to be *pratibhā*, equal to intuition. This flash of understanding of the purport of the whole sentence is different from the meaning of the individual words, sometimes understood even before the

18. Rath, 2000, p. 152.

whole sentence has been uttered. It is not easy to explain this flash of understanding to others. But one cannot deny its existence. Everybody experiences it without being able to define it. The same sentence could convey different meanings to different people. For instance, *gato 'staṁ arkaḥ* simply means that the sun has set. But to a thief, this means that he may start his work, to a student, that he may start his evening prayers and to a damsel, that she may set out to meet her lover! Thus the import of the sentence is not mechanically conveyed by the words themselves, but is synthesised by the *pratibhā* of the speaker and the hearer. This is the basis of *vyañjanā*

> विच्छेदग्रहणेऽर्थानां प्रतिभान्यैवोपजायते ।
> वाक्यार्थ इति तामाहुः पदार्थैरुपपादितम् ॥१४३॥
> इदम् तदिति सान्येशमानाख्येया कथञ्चन ।
> प्रत्यात्मवृत्तिसिद्धा सा कर्त्रापि न निरूप्यते ॥१४४॥
> यथा द्रव्यविशेषाणां परिपाकैरयत्नजः ।
> मदादिशक्तयो दृष्टः प्रतिभास्तद्वताम् तथा ॥१४८॥
> स्वरवृत्तिं विकुरुते मधौ पुंस्कोकिलस्य कः ।
> जन्त्वादयाः कुलयादिकरणे केन शिक्षिताः ॥१४९॥

> *vicchedagrahaṇe 'rthānāṁ pratibhānyaivopajāyate* ।
> *vākyārtha iti tāmāhuḥ padārthairūpapāditam* ॥143॥
> *idam taditi sānyeśamānākhyeyā kathañcana* ।
> *pratyātmavr̥ttisiddhā sā kartrāpi na nirūpyate* ॥144॥
> *yathā dravyaviśeṣāṇāṁ paripākairayatanjaḥ* ।
> *madādiśaktayo dr̥ṣṭaḥ pratibhāastadvatām tathā* ॥148॥
> *svaravr̥ttiṁ vikurute madhau puṁskokilasya kaḥ* ।
> *jantvādayāḥ kulayādikaraṇe kena śikṣitāḥ* ॥149॥
>
> —*VP*, II

Pratibhā arises spontaneously in all beings. It is like the power of intoxication which develops in certain substances on fermentation, without anything external done to them. Birds, for example, have no prompting from anybody to build their nests, or cuckoos to sing in spring. *Pratibhā* is something very comprehensive. It includes intelligence of a high order, intuitive knowledge, the instinct of animals and birds and the spontaneous activities of new-born babies. According to Bhartṛhari there is no knowledge which is not entwined with the word. By *śabda*, he does not mean, in this context, the manifest word of any particular language which is uttered by the speaker and heard by the hearer. The baby is born with the residual *śabda bhāvanā*, the latent capacity for human language. It is emphasised that no human effort can impart this *pratibhā* to the baby.

The Development of Sphoṭa

The grammarian tradition holds that *sphoṭa* is the true language — the real vehicle of meaning. The theory of *sphoṭa* has been acclaimed as one of the most important contributions to the central problem of general linguistics as well as philosophy of language.

For Bhartṛhari, however, this is a wrong term: meaning bearing unit. *Sphoṭa* is the real substratum, proper linguistic unit, which is identical also with its meaning. Language is not the vehicle of meaning or conveyor-belt of thought. Thought anchors language, and language anchors thought. *Śabdanā*, language is thinking; and thought vibrates through language. In this way of looking at things, there cannot be any essential difference between a linguistic unit, its meaning or the thought it conveys. *Sphoṭa* refers to this non-differentiated language principle. Thus I believe that it is sometimes even incorrect to ask whether *sphoṭa* is or is not the meaning bearing speech unit in Bhartṛhari's system.[19]

19. B.K. Matilal, 1990, p. 85.

Although the concept of *sphoṭa* is found in very early writings such as Āgama,[20] it was after Bhartṛhari's exposition that it came to be discussed systematically in Śāstra. All important writers quote Bhartṛhari and add to the arguments on the subject. The Mīmāṁsakas and Naiyāyikas denounce it as an unnecessary fictitious and even illogical proposition while the grammarians point out the untenability and inadequacy of process of *śābdabodha* without *sphoṭa*. In the Sphoṭavāda chapter of *Ślokavārttika*, the great writer Kumārila Bhaṭṭa pointed out the defects in upholding *sphoṭa* as meaning-bearing unit and showed *varṇa*s to be quite adequate to convey sense. Maṇḍana Miśra was a notable exception among Mīmāṁsakas, who accepted *sphoṭa* and argued in its favour, showing that even Kumārila was arguing under mistaken notions on the matter. He pointed out the shortcomings of Kumārila's arguments and upheld *sphoṭa* in the *Sphoṭasiddhi*. Jayanta Bhaṭṭa painstakingly explained the concept of *sphoṭa* according to Vaiyākaraṇas and the objection of Mīmāṁsakas, before presenting his own view according to the Nyāya philosophy school, in the sixth *āhnika* of the *Nyāyamañjarī*. The last chapter of the *Vyākaraṇa-Laghu-Mañjūṣa* of Kauṇḍa Bhaṭṭa, named Sphoṭa Nirṇaya, elaborates on the division of *sphoṭa*. Following is a brief sketch of the main points in development of *sphoṭa* across the centuries.

In the *Nirukta* of Yāska, there is a reference to the word in the mind in the first chapter.

इन्द्रियनित्यं वचनमिति औडुम्बरायणः ।

indriyanityaṁ vacanamiti auḍumbarāyaṇaḥ ।

It is explained as stating that a sentence is actually in the mental faculties of the language — users, the speaker and

20. G.N. Sasrti gives details in *Philosophy of Bhartṛhari.*

the hearer.[21] To even classify words into categories, some sort of permanence has to be attribued to them. This debate is evident even in the *Nirukta* as an objection raised by the camp of Auḍumbarāyaṇa who says that since *śabda* is *anitya*, classification into four types does not make sense. Durgācārya[22] explains this viewpoint clearly that since the *śabda* lasts in the speaker's mind or hearer's mind only in the duration of utterance, it is *anitya*. Since the sentence never exists intact at any instant of time and we cannot count words that are being uttered with those that have already ceased to exist, we cannot divide words into groups as if they are permanent entities.[23] The answer to these objections follows in the next section of *Nirukta*.[24]

Durgācārya explains that the words, though uttered in sequence, are connected. Grammar joins the parts together to form a whole, just as *upasarga-dhātu* or stem and suffix are joined together when uttered together. Although the *śabda* is produced in the mouth, once it comes out, it encompasses all the space around it. When a person hears it after it is uttered and still understands, there is a permanence associated with the *śabda*. Durgācārya explains that since words are short and more efficient than other methods such as miming or gestures, it is the preferred mode of precise communication.

Patañjali's enunciation of *sphoṭa* is also different to the

21. Matilal, p. 79.

22. Durgā in *Ni*. 1.1.17 — इन्द्र आत्मा स येन ईयते लिङ्ग्यते अनुमीयते च - इति तदिन्द्रियम्। तस्मिन्नित्यमिन्द्रियनित्यम् ।

23. शृणु - यावदेव वक्तुर्वागिन्द्रिये श्रोतुश्च श्रोत्रेन्द्रिये वचनं तावदेव तदस्तीति शक्यते वक्तुं प्रच्युतं च नास्ति । वाक्यं समस्तमुद्भूतं तदिन्द्रिये नावतिष्ठते यावदवयवभूतानि पदान्यवयवस्थितानि परिसङ्ख्यातुम्।

24. अयुगपदुत्पन्नानां वा शब्दानामितरेतरोपदेशः ॥२॥ शास्त्रकृतो योगश्च ॥३॥ व्याप्तिमत्त्वात्तु शब्दस्य ॥४॥ अणीयस्त्वाच्च ॥५॥ शब्देन संज्ञाकरणं व्यवहारर्थं लोके ॥५॥

concept of later writers. At one place he says that *sphoṭa* is the speech or language, *śabda* while the noise or sound, *dhvani,* is a quality, a feature of the speech or language. It is explained that the noisy element in language, the audible part, can be soft or loud, or long or short, but the *sphoṭa* is what remains constant or the same, unaffected by the peculiarities of individual speakers. Śabara Svāmi also discusses the concept in rejecting it in the *Tarka Pāda,* without mentioning *sphoṭa* explicitly; he mentions the word *saṅghāta* which Patañjali also uses. This shows that the concept of the unspoken word was current in philosophy since very early times.

Within the grammatical tradition itself, the concept of *sphoṭa* has undergone much change. Patañjali, Bhartṛhari and later grammarians notably represented by Nāgeśa and Kauṇḍa Bhaṭṭa, were perhaps more influenced by the Tantra schools. In the *Paspaśāhnika,* Patañjali discusses *śabda, dhvani* and *sphoṭa.* While examining the ultimate building blocks or unit of language, he asks whether phonemes have meaning or not. We may assume the ultimate meaning-bearing unit, as in the example of *kūpa yūpa sūpa,* the difference in meaning is due to a single *varṇa,* all others being identical. The whole can only be an aggregate of its parts; so unless each *varṇa* is meaningful, how can the word as a whole have meaning? Patañjali's answer is that in the case of verbal roots, stems, suffixes and particles consisting of a single phoneme are considered as meaning-bearing units. But if a word consists of more than one phoneme, meaning is not apprehended from each phoneme separately.

Patañjali maintains that the significance of phonemes lies in differentiating one word from another; but, according to him, the differentiating unit is not necessarily the significant unit. His view is that the isolated phonemes are not directly connected with meaning. As far as the meaning is concerned, the words are indivisible into phonemes. Therefore, Patañjali thinks that it is necessary to postulate a single entity, *saṁghāta*, as conveying the meaning. The whole should be looked upon as a unit different from its parts, from the standpoint of function or purpose and should not necessarily be considered as belonging to the parts like a chariot, each of whose part does not by itself possess the capacity to move on a road, the word as a whole is efficient in its function.

As far back as the *Mahābhāṣya*, it is shown that the level at which utterance and meaning have one-to-one relation depends on the function at that level, on what is relevant at that point of analysis, that is, the *apoddhāra* that Bhartṛhari later talks about. The function of language at sound level is to distinguish between significant units. The function of language at the word level is to signify meaning. The later grammarians identify the significative level of the language as one with *sphoṭa*.[25]

Patañjali does not identify *sphoṭa* with the meaning-bearing nature of language. When Patañjali says that *saṅghāta* is one and indivisible, he means to say that it cannot be divided into phonemes as far as the meaning is to be conveyed. In other words, a word undivided into phonemes conveys meaning. When the later grammarians say that the word is indivisible, they mean that it cannot be divided into a sequence of either morphemes or phonemes.

Patañjali always maintains the hierarchy of linguistic units and does nor reduce them to indivisible entities. While the loophole in the Mīmāṁsā position stems from the temporal sequence of utterances, Patañjali's reason for accepting the whole as a single entity is not based on the unaccountability of the sequence. On rule 1.4.109 (*paraḥ sannikarṣaḥ saṁhitā*),

25. S.D. Joshi, p. 5.

Patañjali says that since the phonemes or *varṇa*s cannot be articulated simultaneously, we have to consider that the unity of the word exists only in our mind. In the conceptual word we have succession of phonemes; the sequence has to be understood as a mental one. Patañjali admits the three propositions: (i) *saṅghāta* is divisible into phonemes structurally, (ii) the sequence of phonemes can exist in our mind and it forms the *saṅghāta*, and (iii) the meaning-bearing nature of *saṅghāta* cannot be assigned individually to each phoneme.[26]

But the later grammarians do not admit the mental sequence, the sound pattern, that forms the permanent aspect of a word. They use the unaccountability of the succession of phonemes as the main argument in establishing *sphoṭa*. In Patañjali's explanation, the phonemes are structurally part of the *saṅghāta*, although they lack its significative power. The later grammarians assume that *sphoṭa* is revealed by the phonemes, but is beyond association with any structure, neither connected with isolated phonemes nor series thereof.

S.D. Joshi writes that later grammarians read more into the concept of *sphoṭa* than what even Bhartṛhari intended. His contention is that Bhartṛhari nowhere explicitly states in the *VP* that *sphoṭa* is the meaning-bearing unit. He cites the nine instances where the word *sphoṭa* is mentioned in the *VP* and illustrates that every time it is connected with sound pattern and not meaning.

In *kārikā* (*VP*) I.44, Bhartṛhari says that word is of two kinds — one is the cause of articulate sound and the other that of meaning. This means that linguistic utterances can be analysed at two levels — phonetic and semantic. The later grammarians take this significative work, *śabda*, as *sphoṭa*.

---

26. S.D. Joshi, p. 13.

Since it is at the mental level of meaning, it cannot be divided further into parts along any criterion. S.D. Joshi writes:

> The linguistic utterance which is directly related to meaning is *sphoṭa*. Accordingly it cannot be divided into smaller constituents, because in conformance with the established opinion, *sphoṭa* is the single partless utterance. In the context of meaningful speech unit, Bhartṛhari has never used the term *sphoṭa*. He has strictly reserved it for indicating the distinctive function of language possibly from the point of auditory perception of sounds that reach the listeners' ears. — *VP*, I.81, 97

Bhartṛhari's statements clearly point out that any sound, revealed to the listener's ear through the process of articulation, is the *sphoṭa*, which need not necessarily involve the notion of meaning. In other words he has used the term *sphoṭa* in the context of distinctive function of language. On the other hand, the later grammarians use the term *sphoṭa* with reference to significative aspect of language. The later grammarians have gone so far as to identify *sphoṭa* with the Vedāntic *Brahman*.

The metaphysical aspect of the word doctrine has been wrongly attributed to the doctrine of *sphoṭa*. The higher reality of the *Śabda-Brahman* is confused with the lower reality of *sphoṭa*. The identity between *śabda* and the *Brahman* conceived by the later grammarians is based on the misunderstanding of the real nature of *sphoṭa*. This ultimately leads to the misunderstanding of the modern Sanskritists that the *sphoṭa* doctrine is mysterious.[27]

The importance of the *sphoṭa* theory, from the point of linguistic interpretation, has been overlooked and neglected by later commentators. It will be interesting to note here that Bhaṭṭojidīkṣita, in his *Śabda-Kaustubha* anticipates that the

27. J. Brough, pp. 41-42.

linguistic theory of *sphoṭa* has no direct connection with the metaphysical doctrine of *Śabda-Brahman*. He states that Bhartṛhari, dealing with the nature of linguistic utterance, incidentally discusses the illusory creation of the world. It is also interesting that Śaṅkara criticises the doctrine of *sphoṭa* and spares the doctrine of *Śabda-Brahman* which generally agrees with his philosophical thinking. By identifying the doctrine of *śabda* with *sphoṭa*, the later grammarians have subjected the theory of *sphoṭa* to a great deal of unnecessary mystification, and as a result, the importance of linguistic interpretation has been sidetracked.[28]

From B.K. Matilal: *The Word and the World: Early Indologists* (Keith, 1928, 387; De, 1925, 180) described *sphoṭa* as a mysterious or mystical entity, and this was probably due to its association with Bhartṛhari's notion of *Śabda-Brahman* or the eternal verbum (Sastri, 1959). But this was a mistake. In spite of its metaphysical underpinning which M. Biardeau (1964: 268) rightly emphasised, there is a linguistic treatment of the concept well documented by Bhartṛhari himself, and other grammarians. Brough (1951: 34) and Kunjunni Raja (1969: 97-148) were right to stress the point that *sphoṭa* was not a mysterious entity. There is another dispute that is connected with it, whether the *sphoṭa* in Bhartṛhari is simply the linguistic sign in its aspect of meaning-bearer (Brough, Kunjunni Raja) or whether it represents an abstract class of sounds sorted out and extracted by the listeners from gross matter (Joshi, 1967: 40), Cardona (1976: 302) thinks that Brough's thesis should be modified since Bhartṛhari also talks about *varṇa sphoṭa*, which refers to a sound unit of the language system, not to any meaning-bearing unit. Iyer (1969: 158-59) has, however, refuted Joshi's rather sweeping comment that

28. S.D. Joshi, p. 43.

Bhartṛhari's *sphoṭa* had nothing to do with the meaning-bearing speech unit. In *Mahābhāṣya-dīpikā*, Bhartṛhari reinterpreted Patañjali's use of the word *śabda*. This was noted by Patañjali as the meaning-bearing element in the Paspaśa section. Bhartṛhari glossed this as *sphoṭa* and characterised it as eternal.[29]

The Sphoṭavāda of Kumārila Bhaṭṭa

The Mīmāṁsakas regard the phonemes in cluster as expression of meaning, while the grammarians refute the view. The Sphoṭavāda starts with a discussion of *śabda* and sound; *sphoṭa* is discussed in the latter portion. Continuing the discussion on what is meant by a word, Śabara is quoted by Kumārila's commentator Pārthasārathi Miśra in the *Nyāyaratnākara*: *gakāra*, *aukāra* and *visarjanīya* form what is called the word, *gauḥ*. The whole is a sum of its parts. Only when the *avayavas*, the parts, coexist simultaneously can they together form the whole, the *avayavin*. Letters of a word are evanescent; no two exist simultaneously: how then can they be parts of a unit such as word. Although the *varṇas* are eternal and all-pervading, they are manifested one by one. Otherwise, they would manifest all words at all times! Also, the whole has to be greater than the parts; how can anything be greater than the *varṇas*, each of which is *nitya* and *vibhu*? Therefore, the word as a separate entity is not composed of the letters. Therefore, since the word *go* as an entity is itself not established, how can the *sāmānya*, *gotva*, which would reside in the word by *samavāya*, be accepted?

विच्छिन्नयत्नव्यङ्ग्यैश्च नित्यैः सर्वगतैरपि ।
व्यतिरिक्तपदारम्भो वर्णैर्नात्रोपपद्यते ॥६५॥
अनारब्धे च गोशब्दे गोशब्दत्वम् कथम् भवेत् ।
वर्णसामान्यवच्चापि न तत्कल्पनमर्हति ॥६६॥

29. Matilal, 1990, p. 84.

vicchinnayatnavyaṅgyaiśca nityaiḥ sarvagatairapi ।
vyatiriktapadārambho varṇernetropapadyate ॥65॥
anārabdhe ca gośabde gośabdatvam katham bhavet ।
varṇasāmānyavaccāpi na tatkalpanamarhati ॥66॥

If the go *śabda* is recognised as such, the Mīmāṁsaka says that it is because *śabda* is one and eternal. But the opponent points out that every individual utterance is unique and different, so *sāmanya* or *jāti* as to be conceded. But Kumārila's answer is that this can be achieved by taking the *varṇa*s as the same; there is no need to postulate the word as a separate entity or *samudāya* or collection of sounds. By not accepting the *samudāya* as a separate entity, the nature of *śabda* or its effectiveness in conveying meaning is in no way affected.

वर्णात्मनामभेदाच्च सिद्धा सामान्यधीरपि ।
समुदायोऽपि तेभ्योऽस्य वारणीयोऽनया दिशा ॥६७॥
अभेदसमुदायस्तु तेषाम् धर्मो न दुष्यति ।
तेषामस्ति हि सामर्थ्यमर्थप्रत्यायनम् प्रति ॥६८॥

varṇātmanāmabhedācca siddhā sāmānyadhīrapi ।
samudāyo 'pi tebhyo 'sya vāraṇīyo 'nayā diśā ॥67॥
abhedasamudāyastu teṣām dharmo na duṣyati ।
teṣāmasti hi sāmarthyamarthapratyāyanam prati ॥68॥

As to the question how, when each *varṇa* cannot convey sense, can they together convey meaning, two analogies are popular in Śāstra. The *pūrvapakṣin* says that just as a single grain of sand cannot yield any oil, neither can a whole pile of sand. The answer is that the letters do not collectively function like a heap of sand, but rather like the parts of a chariot. Although each part such as wheel, axle, beam, etc., does not have the capacity to perform the function individually, they collectively co-operate to form the chariot. So each component has a part of the total capacity to which it contributes. This aspect, Kumārila points out, if viewed as a drawback among the sequential *varṇa*s, can equally be shown relevant in the grammarians formulation of *sphoṭa*, which is formed collectively by the *varṇa*s.

अथ यत्किञ्चिदुच्येत वहने तदिहापि नः ।
स्वात्मप्रत्ययहेतुत्वं वर्णेष्वर्थेऽपि वा क्वचित् ॥९०॥
यस्यानवयवः स्फोटो व्यज्यते वर्णबुद्धिभिः ।
सोऽपि पर्यनुयोगेन नैवैतेन विमुच्यते ॥९१॥
तत्रापि प्रतिवर्णं हि पदस्फोटो न गम्यते ।
न चावयवशो व्यक्तिस्तदभावान्न चात्र श्रीः ॥९२॥
प्रत्येकं चाप्यशक्तानां समुदायेऽप्यशक्तया ।
तत्र यः परिहारस्ते स नोऽत्रापि भविष्यति ॥९३॥

atha yatkiñciducyeta vahane tadihāpi naḥ ।
svātmapratyayahetutvaṁ varṇeṣvarthe 'pi vā kvacit ॥90॥
yasyānavayavaḥ sphoṭo vyajyate varmuddhibhiḥ ।
so 'pi paryanuyogena naivaitena vimucyate ॥91॥
tatrāpi prativarṇaṁ hi padasphoṭo na gamyate ।
na cāvayavaśo vyaktistadabhāvānna cātra śrīḥ ॥92॥
pratyekaṁ cāpyaśaktānāṁ samudāye 'pyaśaktayā ।
tatra yaḥ parihāraste sa no 'trāpi bhaviṣyati ॥93॥

The *Nyāyaratnākara* explains further that even in the Vyākaraṇa process of the *dhvani*s manifesting *sphoṭa*, their sequence is inevitable. They can neither manifest *sphoṭa* singly nor exist collectively. When each is incapable of conveying the *sphoṭa*, wherefrom do they gain the ability collectively? If one *dhvani* can suffice, then the others are rendered superfluous. If the reply is that the earlier *dhvani*s manifest *sphoṭa* indistinctly while the latter distinctly, then we may as well dispense with these that come earlier! Also, if later phonemes take the help of earlier ones for clear manifestation of *sphoṭa*, how is the grammarians theory any improvement on that of the Mīmāṁsā? Since anyway, each syllable takes the help of the others to convey meaning, to overcome the lack of simultaneity, we have to postulate *saṁskāra* or the impressions left by the preceding *varṇa*s that, along with the final *varṇa, caramavarṇa*, convey meaning. There is some unseen merit or capacity, that is created by the earlier *varṇa*s that enable the last one to flash the meaning.

एष एव तु संस्कार इति केचित् प्रचक्षते ।
अदृष्टकल्पनातीतम् तावन्मात्रम् हि दृश्यते ॥९८॥
अथ वा वासनैवास्तु संस्कारः सर्व एव हि ।
दृढज्ञानगृहीतेऽर्थे संस्कारोऽस्तीति मन्वते ॥९९॥

eṣa eva tu saṁskāra iti kecit pracakṣate ।
adṛṣṭakalpanātītam tāvanmātram hi dṛśyate ॥98॥
atha vā vāsanaivāstu saṁskāraḥ sarva eva hi ।
dṛḍhajñānagṛhīte 'rthe saṁskāro 'stīti manvate ॥99॥

So, the grasp of meaning is a composite cognition, *citrarūpā buddhiḥ*, consisting of the existing final *varṇa* and those that have been already uttered. As syllables are evanescent, at the moment of utterance of a particular *varṇa*, the preceding ones have passed into the hearer's memory.

Together they produce meaning directly, as it is in their nature to do so. There is no use of *paryanuyoga*, or questioning the nature of things. We cannot always furnish a logical reason for everything, such as the hotness of fire or the force of gravity and have to accept certain things as they are!

अन्त्यवर्णेऽपि विज्ञाते पूर्वसंस्कारकारितम् ।
स्मरणं यौगपद्येन सर्वेष्वन्ये प्रचक्षते ॥११२॥
सर्वेषु चैवमर्थेषु मानसं सर्ववादिनाम् ।
इष्टम् समुच्चयज्ञानं क्रमज्ञानेषु सत्स्वपि ॥११३॥

antyavarṇe 'pi vijñāte pūrvasaṁskārakāritam ।
smaraṇaṁ yaugapadyena sarveṣvanye pracakṣate ॥112॥
sarveṣu caivamartheṣu mānasaṁ sarvavādinām ।
iṣṭam samuccayajñānaṁ kramajñāneṣu satsvapi ॥113॥

When the opponents ask how a single word such as "cow" flashes when there is no such entity, but only the component syllables, Kumārila says that we do not deny the fact that the three letters lead to the cognition of a single word "cow". The very fact that the three different syllables serve one purpose, i.e. the concept of cow is adequate to convey meaning; there is no need to postulate a separate entity as the word "cow".

गौरित्येकमतित्वं तु नैवास्माभिर्निवार्यते ।
तद्ग्राह्यैकार्थताभ्यां च शब्दे स्यादेकतामतिः ॥१२०॥

gaurityekamatitvaṁ tu naivāsmābhirnivāryate ।
tagdrāhyaikārthatābhyāṁ ca śabde syādekatāmatiḥ ॥120॥

If we consider the process to be as follows: cognition of *śabda*, word or sound, leading to *saṁskāra* revealing *sphoṭa* which then causes cognition of meaning, then there are too many intervals between *śabda* and *arthapratyaya*. Then *śabda* may become secondary cause for meaning, which it is not.

शब्दज्ञानादिसंस्कारव्यक्तस्फोटकृतेऽथ वा ।
प्रत्यये शब्दजन्यत्वमिति गौणं प्रसज्यते ॥१२७॥

śabdajñānādisaṁskāravyaktasphoṭakṛte 'tha vā ।
pratyaye śabdajanyatvamiti gauṇaṁ prasajyate ॥127॥

If we say that even *varṇa*s giving meaning through *saṁskāra*s have the same defects of having intervening steps or intervals, then the reply is that word is not uttered with the purpose of creating *saṁskāra*, the purpose of uttering *śabda* is to communicate import. So the import is the result with *śabda* as its cause, as that is the very purpose of utterance. And since the *saṁskāra* operates along with the last letter, the direct cause and effect relation between *śabda* and *artha* is preserved intact.

संस्कारजननार्थम् च न शब्दोच्चारणम् मतम् ।
अर्थप्रतीतिमुद्दिश्य प्रयुक्तस्य क्रमादयम् ॥१२८॥

तस्मात् तादर्थ्यतः शब्दः फलेन व्यपदिश्यते ।
समुच्चयावबोधे तु व्यवधानम् न केनचित् ॥१२९॥

saṁskārajananārtham ca na śabdoccāraṇam matam ।
arthapratītimuddiśya prayuktasya kramādayam ॥128॥
tasmāt tādarthyataḥ śabdaḥ phalena vyapadiśyate ।
samuccayāvabodhe tu vyavadhānam na kenacit ॥129॥

Just as in Vedic *yajña* the result, *phala,* is obtained by *apūrva* caused by the rituals performed in sequence, so also the various functions in sequence with the final syllable leading directly to meaning. This makes the word the principal cause for *artha jñāna*. In a direct reference to the verses in *VP*, Kumārila says that whether we consider the eternal *varṇa*s or ephemeral *dhvani*s as instrumental in conveying meaning, still, there is no *sphoṭa* of word or sentence that is manifested like the lamp and its light.

वर्णा वा ध्वनयो वापि स्फोटं न पदवाक्ययोः ।
व्यञ्जन्ति व्यञ्जकत्वेन यथा दीपप्रभादयः ॥१३१॥

varṇā vā dhvanayo vāpi sphoṭaṁ na padavākyayoḥ ।
vyañjanti vyñjakatvena yathā dīpaprabhādayaḥ ॥131॥

There is nothing such as *sphoṭa* other than the *varṇa*s themselves; we do not come across any such entity. We only talk about the properties of what we do come across, such as *ghaṭa*.

सत्त्वाद् घटादिवच्चेति साधनानि यथारुचि ।
लौकिकव्यतिरेकेण कल्पितेऽर्थे भवन्ति हि ॥१३२॥
नार्थस्य वाचकः स्फोटो वर्णेभ्यः व्यतिरेकतः ।
घटादिवत् न दृष्तेन विरोधी धर्मसिद्धितः ॥१३३॥

sattvād ghaṭādivacceti sādhanāni yathāruci ।
laukikavyatirekeṇa kalpite 'rthe bhavanti hi ॥132॥
nārthasya vācakaḥ sphoṭo varṇebhyaḥ vyatirekataḥ ।
ghaṭādivat na dṛṣtena virodhi dharmasiddhitaḥ ॥133॥

The *vācaka,* i.e meaning-bearing unit, is not the *sphoṭa.* If the opponent denies the effectiveness of the *varṇa*s, in conveying meaning upon utterance, why, it would be like denying what we clearly perceive, just like denying what we see up in the sky is the moon!

प्रतिषेधेत् तु यो वर्णान् तज्ज्ञानानन्तरोद्भवान् ।
दृष्टबाधो भवेत् तस्य शशिचन्द्रनिषेधवत् ।।१३४।।

pratiṣedhet tu yo varṇān tajjñānānantarodbhavān ।
dṛṣṭabādho bhavet tasya śaśicandraniṣedhavat ।।134।।

The flash of meaning unfailingly follows the perception of the *varṇa*s invariably as the cognition of fire follows the perception of smoke. In inference, the *vyāpti* is tightly knit.

वर्णोत्था वार्थधीरेषा तज्ज्ञानान्तरोद्भवा ।
येदृशी सा तदुत्था हि धूमादेरिव वह्निधीः ।।१३५।।

varṇotthā vārthadhīreṣā tajjñānāntarodbhavā ।
yedṛśī sā tadutthā hi dhūmāderiva vahnidhīḥ ।।135।।

Just as a lamp enables one to see things, the syllables *ga*, etc., enable one to understand the word *gauḥ* as there is a cause and effect sequence to utterance and meaning. Citing any cause other than *varṇa* that is linked to conveying meaning would be a roundabout, laborious route. And the parts of a sentence have to be real, for execution of operations such as *ūha, prayoga, tantra* in *prayāja,* etc., in *yajña.* Therefore the denouncing of *sphoṭa* is required and has been addressed.

दीपवद्वा गकारादिर्गवादेः प्रतिपादकः ।
ध्रुवं प्रतीयमानत्वात् तत्पूर्वं प्रतिपादनात् ।।१३६।।
वर्णातिरिक्तः प्रतिषिध्यमानः पदेषु मन्दं फलमादधाति ।
कार्याणि वाक्यावयवाश्रयाणि सत्यानि कर्तुं कृत एष यत्नः ।।१३७।।

dīpavadvā gakārādirgavādeḥ pratipādakaḥ ।
dhruvaṁ pratīyamānatvāt tatpūrvaṁ pratipādanāt ।।136।।

varṇātiriktaḥ pratiṣidyamānaḥ padeṣu mandaṁ phalamādadhāti ।
kāryāṇi vākyāvayavāśrayāṇi satyāni kartuṁ kṛta eṣa yatnaḥ ॥137॥

On the question whether *sphoṭa* is revealed part by part by the succeeding *varṇas*, raised as an objection by Kumārila, Gaurinath Sastri writes:

> It is an established fact that we can speak of the imperfect or doubtful character of any perceptual knowledge, but never so of any non-perceptual knowledge.[30]

Pārthasārathi Miśra's Views in the Śāstradīpikā

Pārthasārathi Miśra elucidates in clear, simple language the tenets of Mīmāṁsā according to Kumārila Bhaṭṭa. In the section dealing with *śabda*, he explains his position under the headings *sphoṭavādasya upanyāsaḥ* and *sphoṭavādakhaṇḍanam*. He echoes Kumārila's main objection. It is not as if any letter singly conveys the meaning, since the utterance is in sequence, simultaneity or concurrence cannot be considered. The answer is that just as different auxiliaries of *yajña*, although performed at different moments in time still accrue to give one result, so due to the different syllables uttered sequentially together convey one meaning.

Each *varṇa* upon utterance leaves some *saṁskāras*, which act together with the last *varṇa* in achieving their purpose. To the objection that rather than creating numerous *saṁskāras* corresponding to numerous *varṇas*, it is better to concede one unified *sphoṭa*, he replies in the negative saying that what is never found has to be denied to exist. The syllables, or *varṇas*, or phonemes are clearly cognised by everybody and nothing beyond them is ever perceived.

Therefore, we conclude that there is nothing beyond the

30. *Dialectics of Sphoṭa*, p. 48.

sounds. Even if we posit a *śabda-tattva* we still have to resort to *saṁskāra* to overcome the problem of temporal sequence.

> तथा हि प्रत्येकवर्णानुभवभवितैः संस्कारैः संहत्य सर्ववर्णगोचरैका स्मृतिर्जन्यते। तस्यां च युगपद् अवभासमाना वर्णा विनैव संस्कारान्तरेण संहत्यार्थप्रत्ययं जनयन्ति।[31]
>
> *tathā hi pratyekavarṇānubhavabhavitaiḥ saṁskāraiḥ saṁhatya sarvavarṇagocaraikā smṛtirjanyate* ।
> *tasyāṁ ca yugapad avabhāsamānā varṇā vinaiva saṁskārāntareṇa saṁhatyārthapratyayaṁ janayanti* ।

Or, when it is explained that each *varṇa* does reveal *sphoṭa* in varying degrees, rendering it clearer and clearer as we go on, it brings in new criteria for differentiating between the sounds, which are not accounted for. He says that the Mīmāṁsā position is simpler, as it does not require a new *saṁskāra* over and above what each *varṇa* causes. Therefore the sounds which sequentially reveal the *varṇa*s cause a string of *saṁskāra*s that enable the hearer to recall all of them at once, upon the utterance of the last letter and this is responsible for cognition of meaning; there is no *śabda* over and above the sounds uttered.

The Sphoṭa Siddhi of Maṇḍana Miśra

It is a tribute to Bhartṛhari that even the criticism of a great genius like Kumārila could not detract from the importance of *sphoṭa* doctrine. Maṇḍana Miśra, a great exponent of Pūrva-Mīmāṁsā, believed to be a disciple of Kumārila himself, explains in the *Sphoṭasiddhi* how the accusations against *sphoṭa* theory are misplaced. He shows that there is no valid reason to deny the existence of *sphoṭa* as a spiritual entity. He carefully examines the arguments in the Sphoṭavāda of Kumārila and concludes in favour of *sphoṭa* theory.

---

31. *Śāstradīpikā*, p. 193.

दुर्विदग्धैरवक्षिप्ते दर्शने पददर्शिनाम् ।
यथागमं यथाप्रज्ञं न्यायलेशे निदर्श्यते ॥२॥

durvidagdhairavakṣipte darśane padadarśinām ।
yathāgamaṁ yathāprajñaṁ nyāyaleśe nidarśyate ॥2॥

Though Maṇḍana has in particular discussed the nature of *pada-sphoṭa*, he has spoken of *vākya-sphoṭa* as well. That being so, each word is shown to be significant and there is ample justification for a change in the wording of a hymn with a corresponding change in the meaning.[32]

निरस्तभेदं पदतत्त्वमेतद् व्यादर्शि युक्त्यागमसंश्रयेण ।
विधूतभेदग्रहमेतयैव दिशापरं संप्रतियन्त्वभेदम् ॥३६॥

nirastabhedaṁ padatattvametad vyādarśi yuktyāgamasaṁśrayeṇa ।
vidhūtabhedagrahametayaiva diśāparaṁ saṁpratiyantva-bhedam ॥36॥

Kumārila's chief apprehension in accepting *sphoṭa* (especially *vākya-sphoṭa*) was that words would be rendered unreal; this is placated by Maṇḍana's discussion of *pada-sphoṭa*.

The Nyāya and Mīmāṁsā hold that letters pronounced in succession produce *saṁskāra*s, which act in cooperation to give import. But the grammarians counter with the objection that *saṁskāra* can only lead to Smṛti, i.e. only revive the same *varṇa*s to the mind. How can Smṛti, memory, lead to a new cognition, viz. the import of the word? Maṇḍana says that a *saṁskāra* is itself a power of or ability to recall; it cannot be endowed with a further power as this could lead to *anavasthā*:

शक्तेः शक्त्यन्तरायोगस्तत्र सत्यप्यदर्शनम् ।
विलक्षणस्योपजनो नाविशेषाच्च कारणात् ॥७॥

śakteḥ śaktyantarāyogastatra satyapyadarśanam ।
vilakṣaṇasyopajano nāviśeṣācca kāraṇāt ॥7॥

---

32. G.N. Sastri, p. 23.

Gopālikā —

न खलु क्रमभेदेऽपि प्रत्येकमक्षरोपलम्भप्रविभक्ताः संस्काराः परस्परमतिशेरते।

na khalu kramabhede 'pi pratyekamakṣaropalambhapra-vibhaktāḥ saṁskārāḥ parasparamatiśerate ।

Since each *varṇa* is one and eternal, Maṇḍana has a valid question in asking whether the *saṁskāras* produced by a *varṇa* in different utterances are in any way different. How can two words with the same letters, but in different order, have different meaning, as there is no reason why impressions produced by the same letters should in any way be different!

अन्यस्य खलु वाङ्गमात्राद्वदतोऽप्रतिभासनम् ।
वाक्ये पदे वा मर्यादा न विद्मः केन कल्पिता ।।२८।।

anyasya khalu vāṅgmātrādvadato 'pratibhāsanam ।
vākye pade vā maryādā na vidmaḥ kena kalpitā ।।28।।

It is not clear why the Mīmāṁsaka maintains that the sounds must be uttered by one speaker and in a particular sequence in order to convey meaning: Even when uttered by a plurality of speakers and in a different order, their residual traces would be the same, but he maintains that it cannot be understood at all. The meaning is supposed to be understood, not directly from the residual traces, but from the phonemes which figure simultaneously in the final cognition, simple or complex. These phonemes would be the same, no matter in what order the manifesting sounds were uttered. As the sequence does not feature in the final cognition, there is nothing to distinguish *nadī* and *dīna*. And yet, the meaning understood is not the same. Moreover, what is there to prevent the understanding of the meaning even when the speakers are many? Nobody ascertains the sameness of the speaker before understanding the meaning. Provided there is similarity of voice and uninterrupted utterances, meaning should be understood even if the speakers are many.

न प्रत्ययः स्यादेकत्वे प्रयोक्तुरविभाविते ।
न च तस्य परिज्ञानमकस्मादवकल्पते ॥१५॥

na pratyayaḥ syādekatve prayokturavibhāvite ।
na ca tasya parijñānamakasmādavakalpate ॥15॥

> There would be no understanding of meaning if the sameness of the speaker is not ascertained and that would be inexplicable without some reason.[33]

For, sequence or order invariably implies distinction (*bheda*). And, when the recollection that is posited as a unified whole, the question of sequence cannot arise in this case as unity and distinction are contradictory in nature and we can hardly speak of them in the same breath with one and the same identity. Thus, Maṇḍana deals a staggering blow to the theory of Naiyāyikas who have been maintaining that the sequence of letters will also appear in the recollection.[34]

निरुद्धबुद्धयो नैव पूर्वे वर्णा विशेषकाः ।
एकबुद्धावुपारोहे क्रमाद्यस्तमुपागतम् ॥१४॥

niruddhabuddhayo naiva pūrve varṇā viśeṣakāḥ ।
ekabuddhāvupārohe kramādyastamupāgatam ॥14॥

> The previous phonemes whose cognitions have already disappeared cannot specify the last phoneme. If they all figure in a single cognition (in the form of remembrance), sequence, etc., disappear.

Jayanta Bhaṭṭa's Criticism of Sphoṭa

The sixth chapter of *Nyāyamañjarī* discusses the Sphoṭavāda in detail, first presenting the grammarian's standpoint on

33. K.A.S. Iyer, *Sphoṭa Siddhi*.

34. *Dialectics of Sphoṭa*, p. 38.

śabda, dhvani, saṁskāra and *sphoṭa*, and then the Mīmāṁsā and Naiyāyika objections to it. Jayanta Bhaṭṭa shows that *sphoṭa* can neither be established by *anumāna* nor *pratyakṣa* and then propounds the Nyāya process of *śabda* conveying meaning directly, without the necessity of a new entity called *sphoṭa*.

As per the Nyāya tenets, that which necessarily precedes something is considered the cause of the latter (i.e the effect). Thus, since utterance in the form of word and sentence, which, when heard, produce word-meaning and sentence-meaning, word and sentence are the cause of meaning. We find this pair always present in unvarying combination and hence it is correct to take *pada* and *vākya* as reason, *nimitta* in *padārtha* and *vākyārtha*.

Nyāyamañjarī (vol. I, 6th Āhnika, p. 107):

किमत्र निरूपणीयम् । यदनन्तरं यद् भवति तत् तस्य निमित्तम् । पदवाक्यश्रवणे च सति पदार्थवाक्यार्थसंप्रत्ययो भवति इति ते एव तत्र निमित्तं ।

kimatra nirūpaṇīyam । *yadanantaraṁ yad bhavati tat tasya nimittam* । *padavākyaśravaṇe ca sati padārthavākyārthasaṁpratyayo bhavati iti te eva tatra nimittaṁ* ।

The grammarians say that since the syllables of a word do not have simultaneous existence, they cannot form a group to act together in any manner. They are evanescent and come into existence in sequence; so, they can neither convey meaning in individual capacity nor collectively. Therefore, we have to ascribe the capacity to convey meaning to a separate entity, viz. *sphoṭa*. But *sphoṭa* being eternal and not composed by a reliable authority, *āpta*, it goes against the Nyāya philosophy to accept *sphoṭa*.

Pūrvapakṣa:

न च वर्णानां व्यस्तसमस्तविकल्पोपहतत्त्वेन वाचकमुपपद्यते तस्मादन्य एव स्फोटात्मा शब्देऽर्थप्रतिपादक इति प्रतिजानते ।

na ca varṇānāṁ vyastasamastavikalpopahatattvena vācakamupapadyate tasmādanya eva sphoṭātmā śabde 'rthapratipādaka iti pratijānate ।

Nyāyasiddhānta:

यस्यार्थप्रतीतिहेतुः स्फोटात्मा शब्दस्य नानित्यत्वं न चाप्तप्रणीतत्त्वमित्यस्थाने नैयायिकाः किष्टा भवेयुः । तस्मादनित्यानां वर्णानामेव वाचकत्वं प्रतिष्ठापनीयं पराकरणीयश्च स्फोट इति ।

yasyārthapratītihetuḥ sphoṭātmā śabdasya nānityatvaṁ na cāptapraṇītattvamityasthāne naiyāyikāḥ kiṣṭā bhaveyuḥ । *tasmādanityānāṁ varṇānāmeva vācakatvaṁ pratiṣṭhāpanīyaṁ parākaraṇīyaśca sphoṭa iti* । — pp. 107-08

THE GRAMMARIANS' VIEW

The grammarians explain the necessity of *sphoṭa* by *anumāna*, inference and by *pratyakṣa*, direct perception. Do the syllables convey meaning individually, or collectively. It cannot be singly, as we do not understand any sense by the utterance of any one syllable of a word; they cannot function *in tandem* as a collection as such does not even exist! Although the *varṇa*s are *nitya* according to Mīmāṁsā, yet there is no criterion as to what group of letters convey what meaning as all syllables are uniformly existent at all times! It is not even clear why there should be necessarily only one speaker uttering the syllables in a particular order, as several speakers uttering different syllables simultaneously only contribute to chaos, *kolāhala*, which conveys no sense. So, it is not clear what kind of collection is intended by Nyāya as cause for conveying sense.

When the Naiyāyikas say that the *saṁskāra*s generated by subsequent *varṇa*s, together with the last letter convey meaning, this explanation is also faulty. The *saṁskāra* produced by any experience is capable of recalling exactly that particular experience by memory; it cannot produce a new cognition. Also there cannot be two cognitions occurring at the same time (*jñānayaugapadya* is not possible). We cannot have both the reception of final syllable and recall of earlier syllables, at once. And how can the recalling of several *varṇa*s recall one single *smṛti*?

> यदुच्यते पूर्वपूर्ववर्णजनितसंस्कारसहितोऽन्त्यवर्णः प्रत्यायक इति तदप्ययुक्तम्। संस्कारो हि नाम यदनुभवजनितस्तद्विषयमेव स्मरणम् उपजनयति न पुनरर्थान्तरविषयम् ज्ञानम् इति। न पुनरेका सर्ववर्णगोचरा स्मृतिः ।
>
> *yaducyate pūrvapūrvavarṇajanitasaṁskārasahito 'ntyavarṇaḥ pratyāyak iti tadapyuktam । saṁskāro hi nām yadanubhavajanitastadviṣayameva smaraṇam। upjanayati na punararthāntaraviṣyam jñānam iti । na punarekā sarvavarṇagocarā smṛtiḥ ।* —p. 109

Also, *saṁskāra* is endowed with capacity to recall a cognition from memory, but not with the power to create a new cognition. This is the major defect in the Nyāya version of *śābdabodha*.

> संस्कारस्य सहचरदर्शनाद्याहितप्रबोधस्य सतः स्मरणमात्रजन्मनि निर्ज्ञातसामर्थ्यस्य इन्द्रियेण व्यापाराभावात् । तस्मान्न वर्णा वाचकाः ।
>
> *saṁskārasya sahacaradarśanādyāhitaprabodhasya sataḥ smaraṇamātrajanmani nirjñātasāmarthyasya indriyeṇa vyāpārābhāvāt। tasmānna varṇā vācakāḥ।*

Again, are the *varṇa*s supposed to convey meaning taken with particular sequence, or without sequence? That is, taking a number of *varṇa*s that form a particular word, do they convey sense taken in some permutation, or will any combination produce the same result? Therefore, by *anumāna*, as some reason is required for the understanding of meaning from utterance, we arrive at *sphoṭa* as the cause.

> कार्यानुमानमिदं अस्तु। परिशेषानुमानं वा अर्थापत्तिर्वा सर्वथा अर्थप्रतीतिलक्षणकार्यवशात् कल्पमानं तत्करणं स्फोट इत्युच्यते।

kāryānumānamidaṁ astu । *pariśeṣānumānaṁ vā arthāpattirvā sarvathā arthapratītilakṣaṇakāryavaśāt kalpamānaṁ tatkaraṇaṁ sphoṭa ityucyate* ।

It is because of the indivisible unity of *sphoṭa* that the word *śabda* is used in the singular. We say that meaning is grasped from the word; *śabdād artho 'vagamyate,* not *śabdebhyaḥ*. It cannot be said that *śabda* is only that which can be grasped by the ear even the *jāti, śabdatva* is grasped by the ear.

Nyāya rule:

येनेन्द्रियेण यद्द्रव्यम गृह्यते, तेनैव तद्गता जातिर भावश्च

yenendriyeṇa yaddravyaṁ gṛhyate, tenaiva tadgatā jātirabhāvaśca.

So *sphoṭa* can also be grasped by the auditory faculty. In fact, the *varṇa*s manifest *sphoṭa* which is directly perceived. We do not say that the syllables are not perceived by the sense of hearing, they are discerned by the ear along with the variation in quality of intonation, speed, loudness, etc. But the indivisible *sphoṭa* manifested by the audible sounds is directly perceived in a flash and this is what conveys meaning.

JAYANTA'S REFUTAL OF SPHOṬA

Jayanta examines the arguments in establishing *sphoṭa* by *anumāna* and *pratyakṣa* and finds both faulty. He says that it cannot be substantiated by inference as it is seen that the aggregate of syllables themselves, qualified by a particular sequence, directly leads to the cognition of meaning.

न तावदनुमानतः स्फोटस्वरूपमुपपादयितुम् पार्यते परिदृश्यमानविशिष्टानुपूर्वीकवर्ण- कलापकरणेन अर्थप्रतीतेर्घटमानत्वात् ।

na tāvadanumānataḥ sphoṭasvarūpamupapādayitum pāryate paridṛśyamānaviśiṣṭānupūrvīkavarṇakalāpakaraṇena arthapratīterghaṭamānatvāt । — p. 120

The syllables give rise to meaning collectively, not individually. This is in opposition to the Vyākaraṇa view that *sphoṭa* being one and indivisible, it is revealed by the utterance of the first syllable of the word itself; so as not to render subsequent *varṇa*s superfluous, they are said to aid in making the revelation of *sphoṭa* more and more clear or unambiguous. Refuting this tenet, Jayanta says that the *varṇa*s do not convey meaning in individual capacity.

> व्यस्तानां तावद् वाचकत्वं नेष्यते वर्णानां समस्ता एव ते वाचकाः ।
>
> *vyastānāṁ tāvad vācakatvaṁ neṣyate varṇānāṁ samastā eva te vācakāḥ* । — p. 120

When we say that a collection or aggregate cannot exist simultaneously, so be it. Even though existing only in sequence, their collective efficiency is still possible, as we see in several examples. Just as the three stones equally bear one vessel during cooking, with the fire lit below the dish in an arrangement like a tripod, so can subsequent entities occurring in sequence equally share the collective efficiency. For example, while eating a full meal, it is a series of mouthfuls that lead to the feeling of satiation; even one less would not give the same feeling of satisfaction.

It is not possible to devour all the mouthfuls at once; in the same way a text of any length has to be recited with sequence in time, but has the capacity to convey sense as a whole.

> यथा युगपद्भाविनः समास्त्रयो ग्रावाण एकाम् उखाम् धारयन्तो दृश्यन्ते तथा क्रमभाविनोऽपि समस्ता ग्रासा एकां तृप्तिमुत्पादयन्तो दृश्यन्ते ।
>
> *yathā yugapadbhāvinaḥ samāstrayo grāvāṇa ekām ukhām dhārayanto dṛśyanto tathā kramabhāvino 'pi samastā grāsā ekāṁ tṛptimutpādayanto dṛśyante* । — p. 120

In Vedic ritual also, this is a very crucial point. It is not possible to perform a *yajña* with all its auxiliaries which may be prescribed over a long time period, all at once. But the *yajña* is said to be complete only when it is fully performed; only then can it lead to result or *phala*. This is the reason *adṛṣṭa*, and *apūrva* are logical necessitates, to knit together events spread over time.

So, in practical situations in the world, we see that sequence in events is not a hindrance to their collective action.

SPHOṬA IS NOT INFERRED

In the case of several mouthfuls of food leading to feeling of satiation and the arrangement of items one by one to form an array, we see the effect brought about gradually. What is achieved by the various auxiliaries of *yajña* performed at separate instances in time? It is the tentative *avāntara apūrva*, which leads to the full *apūrva* that causes the result when all the minor rituals are completed. But one can object that these do not form the parts of the whole in the sense of *avayava* and *avayavin*. But even so, the relationship of cause and effect certainly exists.

> तयोः प्रधानकार्यावयवत्वं नास्तीति चेत् । मा भूदवयवत्वं तदुपयोगिता तु विद्यते एव । अवयवावयविव्यवहारस्तु अवान्तरपरमापूर्वयोरपि दुरुपपादः ।
>
> *tayoḥ pradhānakāryāvayavatvaṁ nāstīti cet । mā bhūdavayavatvaṁ tadupayogitā tu vidyate eva । avayavāvayavivyavahārastu avāntaraparamāpūrvayorapi durupapādaḥ ।* —p. 122

Or, we can take the view that even in the case of syllables uttered in sequence, the mental understanding brought about is of the form of the whole group of letters, which leads to understanding of meaning. Just as we get the idea, "Devadatta has eaten a hundred mangoes."

अथ वा क्रमोपलब्धेष्वपि वर्णेषु मानसमनुव्यवसायरूपमखिलवर्णविषयम् सङ्कलनाज्ञानम् यदुपजायते तदर्थप्रत्यायनाङ्गम् भविष्यति। दृश्यते च विनश्वरेष्वपि पदार्थान्तरेषु क्रमानुभूतेषु युगपदनुव्यवसायो मानसः शतमाम्राणि भक्षितवान् देवदत्त इति ।

atha vā kramopalabdheṣvapi varṇeṣu mānasamanuvyavasāya-rūpamakhilavarṇaviṣayam saṅkalanājñānam yadupajāyate tadarthapratyāyanāṅgam bhaviṣyati । dṛśyate ca vin śvareṣvapi padārthāntareṣu kramānubhūteṣu yugapadanuvyavasāyo mānasaḥ śatamāmrāṇi bhakṣitavān devadatta iti ।

The group of letters functioning together to form a word (or sentence) is not like a bunch (*stabaka*) but also takes into account the serial order of the letters.

विशिष्टानुपूर्वीकवर्णमालानुभवसमनन्तरभावी हि सङ्कलनाप्रत्ययोऽर्थप्रतीतेर्हेतुः।

viśiṣṭānupūrvīkavarṇamālānubhavasamanantarabhāvī hi saṅkalanāpratyayo 'rthapratīterhetuḥ ।

Thus Jayanta veers towards the Mīmāṁsā explanation and says,

यथा पूर्ववर्णजनितसंस्कारसहितोऽन्त्यवर्णः इति तत्रभवता मीमांसाभाष्यकृता वर्णितम् तथा वा वर्णानाम् अर्थप्रत्याकत्वमस्तु।

yathā pūrvavarṇajanitasaṁskārasahito 'ntyavarṇaḥ iti tatrabhavatā mīmāṁsābhāṣyakṛtā varṇitam tathā vā varṇānām arthapratyākatvamastu । — p. 123

The main objection to the method of explaining process of meaning conveyed by words, is that it depends heavily on *saṁskāra* which is crucial in recalling memory, not relevant in cognition occurring at the moment of hearing the word, which is *pratyakṣa* or *anubhava*. To this Jayanta says that it is not a royal order that *saṁskāra* should lead only to *smṛti*; it is only a tenet of Śāstra. We say instead, that Śāstra can allow *saṁskāra* to convey meaning from hearing utterances also.

saṁskāra is an ability to or capacity of the mind that enables it to understand, by practice, repeated attentive study. It is a refinement, some state of mind, that helps in cognition.

किमयम् राजाज्ञा स्मृतिरेव संस्कारेण कर्तव्येति। नेयं राजाज्ञा नयाज्ञा त्वेषा।

kimayam rājājñā smṛtireva saṁskāreṇa kartavyeti । neyaṁ rājājñā nayājñā tveṣā ।

It cannot be said that *saṁskāra* cannot be responsible for current experience, *anubhava*, which is what happens when import is gained from a word that is heard. *Saṁskāra* is not defined as the cause for memory; *saṁskāra* is a quality of *ātman*; nothing prevents it from causing different types of cognition. Just as it causes remembrance, it can also lead to cognition of import of a word. The syllables and their perception are transient and fleeting; there is no need to postulate a separate entity beyond the syllables such as *śabda-tattva*, which is anyway beyond experience. And the cognition of meaning is not without reason: this reason is the *saṁskāra*, so there is no room to infer anything else.

न हि स्मरणशक्तिः संस्कारः किन्त्वात्मगुणो वासनाख्यः । स च स्मृतिमिवार्थप्रतीतिमपि जनयितुमुत्सहते ।
वर्णाश्च तदनुभवाश्च व्यतीताः । अन्यच्च शब्दतत्त्वं नानुभूयत् इति वक्ष्यामः । यदस्याः करणं स संस्कार इति स्मृतिरिवार्थप्रतीतिरपि तत्कार्यत्वात् तदनुमापिका भवत्येव ।

na hi smaraṇaśaktiḥ saṁskāraḥ kintvātmaguṇo vāsanākhyaḥ । sa ca smṛtimivārthapratītimapi janayitumutsahate ।
varṇāśca tadanubhavāśca vyatītāḥ । anyacca śabdatattvaṁ nānubhūyat iti vakṣyāmaḥ । yadasyāḥ karaṇaṁ sa saṁskāra iti smṛtirivārthapratītirapi tatkāryatvāt tadanumāpikā bhavatyeva ।

It is not a rule that what causes remembrance, i.e. the seed of memory, *saṁskāra*, cannot also give rise to perception: it can do both. The *saṁskāra* of the earlier syllables along with the perception of the last syllable, together bring the import of the word to experience.

> स्मृतिबीजमिति यदुच्यते तत् कथमनुभवबीजं स्यात्। नैष नियमः स्मृतेरेव बीजमिति। साक्षाद् अर्थप्रतीतिकारी संस्कारः स्मृतिद्वारेण तां करिष्यति । पूर्ववर्णेषु संस्कारात् स्मरणं अन्त्यवर्णे श्रोत्रेन्द्रियादनुभव इत्येवं स्मर्यमाणानुभूयमानवर्णकरणको अर्थप्रत्ययः स्यात् को दोशः ।
>
> *smṛtibījamiti yaducyate tat kathamanubhavabījaṁ syāt । naiṣa niyamaḥ smṛtereva bījamiti । sākṣād arthapratītikārī saṁskāraḥ smṛtidvāreṇa tāṁ kariṣyati । pūrvavarṇeṣu saṁskārāt smaraṇaṁ antyavarṇe śrotrendriyādanubhava ityevaṁ smaryamāṇānubhūyamānavarṇakaraṇako arthapratyayaḥ syāt ko dośaḥ ।*

In taking *saṁskāra* as leading to *artha pratīti*, there is no new postulation, as the grammarians also concede that the *saṁskāra* of preceding *varṇa*s aid the flash of meaning along with the final letter. But in postulating indivisible *sphoṭa* as distinct from the letters, there is unnecessary and cumbersome artificiality.

Jayanta disapproves the two examples given by Bhartṛhari in showing that although conveying *sphoṭa* singly, every *varṇa* does contribute to progressively clearer revelation of *sphoṭa*, just as repeated examination of a gem or repeated recitation of a hymn leads to more lucid understanding. Jayanta Bhaṭṭa says these two examples are not suitable, as the gem and the hymns have parts, *avayava*s, unlike the *sphoṭa*, which is said to be an indivisible unit. It is also futile to say that *sphoṭa* is revealed by *dhvani* or audible sound. We can clearly perceive *varṇa*s and sounds with our senses, but nothing beyond. How can we say that what we perceive does not exist, but what we do not perceive, actually exists?

Even the view that the sequence itself may be taken as *sphoṭa*, as otherwise the same *varṇa*s in different sequence (in a jumbled up word) can also convey sense, is faulty. Sequence is a property, *dharma*, of *varṇa*s, not an independent entity. It is only an attribute of time — sequence is temporal arrangement, not time itself.

क्रमो हि स नाम कालभेदः न च काल एव स्फोटो भवितुर्महति क्रमोऽपि च न स्वतन्त्रः प्रतिपादकः पदार्थान्तरवृत्तिर्वा किन्तु वर्णाश्रय एव।

kramo hi sa nāma kālabhedaḥ na ca kāla eva sphoṭo bhaviturmahati kramo 'pi ca na svatantraḥ pratipādakaḥ padārthāntaravr̥ttirvā kintu varṇāśraya eva ।

SPHOṬA IS NOT PERCEIVED

When we say that *śabda* conveys meaning, it does not mean that *sphoṭa* conveys meaning. Since the *varṇa*s directly convey import, the word *śabda* only refers to the *varṇa*s.

In opposition to this, the grammarians cite three shortcomings in taking *śabda* to mean *varṇa*. At the outset, every *varṇa* individually cannot convey meaning *śabda* has to refer to the *varṇa*s collectively.

(i) Since *śabda* is a generic word, a *sāmānya*, it cannot refer to several *varṇa*s at a time. Just as we do not say "Devadatta and Yajñadatta are a person" or, "Mango and Banyan are a tree", we cannot say that c, o and w are a word!

(ii) If we take *śabda* to refer to *varṇa*s as a group, *samudāya*, as in the case of a group of trees forming a forest, it is still untenable as even groups can be classified according to category, such as an orchard of mango or a forest of woodapple. But we never speak of a word as a certain group of *varṇa*s.

(iii) If we take *śabda* to be the same as *varṇa*s by *abheda*, or non-distinct, the forest as a whole is still distinct from a single tree, the two are not equated. Here, *śabda* would mean each *varṇa* individually and also the aggregate as a whole (the word). This is not logical. So the parallel is incorrect. To this, Jayanta says that it does not matter if the grammarians find the definition of *śabda* incorrect; things in the world are not obliged to follow the definition of *śāstrakāra*s, those who write Śāstras.

There is no way that we can acknowledge *sphoṭa*, neither by perception nor by inference. Since the primary definition of *śabda* (sound) is *śrotragrāhyatva*, we take *varṇa*s to mean *śabda* (language).

श्रोत्रग्राह्यत्वञ्च वर्णेष्वेव नार्थान्तरस्येति वर्णा एव शब्दः ।

śrotragrāhyatvañca varṇeṣveva nārthāntarasyeti varṇā eva śabdaḥ ।

If we conceded class concept in *śabda*, namely *sphoṭa*, we should be able to recognise it at utterance of every single phoneme. In the case of *jāti* such as *gotva*, we are able to cognise the whole class concept each time we see an individual cow. Upon seeing one cow, we perceive the class property of being a cow, i.e. *gotva jāti*. But on hearing each *varṇa* of a word or sentence, the cognition that it is part of such and such word or such and such sentence, does not occur; neither is *sphoṭa* formed by *varṇa*s like a cloth is formed by its threads. So *sphoṭa* does not exist.[35]

---

35. This section was presented in paper titled, "The Significance of Temporal Sequence in Language Study in Śāstra" in Seminar on Indian Linguistics at Dept. of Philosophy, University of Delhi, in March, 2007. It has also been selected for publishing in Journal of ICPR.

Summary

From the permanent acoustic pattern of Patañjali to the *śabda-tattva* of Nāgeśa and eight divisions with varying relative validity discussed by Kauṇḍa Bhaṭṭa, the concept of *sphoṭa* has undergone much evolution. Accordingly, the tone of refuting from other schools is also different in the writing of different eras.

From the linguistic point of view, *sphoṭa* seems the most reasonable answer to process of *śābdabodha* and is in harmony with the common sense understanding of what a word is. The felt unity of the word corresponds to an objective unit. From G.N. Sastri: The grammarian philosopher justifiably lays stress upon this fundamental character of our knowledge. He shows that the philosophers of other schools have failed to account for the felt unity of the word and that their philosophical exercises are not calculated to carry conviction to an unsophisticated and unbiased student of philosophy in spite of the wealth of ingenuity displayed by them.

In its essence, the *sphoṭa* enunciated by Bhartṛhari is not different from the definition of *śabda* given by Jayanta Bhaṭṭa by Śabara Svāmi. But Nyāya and Mīmāṁsā are adamant that they will not accept *sphoṭa* by name. Jayanta's exposition of *sphoṭa* is so lucid and beautiful that it is hard to believe that he disputes the theory!

The Nyāya and Mīmāṁsā explanations do not have convincing answers to two compelling issues. One is the issue of *śleṣa* or pun. For example,

शारदा शारदाम्भोजवदना वदनाम्बुजे।
सर्वदा सर्वदाऽस्माकं सन्निधिं सन्निधिं क्रियात्।।

śāradā śāradāmbhojavadanā vadanāmbuje।
sarvadā sarvadā'smākaṁ sannidhiṁ sannidhiṁ kriyāt।।

In the above stanza how can two meanings be revealed by the same set of *varṇa*s in the same order? Jayanta himself presents the example of *kāle nadanti nāgaḥ*, in the grammarian's view. G.N. Sastri writes that in the word *ku* refers to "bad" and *māra* means "Cupid", while the word *kumāra* simply means boy. How can we explain this without *sphoṭa*?

The other issue which does not seem to find much mention in the debate on *sphoṭa* is that of language at the silent level, *upāṁśu kathana* or the *maunī śloka* that Bhartṛhari mentions. Since *śabda* is strictly *śrotra grāhya* or audible, by definition in Nyāya and Mīmāṁsā, the grammarian's extension of language to mental level seems the only answer to this. To quote Jayanta, *saṁskāra* of one person cannot cause cognition in another. It is only the word in the mind, when expressed by speaker and heard by the other person, that unites speaker and hearer in *śabda-tattva*.

4

Concept of Jāti in Vākyapadīya

Introduction to Vākyapadīya

THE *Vākyapadīya* (*VP*) of Bhartṛhari is a voluminous treatise written in *kārikā* style spread over three *kāṇḍa*s. The first is called Brahmakāṇḍa or Āgamasamuccaya and contains 155 verses. The second is called Vākyakāṇḍa and has 483 verses. The third *kāṇḍa* is called Prakīrṇakāṇḍa or Padakāṇḍa and has roughly 1430 *kārikā*s arranged topicwise in 14 *samuddeśa*s. This focus of this research is the first of these, the Jāti Samuddeśa. There is an ancient commentary accompanying the *kārikā*s of the first two *kāṇḍa*s, called the *Vṛtti*, composed in prose and believed to be authored by Bhartṛhari himself. If that is as tradition has it, then *VP* consists of *kārikā* and prose elucidation. There is also a very old view that the *VP* consists of only the first two *kāṇḍa*s and that what we have as the third *kāṇḍa* is actually a separate work by Bhartṛhari called *Prakīrṇa* or *Prakīrṇaka*. The last few verses of the second *kāṇḍa* seem to wind up the treatise and suggest that the *VP* ends there.

Bhartṛhari was earlier believed to have lived around CE 650, mainly on the basis of the references made by I-tsing, the Chinese pilgrim. But further research has led to the view among scholars that his period was more likely around CE 450, and that of his teacher Vasurata, probably CE 400, paying homage to his *guru*, Bhartṛhari reverently states that the *VP* was verily composed by his teacher Vasurata. This shows that he must have received most of the concepts in *VP* from the teachings of his *guru,* and in all likelihood even borrowed many phrases from Vasurata's work. This also proves that there was flourishing debate on the topics addressed in the *VP* in Śāstra at that time.

Other than the *Vṛtti,* there are several commentaries on the *VP* that have come down to us over the centuries. Some doubt as to Bhartṛhari's authorship on the *Vṛtti* does arise in the student's mind. Can it really be possible to add so much meaning, that is actually distilled from the developing tradition, at places, to the *kārikā*? While the tradition that Bhartṛhari himself composed the *Vṛtti* is supported by most writers, notably K.A.S. Iyer and Raghunath Sarma, Madeleine Biardeau has concluded upon careful observation that the author of *kārikā*s and *Vṛtti* could not have been the same. Iyer presents her arguments, refutes them and shows that we do not have enough evidence to dispute the tradition.

While discussing the *Vṛtti,* Iyer notes that the language is very obscure at many places, with unnecessarily long, complicated sentences that actually convey a simple point sometimes. The *Vṛtti* represents a rather peculiar style of writing. It is a fact that we hardly have any text on Śāstra from that period, certainly no other in Vyākaraṇa. The manner in which the *Vṛtti* elucidates on the *kārikā*s definitely points to the fact that the *kārikā*s were composed in an environment where the issues being discussed were well known. The manner in which Bhartṛhari enunciates his views, though showing a lot of originality, still do not seem to insist on one writer's views but rather represent a tradition. Like several other great innovative writers Bhartṛhari takes pains to show that he is only continuing a long line of thinking that has come down from Vedic times.

In the course of discussing various topics, Bhartṛhari mentions many diverse views, using words such as *eke, apare, keśāñcit, anyaiḥ,* etc. No specific school is explicitly mentioned, though it can be sometimes guessed. Many of these views are in agreement with Bhartṛhari's and many are not. The trouble is that he does not mention clearly which way it is. This occasionally leads to confusion as to whether the statement is to be interpreted according to his philosophy or not. A good example is *kārikā* I.93. Even when he clearly disagrees or confronts another's view, Bhartṛhari does not necessarily even state that it is somebody else's position. While words such as *apare, kaiścit,* etc., definitely help in the metre of composition, they also illustrate Bhartṛhari's spirit of accommodation in showing how different viewpoints can be explained by language.

The ancient commentaries often help[1] in telling us who is meant by words such as *kecit*. Iyer gives the example of *Jāti Sam.* 19, where the point as to how words like, *ākāśa, kāla, dik,* etc., can explain universal, is understood only with the help of Helārāja's commentary. The observations of Bhartṛhari are not to be taken as mutually exclusive definitions, but as adding to the enunciation of the concept.

It is interesting that while remarking on the strangeness and obscure nature of the *Vṛtti,* which makes it essential to know the full background of the issue at hand, before an accurate interpretation is possible, Iyer gives two specific examples and both discuss the issue of *jāti.*[2]

Even when the sentence is not long, its meaning may not be clear. In the last sentence of the *Vṛtti* on I.60, the author wants to say that the *sūtra P.* 1.1.68 makes the word *agni* found

1. Iyer, *Bhartṛhari,* p. 53.

2. Iyer, 1965, *VP* with *Vṛtti,* tr. p. xiii.

in *P.* 4.2.33 the name *saṁjñā* of the word *agni* actually used in speech, to which the suffix *ḍhak* is to be added. The sentence reads as follows:

> तस्माद् अग्निशब्दो । येनार्थभूतेनाभिन्नरूपेणाग्निशब्दार्थवान् तम् अग्नि-शब्दान्तराभिधे-यस्य तुल्यश्रुतेर अग्निशब्दस्य संज्ञाभावं प्रतिपादयतीति ।
> *tasmād agniśabdo yenārthabhūtenābhinnarūpeṇāgniśabdārthavān tam agniśabdāntarābhidheyasya tulyaśruter agniśabdasya saṁjñābhāvaṁ pratipādayatīti*।

The obscurity of this sentence is due to the following:

(1) It is not made clear that *agniśabdaḥ* means the word *agni* found in a *sūtra* like *agnerḍhak*.

(2) *abhidheyasya* is a repetition of *arthabhūtena* and *tulyaśruteḥ* of *abhinnarūpeṇa*.

(3) It seems that *agniśabdaḥ* is the agent of the verb *pratipādayati* but on reflection, it is clear that it is the *sūtra svaṁ rūpaṁ śabdasya* which is the agent. Similarly, *na hyabhivyaktimatām abhivyañjakair āśritānām evābhivyaktir niyamena kriyate* does not mean anything more than that suggestors (manifestors) do not necessarily suggest (manifest) what inheres in them, but this meaning does not come out quickly.

The second sentence quoted here is very typical and representative of discussions in Śāstra on the nature of universal or class concept. Familiarity with such discussions in Nyāya or Mīmāṁsā helps to put such statements in Vyākaraṇa in context.

Brahmakāṇḍa

The first four *kārikā*s of the Brahmakāṇḍa summarise the philosophy of Bhartṛhari. *Brahman* is equated to *śabda-tattva*, *śabdaḥ tattvam yasya*, whose manifestation is Veda. From *kārikās* 5 to 10, the Vedas are praised as supreme knowledge in their pristine glory. In *kārikā* 11, *Vyākaraṇa* is venerated as the closest aid to study Veda. The importance of Vyākaraṇa is explained up to *kārikā* 22.

Kārikā 15:

यथार्थजातयः सर्वाः शब्दाकृतिनिबन्धनाः ।
तथैव लोके विद्यानामेषा विद्या परायणम् ॥१५॥

yathārthajātayaḥ sarvāḥ śabdākṛtinibandhanāḥ I
tathaiva loke vidyānāmeṣā vidyā parāyaṇam II25II

Just as all the universals of things depend upon the form of their words for their communication, so is this science the basis of all other sciences, translated by K.A.S. Iyer any entity is understood by the mention of its name. The name is *śabdajāti*, the same word repeated at every mention. The content of the word, the referent, is *arthajāti*. Thus the knowledge of all entities is associated with the form of the word — grammar is indeed a supreme branch of learning. The *Ambākartrī* points out that *arthagata jāti śakyā, śabdagatā jātisca śaktā, lāghavāt.*[3]

Kārikā 23:

नित्याः शब्दार्थसंबन्धास्तत्राम्नाता महर्षिभिः ।
सूत्राणां सानुतञ्त्राणां भाष्याणां च प्रणेतृभिः ॥२३॥

nityāḥ śabdārthasaṁbandhāstatrāmnātā maharṣibhiḥ I
sūtrāṇāṁ sānutañtrāṇāṁ bhāṣyāṇāṁ ca praṇetṛbhiḥ II23II

The *nityatva* of *śabda* is stated here, as the foundation on which the fundamentals of grammar are built. The *nityatva* is of the form of *jāti* or *ākṛti* and also of the nature of *pravāhanityatva*.

3. *VP*, Brahmakāṇḍa, p. 38.

The *Vṛtti* says here that *ākṛti* refers to the form of the word.

तत्र हि शब्द इत्यनेन शब्दाकृतिरभिधीयते ।

tatra hi śabda ityanena śabdākṛtirabhidhīyate ।

Vārttika:

आकृतिनित्यत्वान्नित्यः शब्दः । वा ।

ākṛtinityatvānnityaḥ śabdaḥ । *vā* । — 1.1.19

The *Vṛtti* explains very clearly that *VP* I.23 refers to word being enduring as its form is enduring. Both the concept of *sphoṭa* and *pravāhanityatā* are essential to understand this perspective. This *kārikā* establishes *jāti* at different levels in language, just as the higher and lower *sāmānya*s help cognise *dravya*s in the external world.

Vṛtti

शब्दाकृतिविशेषा हि वृक्षशब्दत्वादयः सति वस्तुसंप्रमोहे निमित्तसरूपतामापन्ना अभिव्यक्ताः शब्दा इत्यपदिश्यते ।

यथा हि घटे द्रव्यत्व-पृथिवीत्व-घटत्वादीनम् अविरुद्धः समवायः, तथा वृक्षशब्देऽपि गुणत्व-शब्दत्व-वृक्षशब्दत्वादीनाम् आकृतिविशेषाणाम् अविरुद्धः समवायः ।

śabdākṛtiviśeṣā hi vṛkṣaśabdatvādyaḥ sati vastusaṁpramohe nimittasarūpatāmāpannā abhivyaktāḥ śabdā ityapadiśyate ।

yathā hi ghaṭe dravyatva-pṛthivītva-ghaṭtvādīnam aviruddhaḥ samavāyaḥ, tathā vṛkṣaśabde 'pi guṇatva-śabdatva-vṛkṣaśabdatvādīnām ākṛtiviśeṣāṇām aviruddhaḥ samavāyaḥ ।

— p. 42

Ambākartrī explains that *abhidhāna* also refers to class concept in a word.

अतोऽभिधानमपि शब्दाकृतिरूपमेव युक्तम् ।

ato 'bhidhānamapi śabdākṛtirūpameva yuktam । — p. 41

The issue of eternality of *śabda* has been discussed earlier in chapter 2.

The class concept as universal in words is clearly illustrated when the same word is uttered by parrot, man, boy, lady, etc. The *Ambākartrī* commentary of Pt. Raghunath Sarma adds — When we start uttering *vakāra* with the intention of pronouncing *vṛkṣa-śabda*, the effort is different to that when uttering *vakāra* with the intention of pronouncing *vṛka-śabda*, even though *vṛka* and *vṛkṣa* are very close in form. Even though there is difference in effort, we categorise both as *vakāra*, as we do not see any tangible difference in class category. But the difference is certain, due to difference in effort, and it is very hard to discern.

Vṛtti

तस्यास्तु शब्दाकृतेरस्तित्वं शुकशारिकामनुष्यादिप्रयुक्तेषु वृक्षादिशब्दव्यक्ति विशेषेषु स एवायमिति प्रत्ययाभेदात् अनुमीयते ।

tasyāstu śabdākṛterastitvaṁ śukaśārikāmanuṣyādiprayukteṣu vṛkṣādiśabdavyakti viśeṣeṣu sa evāyamiti pratyayābhedāt anumīyate ।

Ambākartrī

यद्यपि वृक्षवृकादिशब्देषु वृक्षशब्दं उच्चारयानीति अभिप्रायेण वृक्षशब्दोच्चारणे अन्यः प्रयत्नः, वृकशब्दमुच्चारयाणीति अभिप्रायेण च वृकशब्दोच्चारणे च अन्यः प्रयत्नः । एवं प्रयत्नभेदे सत्यपि वृक्षवृकशब्दयोर्वकारस्य भेदो नोपलभ्यते, जनकप्रयत्नभेदात् तु भेदोऽस्त्येव । स तु दुरवधारः । तदनवधारणाच्च वकारमात्रश्रुतौ वृक्षशब्दत्वरूपजातिविशेषपरिच्छेदो वृकशब्दत्वरूपजातिविशेषपरिच्छेदो वा नास्ति ।

किञ्च, वृक्षशब्दत्वादिरूपा शब्दत्वादपरा जातिर्नाङ्गीकृता व्यक्तौ जातिसंसर्गं अङ्गीकुर्वद्भिरिति चेत्, न, यतः शास्त्रान्तरे परिदृष्टा जात्यभिव्यक्ति प्रक्रिया नावश्यं वैयाकरणैः परिगृह्यते ।

yadyapi vṛkṣavṛkādiśabdeṣu vṛkṣaśabdaṁ uccāryānīti abhiprāyeṇa vṛkṣaśbdoccāraṇe anyaḥ prayatnaḥ, vṛkaśabdamuccārayāṇīti abhiprāyeṇa ca vṛkaśabdoccāraṇe ca anyaḥ prayatnaḥ । *evaṁ prayatnabhede satyapi*

vṛkṣavṛkaśabdayorvakārasya bhedo nopalabhyate, janakaprayatnabhedāt tu bhedo 'styeva । *sa tu duravadhāraḥ* । *tadanavadhāraṇācca vakāramātraśrutau vṛkṣaśabdatva-rūpajātiviśeṣaparicchedo vṛkaśabdatvarūpajātiviśeṣaparicchedo vā nāsti* ।
kiñca, vṛkṣaśabdatvādirūpā śabdatvādaparā jātirnāṅgīkṛtā vyaktau jātisaṁsargaṁ aṅgīkurvadbhiriti ceta, na, yataḥ śāstrāntare paridṛṣṭā jātyabhivyaktiprakriyā nāvaśyaṁ vaiyākaraṇaiḥ parigṛhyate ।

Bhartṛhari then indicates what topics are discussed in the *VP* and what we mean by *apoddhāra*.

अपोद्धारपदार्था ये ये चार्थाः स्थितलक्षणाः ।
अन्वाख्येयास्च ये शब्दा ये चापि प्रतिपादकाः ।।२४।।
कार्यकारणभावेन योग्यभावेन च स्थिताः ।
धर्मे ये प्रत्यये चाङ्गं संबन्धाः साध्वसाधुषु ।।२५।।
ते लिङ्गैश्च स्वशब्दैस्च शास्त्रेऽस्मिन्नुपवर्णिताः ।
स्मृत्यर्थमनुगम्यन्ते केचिदेव यथागमं ।।२६।।

apoddhārapadārthā ye ye cārthāḥ sthitalakṣṇāḥ ।
anvākhyeyāsca ye śabdā ye cāpi pratipādakāḥ ।।24।।
kāryakāraṇabhāvena yogyabhāvena ca sthitāḥ ।
dharme ye pratyaye cāṅgam saṁbandhāḥ sādhvasādhuṣu ।।25।।
te liṅaiśca svaśabdaisca śāstre 'sminnupavarṇitāḥ ।
smṛtyarthamanugamyante kecideva yathāgamaṁ ।।26।।

These *kārikā*s list the eight important topics that grammar chiefly concerns, which are discussed in the *VP*. These are: (i) two kinds of *artha*: the meanings which have been fixed by abstraction, *apoddhārapadārtha*, and those that have a fixed character *sthitalakṣaṇa*; (ii) two kinds of *śabda* forms, those which have to be grammatically analysed *anvākhyeya* and those used for this purpose, *pratipādaka*; (iii) two relations of causality *kāryakāraṇabhāva* and fitness or suitability *yogyatā*; and (iv) two goals or purposes — that which leads to merit and that which leads to understanding of meaning in the case of correct or incorrect forms.

These concepts have already been enunciated in tradition and are dealt with here for the sake of revision so that they may be fixed in memory. Bhartṛhari recalls the long tradition of *sūtrakāra, vṛttikāra* and *bhāṣyakāra* whose illustrious tradition his own work furthers.

*Kārikā*s 27, 28 and 29 say that the correct forms of words have down by long tradition of the *śiṣṭa*s; those who know Vedic matters correctly and whatever be the nature of the words they are eternal. Nobody can question the validity of this learning that has come down to us from the wise sages of yore and is codified in Vyākaraṇa. From *kārikā*s 30 to 43, Bhartṛhari enunciates the importance of *śabda-pramāṇa* embodied by Veda, as the only valid means to understand *dharma* which is the chief purpose of Vedas. All other *pramāṇa*s are shown to be inadequate and unreliable for obtaining true knowledge. Hence it is of utmost importance to understand *śabda* properly.

From *kārikā*s 44 to 117, the serious discussion on the nature of *śabda* is presented. In *kārikā* 44 Bhartṛhari straightaway plunges into the different levels of *śabda*.

द्वावुपादानशब्देषु शब्दौ शब्दविदो विदुः ।
एको निमित्तं शब्दानामपरोऽर्थे प्रयुज्यते ॥४४॥

dvāvupādānaśabdeṣu śabdau śabdavido viduḥ ।
eko nimittaṁ śabdānāmaparo 'rthe prayujyate ॥44॥

When it comes to articulate sound or words that convey sense, there are two kinds or two levels — one audible and the other at the mental level. This is the *sphoṭa*. Taking the two phenomena of speaker articulating a word to convey some meaning and the hearer receiving the sound and then discerning the meaning, we consider the *sphoṭa* to be the cause and the audible sound to be the effect and vice versa. The heard sound does not directly convey meaning to the hearer, but through the *sphoṭa* level in the hearer's mind. This is the fundamental difference between Vyākaraṇa and Mīmāṁsā schools on the process of *śābdabodha*.

Since *sphoṭa* has to be meticulously established, many parallels from everyday life are given. As in the normal process of communication the common man never pauses to think about the subtle levels, the grammarian points out the different stages in the seemingly simple process of one person saying something to another.

Before the spoken word is uttered, its concept comes to mind. Some people say that there are two different qualities and some that they are one. Just as the flame in the kindling sticks or tinderbox leads to another light, so is the *śabda* in the mind the spark from where the uttered sound flashes forth. Shri Vamdeva Acharya rightly mentions that a modern equivalent is matches; just as a match can light another flame in a *dīyā* (candle) so does the *sphoṭa* in the mind initiate the manifest word.

अरणिस्थं यथाज्योतिः प्रकाशान्तरकारणम् ।
तद्वच्छब्दोऽपि बुद्धिस्थः श्रुतीनां कारणं पृथक् ।।४६।।

araṇisthaṁ yathājyotiḥ prakāśāntarakāraṇam ।
tadvacchabdo 'pi buddhisthaḥ śrotīnāṁ kāraṇaṁ pṛthak ।।46।।

Before an utterance is fully manifest with sequence, it is there in seed form in the mind. That is, in normal operation of the mind, one is aware or conscious of what one is going to say the next moment. This word in the mind has no structure or form, no temporal sequence and certainly no characteristics such as speed of utterance, high or low volume! This is in the germ form, like the peahen's egg with its latent potential for the myriad hues. The attributes of *dhvani* or *nāda*, such as temporal sequence, speed, accent, etc., are imputed onto the *sphoṭa*, just as when there are ripples in the water, any reflection in it also appears to quiver, although the original object, say moon, is quite still.

Although *ākṛti* or *jāti* is quite important in all schools of philosophy, Vyākaraṇa gives unique significance to the *ākṛti* form of the word itself, as it deals with linguistics. This is the new concept that Bhartṛhari establishes in this section from *kārikā*s 50 to 69. Just as in a cognition, we are aware of the cognition and its content as two distinct entities, so it is with a word also. The word has its own form and content, although people tend to perceive word and meaning as identical in everyday use.

आत्मरूपं यथा ज्ञाने ज्ञेयरूपं च दृश्यते ।
अर्थरूपं तथा शब्दे स्वरूपं च प्रकाशते ।।५०।।

ātmarūpaṁ yathā jñāne jñeyarūpaṁ ca dṛśyate ।
artharūpaṁ tathā śabde svarūpaṁ ca prakāśate ।।50।।

Just as light has two abilities, that of revealing itself and revealing other objects, in the same way, *śabda* also has the capacity to convey itself to the hearer, and also to convey its import. When we switch on a lamp at night, we are able to see other objects illuminated by the light, such as jar, table, book, etc. But the light by itself is also visible. In the same way, when we hear a foreign language spoken and cannot understand its import, we grasp only the form of the *śabda*. Words do not convey meaning by their mere presence, but only if they are comprehended. This again points to the *sphoṭa* level being required for communication.

ग्राह्यत्वं ग्राहकत्वं च द्वे शक्ती तेजसो यथा ।
तथैव सर्वशब्दानामेते पृथगवस्थिते ।।५५।।

विषयत्वमनापन्नैः शब्दैर्नार्थः प्रकाश्यते ।
न सत्तयैव तेऽर्थानामगृहीताः प्रकाशकाः ॥५६॥

grāhyatvaṁ grāhakatvaṁ ca dve śaktī tejaso yathā |
tathaiva sarvaśabdānāmete pṛthagavasthite ||55||
viṣayatvamanāpannaiḥ śabdairnārthaḥ prakāśyate |
na sattayaiva te 'rthānāmagṛhītāḥ prakāśakāḥ ||56||

Thus, when the form of the word is not heard distinctly, we ask, "What did (you) say?" If only the indistinct sound is heard, but the actual form of the word not clearly distinguished, we cannot get the import. This can happen if the speaker is shouting from afar or over a poor telephone connection. The form of a word should be clearly discerned for proper one-to-one cause-effect relation of word and meaning. In this way, a word has two functions, that of conveying itself, *grāhyatva* and that of conveying meaning, *grāhakatva*. These two functions coexist, one in no way impeding the other.

भेदेनावगृहीतौ द्वौ शब्दधर्मावपोद्धृतौ ।
भेदकार्येषु हेतुत्वमविरोधेन गच्छतः ॥५८॥
वृद्ध्यादयो यथा शब्दाः स्वरूपोपनिबन्धनाः ।
आदैच्प्रत्यायितैः शब्दैः सम्बन्धं यान्ति संज्ञिभिः ॥५९॥

bhedenāvagṛhītau dvau śabdadharmāvapoddhṛtau |
bhedakāryeṣu hetutvamavirodhena gacchataḥ ||58||
vṛddhyādayo yathā śabdāḥ svarūpopanibandhanāḥ |
ādaicpratyāyitaiḥ śabdaiḥ sambandhaṁ yānti saṁjñibhiḥ ||59||

It is only the linguist who is concerned with these aspects. Just as the label *vṛddhi* has its own form and is a *samjñā*. It is also associated with *ādaic* which are the *saṁjñin*s in this case. Bhartṛhari takes such an example to make the illustration clear, rather than one in which the form is *ghaṭa* and the import is also *ghaṭa*.

In this manner, the word *agni* also recalls to the mind other words of same form *agni*, or, other instances where the word *agni* is employed in communication. Hearing the word *agni*, we know that it stands for the instances when the word *agni* is to be used.

The *Vṛtti* explains that in the *sūtra svam rūpam śabdasya*, Pāṇini refers to two aspects of the word. *Svam rūpam* refers to the form that belongs to the word, *śabdasya*. So the word has two aspects, *saṁjñā* and *saṁjñin*, form and meaning or content. So when a word is mentioned in grammar, since the operations are performed on the structure of the word, that is what is intended, not its import. For example, a case ending form applicable to *ākārānta strīliṅga* such as *latā, bālā, ramā,* etc. will yield forms *latāyai, bālāyai, ramāyai*, no matter what be the meaning of each word. In the same way, when *agni śabda* is mentioned in grammar, it stands for all *agni* utterances that are actually used in communication.

The *Ambākartrī* explains: Just as *vṛddhi śabda* refers to *ādaic*, in this case, the *agni śabda* uttered in saying *agnerḍhak* is defined by its form of *agni śabda* is intended to convey others of the same form, on which grammatical operation *ḍhak pratyaya* is intended.[4]

अयमर्थः

तथैव वृद्ध्यादिशब्दवदेव अयमग्निशब्दः अग्नेर्ढक्इति उच्चार्यमाणोऽग्निशब्दः अग्निशब्दनिबन्धनः स्वरूपप्रवृत्तिनिमित्तकः अग्निशब्दाभिधेया सूत्र-घटकाग्निशब्दवाच्यया अग्निश्रुत्या प्रयोगघटकाग्निशब्देन सह संबन्धं संज्ञासंज्ञिसंबन्धं एति गच्चति अनुभवतीति यावत् ।

ayamarthaḥ

tathaiva vṛddhyādiśabdavadeva ayamagniśabdaḥ agnerḍhak iti uccāryamāṇo 'gniśabdaḥ agniśabdanibandhanaḥ svarūpapra-

4. *VP*, p. 108.

vṛttinimittakaḥ agniśabdābhidheyā sūtraghaṭakāgni-śabdavācyayā agniśrutyā prayogaghaṭakāgniśabdena saha saṁbandhaṁ saṁjñāsajñi-saṁbandhaṁ eti gaccati anubhavatīti yāvat ।

Whichever word is uttered is not always the one which executes the direction or action. This doesn't hinder its ability to recall other instances (of the same word) which it represents.

यो य उच्चार्यते शब्दो नियतम् न स कार्यभाक् ।
अन्यप्रत्यायने शक्तिर्न तस्य प्रतिबध्यते ॥६९॥

yo ya uccāryate śabdo niyatam na sa kāryabhāk ।
anyapratyāyane śaktirna tasya pratibadhyate ॥69॥

When a word is uttered for the purpose of illustrating another, the grammatical operations are to be performed on the other of same form. When the uttered word is for the sake of indicating the other exists in the hearer's mind, it no way obstructs its power to convey another similar word. This is the nature of all words that are uttered.

The reason for this is given in the next verse. As the uttered words are only for conveying something else, they are not themselves connected with the action, being secondary to the meaning. The action is connected with the purport of words.

उच्चरन् परतन्त्रत्वाद् गुणः कार्यैर्न युज्यते ।
तस्मात् तदर्थैः कार्याणां संबन्धः परिकल्प्यते ॥६२॥

uccaran paratantratvād guṇaḥ kāryairna yujyate ।
tasmāt tadarthaiḥ kāryāṇāṁ saṁbandhaḥ parikalpyate ॥62॥

The *Vṛtti* explains that just as in *gām ānaya*. The action is connected with the object, cow, not the word, "cow," the when a word is uttered to illustrate another, the grammatical operations are performed on those indicated, not the first one. *Ambākartrī* adds that external objects grasped by the eyes and word forms grasped by ear are employed in our operations, not the initial word uttered for indication.

तस्मात् सर्वस्य प्रत्याय्यस्यार्थस्य चक्षुरादिग्राह्यस्य च क्रियासाधनत्वं विज्ञायते ।

tasmāt sarvasya pratyāyyasyārthasya cakṣudigrāhyasya ca kriyāsādhanatvaṁ vijñāyate ।

In *kārikā* 66, Bhartr̥hari says that before the word is associated with its import, it is first associated with its own form. That is how it obtains a *vibhakti pratyaya*, such as *ṣaṣṭhī* in *agnerḍhak*.

प्राक् संज्ञिनाभिसंबन्धात् संज्ञा रूपपदर्थिका ।
षष्ठ्यास्च प्रथमायास्च निमित्तत्वाय कल्पते ।।६६।।
तत्रार्थवत्वात् प्रथमा संज्ञाशब्दात् विधीयते ।
अस्येति व्यतिरेकश्च तदर्थादेव जायते ।।६७।।
स्वं रूपमिति कैश्चित् व्यक्तिः संज्ञोपदिश्यते ।
जातेः कार्याणि संस्ष्टा जातिस्तु प्रतिपद्यते ।।६८।।

prāk saṁjñinābhisaṁbandhāt saṁjñā rūpapadarthikā ।
ṣaṣṭhyāsca prathamāyāsca nimittatvāya kalpate ।।66।।
tatrārthavatvat prathamā saṁjñāśabdāt vidhīyate ।
asyeti vyatirekśca tadarthādeva jāyate ।।67।।
svaṁ rūpamiti kaiścit vyaktiḥ saṁjñopadiśyate ।
jāteḥ kāryāṇi saṁsr̥ṣṭā jātistu pratipadyate ।।68।।

With a preamble, so to speak, *kārikā* 68 hits the nail on the head by calling each utterance a manifestation of the *jāti*, or prototype of the word. Two different interpretations of Pāṇini *sūtra* 1.1.68 *svam rūpam śabdasya aśabdasaṁjñā*, are alluded to.

The uttered word has two aspects, form and content. There are variant views on the nature of this form itself. Some people hold that the particular utterance *vyakti* constituted by the sequence of letters is the *saṁjñā* or name referred to by *svam rūpam*. The referent of the particular utterance is the general form, or *jāti*, by which the word is understood, in other particular instances wherein the grammatical operation is performed.

According to some people's view, the *vyakti* is referent as *saṁjñā*, in the *sūtra svaṁ rūpam śabdasya aśabdasaṁjñā* and since the individuals are invariably associated with the universal, *jāti*, that becomes implied. Others say that the *vyakti* is to be taken as the named, the label *saṁjñā* referring to *jāti*. In particular instances, the form, which is recognised by the *jāti*, stands for grammatical operations. Iyer writes: While explaining the *sūtra svaṁ rūpam śabdasya*, etc., some commentators say: the own form of a word is the expressor, the illuminator, the conveyor of the word, while others say, the own form of the word is the expressed, the illuminated, the conveyed. These two views have been set forth by these two verses. He continues to explain that in discussions on the very nature of universal of *śabda*, many diverse views are current. Some people hold that each particular has its own form, call it *ākṛti* or configuration. It is by this form and the similarity or commonness among these forms that *sāmānya* or *jāti* is recognised. The other view is that there is only one *jāti* and the several individuals are different manifestations.

Vamdeva Acharya writes that there are small variations in the views of the early grammarians on the explanation of this *sūtra*.

शब्दस्य स्वं रूपं ग्राहकं द्योतकं प्रत्यायकं वा भवति ।

śabdasya svaṁ rūpaṁ grāhakaṁ dyotakaṁ pratyāyakaṁ vā bhavati ।

One view is that the form of the word is what conveys the meaning. The other view is that the form of the word is itself what is conveyed by the utterance of the word. Here *saṁjñā* is to be taken as *grāhaka*, *pratyāyaka* or *dyotaka* and *saṁjñin* is to be taken as *grāhya, dyotya* or *pratyāyya*. This *sūtra* again refers to two aspects of the word, *śabdajāti* and *arthajāti*.

> अनेकव्यक्त्यभिव्यङ्ग्या जातिः स्फोट इति स्मृता ।
> कैश्चिद् व्यक्तय एवास्या ध्वनित्वेन प्रकल्पिताः ।।९३।।
>
> *anekavyaktyabhivyaṅgyā jātiḥ sphoṭa iti smṛtā* ।
> *kaiścid vyaktaya evāsyā dhvanitvena prakalpitāḥ* ।।93।।

Although there is more to *sphoṭa* than the phonological structure alone, the case is stated very simply and clearly here. Those who uphold the eternality of *śabda* because of universal, illustrate that the *sphoṭa* is the *jāti* and that individual utterances, *dhvani*s are the manifestations. This *jāti* is different from the superset of *śabdatva* and is sentence-specific or word-specific. K.A.S. Iyer writes that earlier, in verse 69, it was declared that the universal is the name and the individual is the named and here, the view that the universal is the *sphoṭa* is set forth.

Vākyakāṇḍa

The Sentence: In Bhartṛhari's philosophy, the sentence as a unified whole is the real language, the significant utterance. It is an indivisible unit, with no real parts. We must not confuse the myriad forms of individual sentences or their diversity with the true indivisible nature of the cognition arising from the divisions which are only practical abstractions. The *vācaka*, the true sentence is the *sphoṭa*, of the form of *akhaṇḍa-vākya* or *vākya-sphoṭa,* which is the ultimate level of language. All lower levels are only practical devices that aid in reaching this level and have no real significance of their own. The idea in the mind which is the seed of the expression that manifests, has no form or structure. The urge to communicate is not language specific.

The idea in the mind, the flash of understanding, *pratibhā*, is the true *śabda*. All modes of communicating it — full sentence, half sentence (elliptic) or single word, Sanskrit or Apabhraṁśa, are all incidental details. While analysing the manner in which a language is learnt, other schools such as Mīmāṁsā and Nyāya describe what happens in society. *Vr̥ddha-vyavahāra, anvaya-vyatireka, śaktigraha,* etc. are used to explain the cause-effect theory of language. It is only Bhartr̥hari who takes the process deeper within the mind and talks of *śabda-bhāvanā,* intuition within the child which prompts him to use language.

The focus of the second *kāṇḍa* is the sentence. Bhartr̥hari upholds the *akhaṇḍa-vākya-pakṣa* against the *sakhaṇḍa-pakṣa* and explains his viewpoint over 490 *kārikā*s. Certain details of grammar such as meaning of word as *mukhya-viśeṣya, karmapravacanīya, kāraka, samāsa* and elliptical construction and their significance to sentence meaning are also discussed. The *kāṇḍa* ends with a very brief history of study of grammar prior to Bhartr̥hari. This section of this research project selects out the references to the concept of universal in the second *kāṇḍa* and presents a brief sketch.

The first two *kārikā*s list eight ways of looking at the sentence broadly current. Of these, three are in harmony with Bhartr̥hari's view, viz. (i) *jātiḥ saṁghātavartinī,* (ii) *eko anavayavaḥ,* (iii) *buddhyanusaṁhr̥ḥ.*

आख्यातशब्दः सङ्घातो जातिः सङ्घातवर्तिनी ।
एकोऽनवयः शब्दः क्रमो बुद्ध्यनुसंहृतिः ॥१॥
पदमाद्यं पृथक् सर्वं पदं साकाङ्क्षमित्यपि ।
वाक्यं प्रति मतिर्भिन्ना बहुधा न्यायवादिनाम् ॥२॥

ākhyātaśabdaḥ saṁghāto jātiḥ saṁghātavartinī ।
eko 'navayaḥ śabdaḥ kramo buddhyanusaṁhr̥tiḥ ॥1॥
panamādyaṁ pr̥thak sarvaṁ padaṁ sākāṅkṣamityapi ।
vākyaṁ prati matirbhinnā bahudhā nyāyavādinām ॥2॥

(i) When many sentences utterances of the same sentence are heard and perceived as such, it is the *jāti*, universal in the group of words that is recognised. The understanding of the commonality, *sāmānya* is the basis for the understanding of class concept.

(ii) The sentence is one unified complete utterance, without any parts that it can be broken into.

(iii) A third way in which a sentence can be viewed is *buddhyanusaṁhṛtiḥ*, that is, a cognition in the mind without explicit structure or sequence, in which form and meaning are merged. The external sentence conceived as a single entity (*eko anavayaḥ śabdaḥ*) or as a persisting common factor *jāti* is only a symbol of this inner sentence, just as the written alphabet is a symbol of the alphabet which is uttered.[5]

सामान्यार्थस्तिरो भृतो न विशेषेऽवतिष्ठते ।
उपात्तस्य कुतस्त्यागो निवृत्तः क्वावतिष्ठताम् ।।२५।।

sāmānyārthastiro bhṛto na viśeṣe 'vatiṣṭhate ।
upāttasya kutastyāgo nivṛttaḥ kvāvatiṣṭhatām ।।25।।

According to the *abhihitānvaya* view of Mīmāṁsā, the import of a word is in *ākṛti*, or *jāti*. When employed in a sentence, it gives rise to particular cognition in association with the other words. Bhartṛhari criticises this view. How can the general meaning simply disappear and give rise to a particular cognition?

विशेषशब्दाः केषाञ्चित् सामन्यप्रतिरूपकाः ।
शब्दान्तराभिसंबन्धात् व्यज्यन्ते प्रतिपत्तृषु ।।

viśeṣaśabdāḥ keṣāñcit sāmanyapratirūpakāḥ ।
śabdāntarābhisaṁbandhāt vyajyante pratipttṛṣu ।।

— *VP*, II.17

5. Iyer, *Bhartṛhari*, p. 161.

This refers to definitions 7 and 8 of the sentence. The *anvitābhidhāna* view says that the particular words, seemingly having the universal form, are revealed to the hearer by virtue of their association with the other words in the sentence and hence convey the particular meaning.

यथा क्षेपविशेषेऽपि कर्मभेदो न गृह्यते ।
आवृत्तौ व्यज्यते जातिः कर्मभिर्भ्रमणादिभिः ॥२०॥
वर्णवाक्यपदेष्वेवं तुल्योपव्यञ्जना श्रुतिः ।
अत्यन्तभेदे तत्त्वस्य सरूपेव प्रतीयते ॥२१॥

yathā kṣepaviśeṣe 'pi karmabhedo na gr̥hyate ।
āvr̥ttau vyajyate jātiḥ karmabhirbhramaṇādibhiḥ ॥20॥
varṇavākyapadeṣvevaṁ tulyopavyañjanā śrutiḥ ।
atyantabhede tattvaya sarūpeva partīyate ॥21॥

Here the class concept or universal in *śabda* is established, using the universal in actions as an analogy. If we analyse an action such as throwing or running moment by moment, i.e. split into a series of actions, each part, as it were, may not reveal the universal. The minute part of the action may be common to several different actions. But upon continuous occurrence or repetition, the *jāti* is revealed by the activity. In the same way, although each utterance is actually different, the sameness is recognised as *jāti* in words, phonemes and sentences.

केवलेन पदेनार्थो यावानेवाभिधीयते ।
वाक्यस्थं तावतोऽर्थस्य तदाहुरभिधायकम् ॥४१॥
संबन्धे सति यत्त्वन्यदाधिक्यमुपजायते ।
वाक्यार्थमेव तं प्राहुरनेकपदसंशयम् ॥४२॥

kevalena padenārtho yāvānevābhidhīyate ।
vākyasthaṁ tāvato 'rthasya tadāhurabhidhāyakam ॥41॥
saṁbandhe sati yattvanyadādhikyamupajāyate ।
vādyārthameva taṁ prāhuranekapadasaṁśayam ॥42॥

The *abhihitānvaya* view of sentence-meaning is referred to here. The word by itself has a direct meaning (called *abhidhā*) which remains in all situations; but when employed in sentence, together with the other words in the sentence, it conveys an additional sense, *vākyārtha*. The *vākyārtha* exists in all the words together.

स त्वनेकपदस्थोऽपि प्रतिभेदं समाप्यते ।
जातिवत् समुदायेऽपि संख्यावत् कल्प्यते परैः ॥४३॥

sa tvanekapadastho 'pi pratibhedaṁ samāpyate ।
jātivat samudāye 'pi saṁkhyāvat kalpyate paraiḥ ॥43॥

The sentence-meaning reveals itself through several words, such as universal, reveals itself through the whole group, not individually, in the same manner that number reveals itself as in the example of six jars. This harks back to the two different modes of a class concept manifesting — *pratyekam parisamāptam* and *vyāsajyavṛtti*. The first implies that although *jāti* is one and eternal, it is contained in entirety by each of the innumerable individuals manifesting it. For example, every individual cow manifests cow-universal completely. The other manner in which an entity is revealed requires all its parts to reveal the whole at once, e.g. a dozen. To illustrate *vākyārtha*, the *Vṛtti* on *kārikā* 43 uses both examples. The first line equates *vākyārtha* to *jāti*, which although revealed fully by one individual, does not cause shortfall in another individual.

तद्यथा जातिवत् सत्तावानेकाधिकरणयोगेऽपि प्रत्यधिकरणमन्यूनकार्या तथायमेकेषां वाक्यार्थ आवृत्तिन्युनतासमतिक्रमेण प्रतिपदमेवाविकलः समाप्यते । अथापरः कल्पः यथैकस्या विंशत्यादिकायाः संख्यायाः प्रत्यधिकरणं तन्निमित्तप्रत्ययहेतुत्वं तथा वाक्यार्थस्य प्रतिपदं प्रत्याय्यत्वेन अवस्थानमिति ।

tadyathā jātivat sattāvānekādhikaraṇayoge 'pi

pratydhikaraṇamanyūnakāryā tathāyamekeṣāṁ vākyārtha āvṛttinyunatāsamatikrameṇa pratipadamevāvikalaḥ samāpyate I *athāparaḥ kalpaḥ yathaikasyā viṁśatyādikāyāḥ saṁkhyāyāḥ pratyadhikaraṇaṁ tannimittapratyayahetutvaṁ tathā vākyārthasya pratipadaṁ pratyāyyatvena avasthānamiti* I

The second line takes the example of a group revealing *jāti*. The sight of one individual does not lead to our cognition of *jāti* — only when a second individual is perceived as the same, do we truly cognise *jāti*. The *Vṛtti* gives the example of the number twenty (say, jars) being manifest only by twenty jars together.

नित्यत्वे समुदायानां जातेर्वा परिकल्पने ।
एकस्यैवार्थतामाहुर्वाक्यस्याव्यभिचारिणीम् ।।५६।।

nityatve samudāyānāṁ jātervā parikalpane I
ekasyaivārthatāmāhurvākyasyāvyabhicāriṇīm ||56||

The *vākya-sphoṭa* view is summarised. While admitting the *jāti* nature of a sentence, it is still held subordinate to the *sphoṭa* nature of sentence. In the case of eternality of the group of words forming a sentence-universal, only one invariable sentence-meaning is admitted.

प्रतिवर्णं असंवेद्यः पदार्थप्रत्ययो यथा ।
पदेष्वेवमसंवेद्यं वाक्यार्थस्य निरूपणम् ।।६०।।

prativarṇaṁ asaṁvedyaḥ padārthapratyayo yathā I
padeṣvevaṁasaṁvedyaṁ vākyārthasya nirūpaṇam ||60||

This further elaborates on the nature of the *vākya-sphoṭa*. Just as the *sphoṭa* of a word is not revealed by each *varṇa* singly, in the same sentence-meaning is also formulated as not revealed by each word singly, but only in tandem with one another.

अविभक्तेऽपि वाक्यार्थे शक्तिभेदादपोद्धृते ।
वाक्यान्तरविभागेन यथोक्तं न विरुध्यते ।।८८।।

यथैवैकस्य गन्धस्य भेदेन परिकल्पना ।
पुष्पादिषु तथा वाक्येऽप्यर्थभेदो विधीयते ॥८९॥

avibhakte 'pi vādyārthe śakti bhedādapoddhṛte ।
vākyāntaravibhāgena yathoktaṁ na virudhyate ॥88॥
yathaivaikasya gandhasya bheden parikalpanā ।
puṣpādiṣu tathā vākye 'pyarthabhedo vidhīyate ॥89॥

The objections of the *padavādin* are answered here. Although the sentence-meaning is an indivisible whole, by virtue of different *śakti* or capacity of the different words, *apoddhāra* or division for analysis, is possible within the sentence. Just as a single entity, scent, when further differentiated as that of flowers, etc., i.e. its components, still retains its identity, in the same way a sentence is divided into words, verb, phrases, clauses, etc.

गवये नरसिंहे वाप्येकज्ञानावृते यथा ।
भागं जात्यन्तरस्यैव सदृशं प्रतिपद्यते ॥९०॥
अप्रसिद्धं तु यं भागमदृष्टमनुपश्यति ।
तावत्यसंविदं मूढः सर्वत्र प्रतिपद्यते ॥९१॥

gavaye narasiṁhe vāpyekajñānāvṛte yathā ।
bhāgaṁ jātyantarasyaiva sadṛśaṁ pratipadyate ॥90॥
aprasiddhaṁ tu yaṁ bhāgamadṛṣṭamanupaśyati ।
tāvatyasaṁvidaṁ mūḍhaḥ sarvatra pratipadyate ॥91॥

Words have only relative reality and are parts of a sentence only as provisional means to comprehend the entirety. Just as in the case where a new animal *gavaya*, similar to cow, is seen, or likening Narasiṁha to Half-man and Half-lion, for the sake of understanding, a strange entity belonging to a different class or universal is understood by its similarity in part to a known species. Since a part of it still unknown, the whole is still beyond the understanding of an ignorant person.

एकस्य भागे सादृश्यं भागे भेदश्च लक्ष्यते ।
निर्भागस्य प्रकाशस्य निर्भागेनैव चेतसा ॥९३॥

ekasya bhāge sādṛśyaṁ bhāge bhedaśca lakṣyate ।
nirbhāgasya prakāśasya nirbhāgenaiva cetasā ॥93॥

Thus, in such examples, we see similarity in part and dichotomy in part. In the same way, the mind which has no part, imputes parts to *prakāśa*, knowledge (or *śabda*) which is also actually indivisible.

तथैव भागे सादृश्यं भागे भेदोऽवसीयते ।
भागाभावेऽपि वाक्यानामत्यन्तं भिन्नधर्मणाम् ॥९४॥

tathaiva bhāge sādṛśyaṁ bhāge bhedo 'vasīyate ।
bhāgābhāve 'pi vākyānāmatyantaṁ bhinnadharmaṇām ॥94॥

In the same way, sentences are compared and thought of as similar in certain ways and dissimilar in other ways, although each has its unique, indivisible meaning of its own.

संहिताविषये वर्णाः स्वरूपेणाविकारिणः ।
शब्दान्तरत्वं यान्तीव शक्त्यन्तरपरिग्रहात् ॥१०४॥

saṁhitāviṣaye varṇāḥ svarūpeṇāvikāriṇaḥ ।
śabdāntaratvaṁ yāntīva śaktyantaraparigrahāt ॥104॥

Although a *varṇa* has its own identity and has a *varṇa sphoṭa* recognisable by the specific *jāti*, say, *ga kāra*, when uttered in combination with other syllables it may appear to be different as it takes on different capacities.

The meaning of a word is discussed from *kārikā*s 118 to 150. *Jāti* is widely accepted as the import of a word, although there are around seven other views. In this discussion, the universal being the import of the word is objected to and criticised, to focus on the opponent's viewpoint.

जातेः प्रत्यायके शब्दे या व्यक्तिरनुषङ्गिणी ।
न तद् व्यक्तिगतान् भेदान् जातिशब्दोऽवलंबते ॥१२२॥

jāteḥ pratyāyake śabde yā vyaktiranuṣaṅiṇī ।
na tad vyaktigatān bhedān jātiśabdo 'valambate ॥122॥

When the class-word has universal as its import and refers to an individual, the word cannot convey any features of the individual entity. So this would become a shortcoming in the *jāti śabda* conveying information about the particular in whose sense it is used.

लोकेऽर्थरूपतां शब्दः प्रतिपन्नः प्रवर्तते ।
शास्त्रे तूभयरूपत्वं प्रविभक्तं विवक्षया ॥१३०॥

loke 'rtharūpatāṁ śabdaḥ pratipannaḥ pravartate ।
śāstre tūbhayarūpatvaṁ pravibhaktaṁ vivakṣayā ॥130॥

The form of the word, *jāti* or *ākṛti* is in the whole word, *saṁghāta*. In the example of the words *kūpa, yūpa, sūpa*, the common syllable contributes nothing common in the meanings of the three words having common sound element for the most part. Only one *varṇa* is different in each of the three words, but the meanings have no connection. The *sphoṭa* of each word is in the total form.

न कूपयूपसूपानामन्वयोऽर्थस्य दृश्यते ।
अतोऽर्थान्तरवाचित्वं सङ्घातस्यैव गम्यते ॥१६९॥

na kūpayūpasūpānāmanvayo 'rthasya dṛśyate ।
ato 'rthāntaravācitvaṁ saṁghātasyaiva gamyate ॥169॥

In worldly transactions, the word is used to identify the thing denoted by it; in grammar, both divisions are intended — the form of the word and its import.

सामन्येनोपदेशाश्च शास्त्रे लघ्वर्थमाश्रितः ।
जात्यन्तरवदस्यापि विशेषाः प्रतिपादकाः ॥१७६॥

sāmanyenodeśāśca śāstre laghvarthamāśritaḥ ।
jātyantaravadasyāpi viśeṣāḥ pratipādakāḥ ॥176॥

For the sake of brevity, in grammar, many words of the same

form, i.e. a whole category, is indicated by one common representative. As in the case of any other universal, the category or class is illustrated by many particulars.

तथा स्वरूपं शब्दानां सर्वार्थेष्वनुषज्यते ।
अर्थमात्रं विपर्यस्तं शब्दः स्वार्थे व्यवस्थितः ॥२५६॥

tathā svarūpaṁ śabdānāṁ sarvārtheṣvanuṣajyate ।
arthamātraṁ viparyastaṁ śabdaḥ svārthe vyavasthitaḥ ॥256॥

This is in the context of words that have several meanings, or polysemy. How do we explain the one-to-one correspondence of word and meaning in instances such as *madhu* or *kara*? Some people say that the same word, e.g. *kara* has different meanings such as tax and hand. Some people say that they are actually two different words, one meaning, hand and the other, tax, mistaken to be the same word due to similarity in form. Bhartṛhari says that the form of the word is associated with all its meanings. Only the objects denoted change. The word permanently remains linked to its (own) form (as its meaning).[6] In this *kārikā* Bhartṛhari clearly makes a distinction between *śabdajāti* and *arthajāti*. While Mīmāṁsā talks of import of a word being in *ākṛti*, or universal, it is silent on the configuration of the word itself. But in Bhartṛhari's system, the word has two functions.

जातिशब्दोऽन्तरेणापि जातिं यत्र प्रयुज्यते ।
संबन्धिसदृशाद्धर्माद् तं गौणमपरे विदुः ॥२७३॥

jātiśabdo 'ntareṇāpi jātiṁ yatra prayujyate ।
saṁbandhisadṛśāddharmād taṁ gauṇamapare viduḥ ॥273॥

This *kārikā* discusses the instance where a word gives suggested sense. Usually, the *jāti* is considered the import of a word. *Jāti* is the *pravṛtti-nimitta* of the word, the reason behind

---

6. Pillai, 1971, p. 96.

the choice of that word. So when a *jātiśabda* is used without intending to convey the idea caused by that *jāti* and since some other idea associated with that *jāti* is intended, we call this secondary sense of the word, e.g. *gaurvāhīkaḥ* or *agnirmāṇavakaḥ*. Puṇyarāja[7] explains that in *gaurvāhīkaḥ*, the word *go* is used without *gotvajāti* being its import; its similarity is stated in *vāhīka*. This is the difference between primary *abhidhā* or *mukhya* sense and secondary or *gauṇa* sense. The *Vṛtti* says further that in the case of proper nouns such as *dittha*, as it is still primary sense as the name does associate with the *ākṛti*, i.e. a permanent sense akin to universal. *Dittha* does not change day-to-day, so the name refers to the same concept.

7. *Vākyapadīya* II [16].

5

The Jāti and Dravya Samuddeśas

The Jāti Samuddeśa

Introduction

THE Jāti Samuddeśa is the first of fourteen sections of the third book of the *Vākyapadīya* called Padakāṇḍa or Prakīrṇaka. For convenience of the readers the *Kārikā*s (*śloka*s) of the Jāti Samuddeśa (as also of Dravya Samuddeśa and the Bhūyo Dravya Samuddeśa) are shown within the text with their English transliteration. The Jāti Samuddeśa has 106 *kārikā*s which may be grouped in the following manner.

*Kārikā*s 1 to 19 discuss the nature of word-meaning and how it corresponds to *jāti*, the universal. *Kārikā*s 20 to 48 discuss cosmology and take a philosophical view of the world with *jāti* at the focus of creation.

*Kārikā*s 49 to 72 discuss the significance of *saṁkhyā*, (number) and how it is to be understood as word-meaning in different contexts.

*Kārikā*s 73 to 91 discuss the issue of substitution of an item that may not be available for *yajña* and how the word-meaning is to be understood so as to obtain the correct substitution or representation. This is of vital importance in practical situations of Vedic ritual and this subject also clearly displays the differences in the method of *śābdabodha* in the two schools of Mīmāṁsā and Vyākaraṇa. Since the chief concern of the former is accurate implementation of Vedic injunctions, any linguistic tenet that disables the justification of substitution would be outright rejected. Therefore it is of vital importance to show that the concept of *akhaṇḍa vākya* is quite harmonious with the selecting of *pratinidhi* without resorting to *padārtha* having real status.

After a lengthy and elaborate preamble that actually forms the main body of the Jāti Samuddeśa, *kārikā*s 92 to 106 quickly sum up the true nature of *jāti* as akin to ultimate reality and also list the different ways of looking at the concept of universal in different schools of thought. It is abundantly clear that Bhartr̥hari subscribed to a monistic view of the world, that, without being partisan, preceded the development of Advaita Vedānta that is best represented at its peak by Ādi Śaṅkara. The importance accorded to *jāti* is in keeping with Bhartr̥hari's philosophy.

Yet, in the Dravya Samuddeśa he says that *dravya* is the Ultimate Reality, showing the relevance of such a view. Rather than any contradiction, this shows the comprehensiveness of Bhartr̥hari's world-view. The means are various, but the truth is one. In using any means to understand the truth, it is equally essential to understand the means as such and not confuse it with the end in itself. In other words, the same concept of *apoddhāra* extends beyond linguistic principles to general philosophy. This astute understanding of the fifth century is valid even today, when we have sophisticated models of the universe put together by the principles of modern science.

उपाया: शिष्यमाणानां बालानामुपलापना: ।
असत्ये वर्त्मनि स्थित्वा तत: सत्यं समीहते ।।

upāyāḥ śiṣyamāṇānāṁ bālānāmupalāpanāḥ ।
asatye vartmani sthitvā tataḥ satyaṁ samīhate ।।

— *VP*, II.238

The philosophy of Bhartṛhari forms a constant backdrop to his linguistics and it is quite inappropriate to interpret any portion of the *Vākyapadīya* in isolation. While the first *kāṇḍa* enunciates *śabda-tattva* and *sphoṭa*, and the second mainly concerned with the indivisible sentence, the third *kāṇḍa* discusses the various aspects of *pada* or word. The first *kāṇḍa* sets the provisional reality of the *pada* in context of true reality of the *vākya* by means of *apoddhāra*. Whereas the sentence meaning as a whole is the purport, the word meanings are understood in part as abstractions of the indivisible whole.

WORD-MEANING IS JĀTI

> द्विधा कैश्चित् पदं भिन्नं चतुर्धा पञ्चधापि वा।
> अपोद्धृत्यैव वाक्येभ्यः प्रकृतिप्रत्ययादिवत्॥१॥
>
> *dvidhā kaiścit padaṁ bhinnaṁ caturdhā pañcadhāpi vā |*
> *apoddhṛtyaiva vākyebhyaḥ prakṛtipratyayādivat | | 1 | |*

The word is an unreal, imagined part abstracted from the sentence, just as *prakṛti pratyaya*, base and suffix, are imaginary parts of a word itself. Words themselves are classified in different ways by different people; some consider a twofold division, some fourfold and some, fivefold, etc. Helārāja discusses the technical implications of these different divisions in grammar. Words are obtained as artificial abstractions of a sentence, which is an indivisible whole, more than just a string of syllables. The abstractions of word depend on how the sentence meaning is analysed, which may be done differently by different schools of thought. It is the sentence which is actually *vācaka*, expressive. The cognition of individual words and their meanings is really an illusion, *vibhrama*.[1]

Sentences are infinite in number and no two are identical.

1. Iyer, 1971, p. 1.

Their artificial parts seem to resemble each other and these parts are abstracted from the sentence as that is the only way we can explain the sentence. while the Mīmāṁsā philosophy builds up the sentence-meaning from the meanings of words which are the constituent parts, Vyākaraṇa holds that the meaning ascribed to the parts depends on the whole indivisible purport of a sentence. The status of the individual word meanings is as unreal as that of the parts into which even a word can be broken, viz., base, stem and suffix.

The views on the nature of the indivisible sentence are varied. It is by artificially imposing our imagination that the words are abstracted. Those who hold the sentence as undivided whole, *vākyavādī*s, consider the different words as provisional abstractions. Those who hold the words as eternal, the *padavādī*s such as Mīmāṁsakas, consider the grammatical parts such as root, affix, prefix, suffix, etc., as the abstracted parts. Both hold the abstractions as provisional means, not true as an end in itself. It is division in meaning that is behind the division of parts. Otherwise, there is the danger of abstracting to the syllable level, having to derive even the alphabets! Within the sentence, the parts and whole are determined by the relation of the action to the different words and the verb.

The twofold division of words takes noun, *nāma* and verb, *ākhyāta* into account. These two categories encompass particles, prefixes and indeclinables, as they only serve to qualify nouns and verbs.

But some people view *nipāta* and *upasarga* as separate categories of words, as they do not directly convey any meaning but only by modifying the meaning of *nāma* and *ākhyāta*. Such is the fourfold division of words.

Some others consider the division as fivefold, taking adverbs or *kriyāviśeṣaṇa* as a separate category. Even there, the verb is explicitly mentioned in some cased and not so in others. Where mentioned, the relationship with the other words (nouns) is also explicit, justifying the construction of the sentence with suitable *vibhakti*s, etc. the uttered verb is directly related to the noun without the aid of a second action. For instance, *mātuḥ smarati*. Others explain the connection introducing one more verb, such as, "As he sets out, *avatiṣṭhate*, makes arrangements with regard to his mother, therefore this remembering is in relation to his mother."

पदार्थानामपोद्धारे जातिर्वा द्रव्यमेव वा ।
पदार्थौ सर्वशब्दानां नित्यावेवोपवर्णितौ ।।२।।

padārthānāmapoddhāre jātirvā dravyameva vā |
padārthau sarvaśabdānāṁ nityāvevopavarṇitau | |2| |

When we consider the import of a word, some people hold that it is *jāti*, universal or class concept; some schools hold that it is the individual or *vyakti*, while some others take it to be the individual qualified by the universal.

Padārtha or import of a word can be any of the three mentioned above. As the *Gautama-Sūtra* also indicates, the import of a word can be universal, individual or even the shape/structure/form.

In the *MBh* Patañjali discusses the meaning of a word along with nature of word, in the *paspaśāhnika*. Vyākaraṇa is built on the premise that *śabda*, *artha* and their *sambandha* are *nitya*. In showing *śabda* to be *nitya*, he introduces the broad sense of eternality — whatever endures is permanent — the concept of *pravāhanityatā*.

तदपि नित्यं यस्मिन्स्तत्त्वं न विहन्यते।

tadapi nityaṁ yasminstattvaṁ na vihanyate | — *MBh.* Pas.

This places the issue of eternality of *śabda* in perspective from the practical context of the grammarian's task without quarrelling over the ontological position of *śabda* in different schools of philosophy. Patañjali shows that the import, *padārtha* is always *nitya*, whether in universal or particular. The universal, *jāti* or *ākṛti* or *sāmānya* is of course *nitya* as discussed earlier. Patañjali explicitly takes even *dravya* as *nitya*.

अथ वा द्रव्यं नित्यम्।

atha vā dravyaṁ nityam ।

When both, universal and particular are conveyed, one may take greater importance than the other in a particular context; therefore only one is actually conveyed. Vājapyāyana taught that the import of a word was in the universal. In the case of verbs, the universal of action conveyed by the verb is connected to the particular which is accomplishing the action and through this, to the universal of the agent. The universal of action is manifested in the different moments in which it occurs, and not at once, as in the case of material objects. This is the fundamental issue referred to by *mūrtivivartta kriyāvivartta* or *sattvapradhāna bhāvapradhāna* pair of words.

The second *vā śabda* in the *sūtra* indicates the third option, viz. individual qualified by the universal as the import of the word. In Pāṇini's school of thought import of a word, i.e. *jāti* and *dravya, padārthau,* is mentioned in dual number. In nouns such as "cow", the universal *gotva* is conveyed as it inheres in the individual that is connected by action that is intended to be performed on "cow". This is effected by the *dravya,* the item.

Verb forms also indicate the universal. Whereas the action might appear to be different in different instants of time, as the meaning of the verb such as "walk" or "cook" covers all the different actions leading to the execution of the same verb, it is the universal that is covering all aspects of *kāraka*, i.e. connections with action, or the *vibhakti*s, is secondary here. Words such as *upasarga*s and others also convey their class-meanings, in conjunction with the impact of noun or verb which they qualify. Qualities such as "white" also convey the universal of "whiteness" being common to all things white. Even proper nouns such as *ḍittha* are established to be conveying universal as import. There is no word that is unique. This is according to Vājapyāyana's school of thinking.

In Vyāḍi's school of thought, all words convey the individual, as action can only be associated with the item. Although the *jāti* is not mentioned, it is suggested by association with the individual, just as a crow that is perched on a rather by chance is pointed out to mark the house from a distance. It is not permanently associated with the house, but serves to identify it. Verbs also convey the individual as being employed in that activity, as there cannot be action without the means, *sādhana*, to execute it. For example, in *devadattaḥ pacati*, the individual is engrossed in the activity of cooking. Pronouns also convey only the individual, such as, "This is it", as every time the word is used, it indicates something. Qualities such as white also indicate some item that is white in colour.

In *kārikā* 13 of Jāti Samuddeśa, Bhartṛhari accepts this view ascribed to Vyāḍi. Helārāja writes the taking *dravya* to mean "substance", all words convey the primordial substance, *Brahman*. Taking *dravya* to be synonymous with *vyakti*, individual every word has at its import *jāti* or *dravya*. So both the views exist and the Jāti Samuddeśa we examine the former view.

Iyer writes: Even though the universal of action is eternal, it becomes a process (*sādhya*) through the particular.

केषाञ्चित् साहचर्येण जातिः शक्त्युपलक्षणम् ।
खदिरादिष्वशक्तेषु शक्तः प्रतिनिधीयते ॥३॥

keṣāñcit sāhacaryeṇa jātiḥ śaktyupalakṣaṇam |
khadirādiṣvaśakteṣu śaktaḥ pratinidhīyate | |3| |

अस्वातन्त्र्यफलो बन्धिः प्रमाणादीव शिष्यते ।
अतो जात्यभिधानेऽपि शक्तिहीनं न गृह्यते ॥४॥

asvātantryaphalo bandhiḥ pramāṇādīva śiṣyate |
ato jātyabhidhāne 'pi śaktihīnaṁ na gṛhyate | |4| |

According to the view of some people, the universal serves to convey the capacity or properties of the thing mentioned, because of its invariable association with those properties. When an item is mentioned, some understanding of the required qualities is also conveyed. Therefore, in the case where the required item is not available, only a substitute having the required qualities is used, not any other. Iyer says: "Those words which express the accessories mainly denote capacity."

Helārāja[2] writes that *upalakṣaṇam* means *upāyaḥ*. The *jāti* serves as a means of conveying certain aspects of what is required for the purpose, *kāryayogāt*.

Some people hold that the mention of *jāti* does not convey *śakti*, but the sense of *jāti* is primarily the word-meaning or *abhidhā*. The next verse explains that in this case also, substitution is easily accomplished. Even when the universal is clearly understood as the primary meaning, a specimen which does not have the required capacity is never used, e.g. in *khadire badhnāti*, etc., a slender twig of the same wood will not be used as binding the animal to the post is followed by slaying it.

2. Jāti samuddeśa.

The sentence-meaning conveyed being binding of the animal to the post, taking a post that can withstand the animal bound to it what is meant.

संश्लेषमात्रं बध्नातिर्यदि स्यात्तु विवक्षितः ।
शक्त्याश्रये ततो लिङ्गं प्रमाणाद्यनुशासनम् ।।५।।

saṁśleṣamātraṁ badhnātiryadi syāttu vivikṣitaḥ |
śaktyāśraye tato liṅgaṁ pramāṇādyanuśāsanam | |5| |

The idea is continued in the next verse by pointing out that even if binding literally means only contact with the sacrificial post, the very fact that killing is the next step indicates that an efficient thing is to be taken.

The sentence-meaning has action as primary. *Kriyā* is *pradhāna* in *vākyārtha*. Therefore, an efficient means is to be taken, which may be indicated by a qualifying word, e.g. *khadire yūpe badhnāti*. If a *khadire* post is unavailable, some other wood may be taken as substitute, but a post is required to execute the action. The means may be substituted, but not the very action, as it is the main thing. If some other action is resorted to, it would be a violation of Vedic injunction, which is to be avoided.

The next *kārikā* explicitly states the idea *Bh* introduces from *kārikā* 66 onwards in the Brahmakāṇḍa, viz. that every word has its own *jāti* distinct from *śabda-tattvajāti*. We recognise a word for what it is because we recognise the prototype and understand the class.

स्वा जातिः प्रथमं शब्दैः सर्वैरेवाभिधीयते ।
ततोऽर्थजातिरूपेषु तदध्यारोपकल्पना ।।६।।

svā jātiḥ prathamaṁ śabdaiḥ sarvairevābhidhīyate |
tato 'rthajātirūpeṣu tadadhyāropakalpanā | |6| |

Kārikā 6 says that every word first conveys its own *jāti* of form, which is then associated with the *jāti* of meaning, *padārtha*.

Since the association is so immediate and strong, we take the two to be one. This is the *duravadhāra* that the *Ambākartrī* discusses in the Brahmakāṇḍa.

> We take the two as one. To understand the one as being superimposed on the other implies that we consider the two to be different. We do this but it is only a fiction, *kalpanā* on our part, because the meaning (object), according to grammar, is only an unreal manifestation, *vivartta* of the word.[3]

Helārāja says:

> प्राक् संज्ञिनाभिसम्बन्धात् संज्ञा रूपपदार्थिका इत्युक्तुम्। रूपं हि स्वरूपं स्वा जातिर्वेति दर्शनभेदेन कथ्यते।
>
> *prāk saṁjñinābhisambandhāt saṁjñā rūpapadārthikā ityuktum* I *rūpaṁ hi svarūpaṁ svā jātirveti darśanabhedena kathyate* I

Svā here means *asādhāraṇī*, that is, one's own, not the common universal, *śabatattva*, common to all words. Every words conveys two *jāti*s, first its own form, then of its import. Kātyāyana writes:

> We understand that the specific *śabda-jāti* is associated with the specific or individual word, not the syllables. Since the syllables do not exist alongside in time and appear only in succession, they do not even directly convey import and certainly cannot be the basis for the *jāti*. Only the true word, *sphoṭa*, exists in the dual forms of *jāti* and *vyakti*; the *vyakti sphoṭa* manifests the *jāti*. This clearly indicates that the *jāti* form of the word is *sphoṭa*.
>
> Helārāja quotes Kātyāyana,
> *ākṛtyabhidānādvaikavibhaktau vājapyāyanaḥ*. *Vā*. 1-264.

यथा रक्ते गुणे तत्त्वं कषाये व्यपदिश्यते ।
संयोगिसन्निकर्षाच्च वस्त्रादिष्वपि गृह्यते ॥७॥

3. Iyer, p. 11.

yathā rakte guṇe tattvaṁ kaṣāye vyapadiśyate |
saṁyogisannikarṣācca vastrādiṣvapi gṛhyate | |7| |

तथा शब्दार्थसंबन्धाच्छब्दे जातिरवस्थिता ।
व्यपदेशेऽर्थजातीनां जातिकार्याय कल्पते ॥८॥

tathā śabdārthasaṁbandhācchabde jātiravasthitā |
vyapadeśe 'rthajātīnāṁ jātikāryāya kalpate | |8| |

*Kārikā*s 7 and 8 explain how, sometimes, a quality is mentioned to denote the object itself, as the two are so intimately and invariably associated. Since the quality cannot exist on its own, even a brief mention such as "the ochre" can refer to the robe and not just the colour. In the same way, a word which is mentioned is directly taken to indicate the *arthajāti*, whereas it actually conveys its own *rūpajāti* first, which is associated with the *arthajāti*.

In Nyāya, this reference to the *dravya* by mention of *guṇa* is accepted because of *samaveta samavāya* of *guṇa* and *dravya*. In the case of words, it is *vācya-vācaka* or *pratyāyya-pratyāyaka bhāva*.

According to Nyāya-Vaiśeṣika, *jāti* cannot exist in *jāti*, but only in *dravya, guṇa, karma*. So how can the concept of *jāti* in words be reconciled in the word *jāti* itself? Also, this correspondence with the *śabdajāti* of the specific word, *jātiśabda* in this case, has to be established with the *arthajāti*, which would be *jāti* of *jāti, sā jātīnām jātiriṣyate*.

जातिशब्दैकशेषे सा जातीनां जातिरिष्यते ।
शब्दजातय इत्यत्र तज्जातिश्शब्दजातिषु ॥९॥

jātiśabdaikaśeṣe sā jātīnāṁ jātiriṣyate |
śabdajātaya ityatra tajjātiśśabdajātiṣu | |9| |

Bhartṛhari clearly states that this is allowed, despite the objections of Vaiśeṣika. For the grammarian, the method by which words convey meaning is of prime importance. Practically, we find that the word *jāti* is understood because every time it is used, it indicates that common property that exists in all kinds of individual *jāti*s such as cow, horse, pot, etc. So without disputing the ontological stand of the Vaiśeṣika on there being no *jāti* in *jāti*, Bhartṛhari intends to explain the use of the word *jāti*.

This means that in the instance when the word *jāti* is used to denote all of its kind, *sā-* that *śabda-jāti* does exist in the use of that word. There is *jāti* in the word, *jāti*. This is clear in the illustration, *jātayaḥ imāḥ*, "these are universals". Although there may not exist a distinct universal in all the different universals indicated, yet, the similarity in words justifies the usage.

Helārāja in *Prakāśa*:

> तथा जातय इमा इत्ययमपि जात्याश्रयापरजात्यभावात् वाचकजात्यध्यासाश्रय उपपद्यते। शब्दगतं च सामान्यं जातिकार्यमुपचरतीति उच्यते न सामान्यं जातिकार्यमुपचरतीति उच्यते न त्वर्थजातिष्वेवेति नियमः केनचित् क्रियते इति ।
>
> *tathā jātaya imā ityayamapi jātyāśrayāparajātyabhāvāt vācakajātyadhyāsāśraya upapadyate। śabdagataṁ ca sāmānyaṁ jātikāryamupacaratīti ucyate na sāmānyaṁ jātikāryamupacaratīti ucyate na tvarthajātiṣveveti niyamaḥ kenacit kriyate iti ।*

Ambākartrī:

> तथा इमा गोत्वादिजातयः इत्ययमपि प्रयोगो जातावन्यज्ञात्यभावेपि अर्थजातिषु गोशब्दत्वादिरूपवाचकजातितादात्म्याध्यासाश्रय उपपद्यते । अभिधानशब्दगतञ्च सामान्यमभिधेयासु शब्दजातिष्वर्थर्थजातिषु वोपचरति–तादात्म्याध्यासरूपेणोपचारेण सम्पादयन्ति ।
>
> *tathā imā gotvādijātayaḥ ityayamapi prayogo jātāvanyajjātyabhāvepi arthajātiṣu gośabdatvādirūpavācakajāti-tādātmyādhyāsāśraya upapadyate । abhidhānaśabdagatañca sāmānyamabhidheyāsu śabdajātiṣvartharthajātiṣu vopacarati-tādātmyāsarūpeṇopacāreṇa sampādayanti ।*

या शब्दजातिः शब्देषु शब्देभ्यो भिन्नलक्षणा ।
जातिस्सा शब्दजातित्वमप्यतिक्रम्य वर्तते ।।१०।।

yā śabdajātiḥ śabdeṣu śabdebhyo bhinnalakṣaṇā |
jātissā śabdajātitvamapyatikramya vartate | |10| |

Iyer writes: According to Vaiśeṣika, *Niḥsāmānyāni sāmānyāni*. And yet we do apply the word *jāti* to a large number of universals. How to explain this? It is explained in this way: the universal for which the word *jāti* stands does the work of such a super-universal which really does not exist.[4]

अर्थजात्यभिधानेऽपि सर्वे जात्यभिधायिनः ।
व्यापारलक्षणा यस्मात् पदार्थाः समवस्थिताः ।।११।।

arthajātyabhidhāne 'pi sarve jātyabhidhāyinaḥ |
vyāpāralakṣaṇā yasmāt padārthāḥ samavasthitāḥ | |11| |

Although it is intended to convey the meaning, *arthajāti*, when a word is uttered, in reality, the word functions by conveying its own form first. Thus it is *jātyabhidhāyī*.

The import of every word is the universal, its *artha-jāti*. Whenever a word is employed, the *śabda-jāti* is also assigned in order to enable the process to happen.

Jan Houben writes:

> In other words, from the point of view of how a word-meaning functions in verbal usage, one may hold that all words directly denote a universal: not only in an unproblematic case like "cow", etc., but also in the case of "universal" simply because language treats "universals" and "cows" in the same way as things which may be referred to through a universal feature. Word meanings being thus defined by the way they function in verbal usage, do not have an absolute, independent status.[5]

4. Iyer, p. 13.
5. Houben, chap 3, p. 90

Iyer writes:

> Grammarians are wont to follow worldly usage than the views and conventions of other systems of thought. To them, *artha* means what words convey and all words convey the universal, because that is a matter of fact. In reality, the universal which a word conveys may or may not exist. But the word in question, through its function called *abhidhā*, does convey it. So that is the meaning of the word.[6]

Both Helārāja and Raghunatha Sarma point out here that grammarians have their own method of explaining words and are not constrained by the ontology of other systems of thought.

> प्रत्यक्षा अपि च पदार्थाः स्वकार्यं विज्ञानादिकं कुर्वन्तः सन्तीति व्यवह्रियन्ते किं पुनः शब्दवाच्याः पदार्थाः अपि सामान्यवचनाद् द्रव्यादयोऽपि शब्दवाच्यत्वेनैव लक्ष्यन्ते। शब्दप्रमाणकानां हि यच्छब्द आह तत् परमार्थरूपम्। तथा चान्वयिरूपेण गुणोऽप्यभिधीयमानो जातिरेव ।
>
> *pratyakṣā api ca padārthāḥ svakāryaṁ vijñānādikaṁ kurvantaḥ santīti vyavahriyante kiṁ punaḥ śabdavācyāḥ padārthāḥ api sāmānyavacanād dravyādayo 'api śabdavācyatvenaiva lakṣyante* । *śabdapramāṇakānāṁ hi yacchabda āha tat paramārtharūpam* । *tathā cānvayirūpeṇa guṇo 'pyabhidhīyamāno jātireva* ।

Further,

> एतच्च लौकिकव्यवहारानुगुण्येन शास्त्रेऽस्मिन् व्युत्पद्यते। शास्त्रान्तरप्रसिद्धा हि व्यवस्था लौकिकविरुद्धा । लोके हि गवि शृङ्गम् वृक्षे शाखा इति व्यवहारः । तथैव च व्याकरणेऽप्याधारसप्तमी । शास्त्रान्तरे त्ववयवेष्ववयवीति शृङ्गे गौः ।
>
> *etacca laukidavyavahārānuguṇyena śāstre 'smin vyutpadyate* । *śāstrāntaraprasiddhā hi vyavasthā laukikaviruddhā* । *loke hi gavi śṛṅgam vṛkṣe śākhā iti vyavhāraḥ*। *tathaiva ca vyākaraṇe 'pyādhāra saptamī* । *śāstrāntare tvavayaveṣva-vayavīti śṛṅge gauḥ* ।

6. Iyer, 1971, p. 15.

जातौ पदार्थे जातिर्वा विशेषो वापि जातिवत् ।
शब्दैरपेक्ष्यते यस्मादतस्ते जातिवाचिनः ॥१२॥

jātau padārthe jātirvā viśeṣo vāpi jātivat |
śabdairapekṣyate yasmādataste jātivācinaḥ | |12| |

Kārikā 12 shows that the word can barely grasp the particular. Whereas the Buddhist view would agree that cognition is very specific and unique every moment and does not admit universal or class concept, Bhartṛhari says that the unique peculiar features of an object cannot be conveyed by words at all. Words function only by conveying the general meanings they stand for.

> At the time of learning the convention about words, it is with the common characteristics of objects that we connect the words. The universals may really differ from one another, but words cannot express them. Even proper names denote the universals. The name of a person stands for that unchanging recognisable element which persists in all the changes that he undergoes.[7]

Helārāja:

भवतु मा वा भूज्ज्ञातिषु जातिः । शब्दैस्तु जातिव्यतिरिक्ततया जात्यैकस्वभावैव अपेक्ष्यते प्रत्याय्यत्वेन अङ्गीक्रियते ।

bhavatu mā vā bhūjjātiṣu jātiḥ| *śabdaistu jātivyatiriktatayā jātyaikasvabhāvaiva apekṣyate pratyāyyatvena aṅgīkriyate*|

द्रव्यधर्मा पदार्थे तु द्रव्ये सर्वोऽर्थ उच्यते ।
द्रव्यधर्माश्रयाद् द्रव्यमतः सर्वोऽर्थ इष्यते ॥१३॥

dravyadharmā padārthe tu dravye sarvo 'rtha ucyate |
dravyadharmāśrayād dravyamataḥ sarvo 'rtha iṣyate | |13| |

While Bhartṛhari follows Vājapyāyana's view that import of the word is in universal, as does Mīmāṁsā, there is the other

7. Iyer, p. 16.

view endorsed by Vyāḍi, that the import of the word is in the substance, or particular. In this case also, Bhartṛhari shows that his method is consistent. If each word refers to the particular, how is it that the word repeatedly refers to different particulars? It is only because the word refers to the common characteristics of the particular when it is repeatedly uttered. Only then can the continuity of, say, 'pot' referring to a pot each time it is uttered, be maintained. The mention of 'pot' recalls to the hearer's mind the qualities a pot would have, and in this way, the cognition of a pot is possible.

Helārāja —

द्रव्यपदार्थपक्षेऽपि द्रव्यधर्मा सर्वोऽर्थ उच्यते। कुतः। शाब्देन योऽर्थ उच्यते सर्वोऽसौ द्रव्यधर्मयुक्त एवेत्यभिप्रायः। तथा ममापि जातिवादिनो मुख्यां जातिमभिदध ति केचित् उपचरितमन्य इति मतद्वयेऽपि साम्यम्।

dravyapadārthapakṣe 'pi dravyadharmā sarvo 'rthe ucyate। kutaḥ। śābdena yo 'rtha ucyate sarvo 'sau dravyadharmayukta evetyabhiprāyaḥ। tathā mamāpi jātivādino mukhyāṁ jātimabhidadha ti kecit upacaritamanya iti matadvaye 'pi sāmyam।

अनुप्रवृत्तिधर्मो वा जातिस्स्यात् सर्वजातिषु ।
व्यावृत्तिधर्मसामान्यं विशेषे जातिरिष्यते ॥१४॥

anupravṛttidharmo vā jātissyāt sarvajātiṣu।
vyāvṛttidharmasāmānyaṁ viśeṣe jātiriṣyate।।14।।

Thus we come to the view that *jāti* or *sāmānya*, is the common characteristic that serves to convey the cognition that a word mentioned refers to its import. This view is akin to the broad explanation of *sāmānya* that Kumārila discusses in the Ākṛtivāda as opposed to a more tightly knit definition of the Nyāya school. In *kārikā* 14, Bhartṛhari says that the enduring features are represented by *jāti* in all universals, whereas in the particular, the *jāti* serves to distinguish it from particulars of other kinds. Houben writes,

> One of the views discussed seems to turn the universal into something mental. The universal is not so much a property of the object but rather of the cognition.[8]

Helārāja discusses the differences with the ontologically real *sāmānya* of Nyāya school.

The feature of every universal is that it inheres in every individual of its class, quite completely. It is the cause of every individual being recognised as of the same kind and being named as of the same kind. It never happens that the universal is partially observed in an individual, e.g. a cow. Even when an animal is only partially visible, we can swiftly see that it is a cow. Although present in full capacity in every individual, the qualities specific to each individual are distinct, i.e. the colour of hide, etc. This serves to distinguish one individual from another of the same class. When we regard different types of animals, for example, the qualities are entirely different and we surmise that the individuals belong to different classes. We cannot decide that the set of qualities alone determine what animal it is the universal is indispensable. To illustrate, when we see an animal with dewlap, horns, hump, hooves, etc., we only cognise such an animal as having these attributes, but not necessarily as, "cow".

This concept is illustrated to modern audiences of science fiction and fantasy movies where technology creates strange creatures on the film screen; similarity to something known is not enough to identify the class or universal of the creature being presented!

Helārāja says:

प्रत्याश्रयं च सर्वात्मना परिसमाप्तिः साधारणो जातिधर्मः । प्रत्याश्रयपरिसमाप्ताऽपि च गुणाः प्रतिद्रव्यं भिन्नाः जातिस्त्वेकैवेत्येवमादयोऽसाधारणा धर्मा वाच्याः ।

8. Houben, p. 90.

pratyāśrayaṁ ca sarvātmanā parisamāptiḥ sādhāraṇo jātidharmaḥ । pratyāśrayaparisamāptā 'pi ca guṇāḥ pratidravyaṁ bhinnāḥ jātistvekaivetyevamādayo 'sādhāraṇā dharmā vācyāḥ ।

संयोगिधर्मभेदेन देशे च परिकल्पिते ।
तेषु देशेषु सामान्यमाकाशस्यापि विद्यते ॥१५॥

saṁyogidharmabhedena deśe ca parikalpite ।
teṣu deśeṣu sāmānyamākāśasyāpi vidyate ।।15।।

अदेशानां घटादीनां देशास्संबन्धिनो यथा ।
आकाशस्याप्यदेशस्य देशस्संबन्धिनस्तथा ॥१६॥

adeśānāṁ ghaṭādīnāṁ deśāssaṁbandhino yathā ।
ākāśasyāpyadeśasya deśassaṁbandhinastathā ।।16।।

From verses 15 to 18, the difference in viewpoint of Vyākaraṇa and Nyāya regarding the status of *ākāśa* is pointed out. According to Nyāya, *ākāśa* is not a *jāti* as there is only one space, common everywhere. To qualify as a *jāti*, any feature requires several individuals in which it is manifested. But in popular usage, we do understand divisions is space, such as atmosphere, outer space, solar system, intergalactic space, American airspace or even inside the room as different to outside the room! Although these divisions are all due to *upādhi*, it still points out to *ākāśa* being a common characteristic differentiated by the different objects it is associated with in each part, space having no inherent divisions.

स्वंयोगिधर्मभेदेन आकाशस्य भेदो भवत्युपाधिकृतो न स्वतः । देशभेदाच्च सामान्यमाकाशस्यापि विद्यते ।

svaṁyogidharmabhedena ākāśasya bhedo bhavatyupādhikṛto na svataḥ । deśabhedācca sāmānyamākāśasyāpi vidyate ।

Helārāja points out that in the case of time also, which is actually one with no inherent divisions, we can understand difference by the events or people associated with the artificial parts. Just as a pot, which is actually an undivided whole entity, is said to have regions, depending on the different things associated in different places.

All material entities that exist in space (*ākāśa*) have contact with *ākāśa*. Space is the locus of all material bodies: *avakāśādānād hi tadākāśam*. *Ākāśa* is that which affords room to every entity. Material bodies exist in mutually exclusive space. "Matter occupies space" is a basic tenet in science that children are taught early. The numerous points where material bodies are in contact with *ākāśa* can serve to differentiate different portions.

भिन्नवस्त्वाश्रया बुद्धिः संयोगिष्वनुवर्तते ।
समवायिषु भेदस्य ग्रहणं विनिवर्तते ।।१७।।

bhinnavastvāśrayā buddhiḥ saṁyogiṣvanuvartate |
samavāyiṣu bhedasya grahaṇaṁ vinivartate | |17| |

अतः संयोगिदेशानां गौणत्वं परिकल्प्यते ।
अविवेकात् प्रदेशेभ्यो मुख्यत्वं समवायिनां ।।१८।।

ataḥ saṁyogideśānāṁ gauṇatvaṁ parikalpyate |
avivekāt pradeśebhyo mukhyatvaṁ samavāyināṁ | |18| |

Bhartṛhari points out the reason for this aspect not being conspicuous. Whereas material objects which have physical contact, *saṁyoga*, can easily be perceived to be different, entities that are associated by inherence, *samavāya* are not discerned to be different. Therefore the parts divided (joined) by *saṁyoga* are secondary whereas the parts constituted by *samavāya* are primary (to the whole) as the latter are not perceived to be different (from the whole).

When we know two objects as distinct, that differentiation continues even when they are in (close) contact. But when two entities are inherent in each other, that distinction is blurred, for instance, when we notice a pot, we do not discern the different parts as distinct. The different parts of entities connected by *saṁyoga* are secondary "parts" whereas those connected by *samavāya* are primary components of the whole. Thus the concept of *jāti* is reconciled with the Vaiśeṣika view of *sāmānya*.

अनुप्रवृत्तिरूपां यां प्रख्याताामाकृतिं विदुः ।
केचिद् व्यावृत्तिरूपां तु द्रव्यत्वेन प्रचक्षते ।।१९।।

anupravr̥ttirūpāṁ yāṁ prakhyātāmākr̥tiṁ viduḥ |
kecid vyāvr̥ttirūpāṁ tu dravyatvena pracakṣate | |19| |

In *kārikā* 19, Bhartr̥hari reminds the reader that there are many views on the nature of *jāti*. Buddhists deny its very existence and take it to be a mental construct. Some people say that the common characteristic which we understand as the import of a word is *jāti* and the distinguishing feature as the *vyakti* or particular.

The *vijñānavādin*s hold that the concept of universal is only in the mind, there is no external entity such as *sāmānya* and so it is pointless to attribute such an idea to *ākāśa*. Whether there be external entities or not, only the state of mind is of importance in their view; some features that continue as attributes and help in identifying the thing as of the same class we call as universal; the distinguishing features that enable cognition as distinct, we call *viśeṣa* or individual.

THE SIGNIFICANCE OF JĀTI

From *kārikā*s 20 to 48, Bhartr̥hari points out the need to postulate the existence of universal.

भिन्ना इति परोपाधिरभिन्ना इति वा पुनः ।
भावात्मसु प्रपञ्चोऽयं संसृष्टेष्वेव जायते ।।२०।।

bhinnā iti paropādhirabhinnā iti vā punaḥ |
bhāvātmasu prapañco 'yaṁ saṁsr̥ṣṭeṣveva jāyate | |20| |

नैकत्वं नापि नानात्वं न सत्त्वं न च नास्तिता ।
आत्मतत्त्वेषु भावानामसंसृष्टेषु विद्यते ।।२१।।

naikatvaṁ nāpi nānātvaṁ na sattvaṁ na ca nāstitā |
ātmatattveṣu bhāvānāmasaṁsṛṣṭeṣu vidyate | |21| |

In accordance with his monistic philosophy, Bhartṛhari points out the unity in diversity that we observe in this varied world. Whenever we speak of something as different, it is always with reference to something else, as is also the case when we say something is the same (as something else). Among all existent entities, it is only by interconnection that this diverse world can exist with all its elaborateness. Unity or diversity, existence or absence of anything is always a relative term, never possible inherently in a lone entity that is not associated with anything else.

We cannot employ a thing with no peculiar attributes or characteristics of its own in our verbal or other transactions; it is only on some basis that every single entity is understood or discussed. And this basis is always dependent on the understanding of yet another entity. All knowledge is interrelated. All existent entities are interrelated. When we say something is of the same kind, it is dependent on oneness; when we say that it is different, it is dependent on variety. Whether an entity exists or perishes is also in comparison to the surrounding reality, be it time or space.

सर्वशक्त्यात्मभूतत्वमेकस्यैवेति निर्णयः ।
भावानामात्मभेदस्य कल्पना स्यादनर्थिका ।।२२।।

sarvaśaktyātmabhūtatvamekasyaiveti nirṇayaḥ |
bhāvānāmātmabhedasya kalpanā syādanarthikā | |22| |

In *kārikā* 22, the Advaita view is clear. All the powers or capacities that we see in different entities actually belong to only One. To imagine divisions in capacity in different entities or to postulate differences is quite unnecessary.

It is *Brahman* alone that is manifest with all the different capacities, which are viewed differently due to *avidyā*. This is only due to the differences in the various capacities and not inherent differentiation.

तस्माद् द्रव्यादयः सर्वाः शक्तयो भिन्नलक्षणाः ।
संसृष्टाः पुरुषार्थस्य साधिका न तु केवलाः ।।२३।।

tasmād dravyādayaḥ sarvāḥ śaktayo bhinnalakṣaṇāḥ |
saṁsṛṣṭāḥ puruṣārthasya sādhikā na tu kevalāḥ | | 23 | |

Therefore, all the different powers such as *dravya*, etc., having different qualities, together in tandem help man achieve his goals, not any singly by itself. Helārāja refers to different entities as *vilakṣaṇa vyapārānumeya*.

The *padārtha*s characterised as *dravya, guṇa, karma, sāmānya, viśeṣa, samavāya* are not separate entities. They are all the different aspects of the One *Brahman*, recognised as different due to their different operations. As the concept of *sāmānya* differs from that of Vaiśeṣikas in the case of *ākāśa*, so also do the concepts of *dravya, karma*, etc. adhere to the principles of Monism or Non-dualism.

Helārāja:

यथा हि वैशेषिकाणां व्यतिरिक्तं सामान्यं मैवमिह केवलं विश्वमूर्तेः पदार्थस्य शक्ति मात्रम् । न केवलं सामान्यमेव यावद् द्रव्यादयोऽपीति प्रसङ्गात्कथितम् ।

yathā hi vaiśeṣikāṇāṁ vyatiriktaṁ sāmānyaṁ maivamiha kevalaṁ viśvamūrteḥ padārthasya śakti mātram । *na kevalaṁ sāmānyameva yāvad dravyādayo 'pīti prasaṅgātkathitam* ।

यथैव चेन्द्रियादीनामात्मभूता समग्रता ।
तथा सम्बन्धिसम्बन्धसंसर्गेऽपि प्रतीयते ।।२४।।

yathaiva cendriyādīnāmātmabhūtā samagratā |
tathā sambandhisambandhasaṁsarge 'pi pratīyate | | 24 | |

Just as the unity of all the senses, etc., comprises the self, so also all the differentiated things associated together comprise the Supreme Being.

The *sāmagrī,* cluster formed of all the components, is not an entity separate from the parts — the same thing is understood at two levels.

न तदुत्पद्यते किञ्चिद्यस्य जातिर्न विद्यते ।
आत्माभिव्यक्तये जातिः कारणानां प्रयोजिका ॥२५॥

na tadutpadyate kiñcidyasya jātirna vidyate |
ātmābhivyaktaye jātiḥ kāraṇānāṁ prayojikā ||25||

कारणेषु पदं कृत्वा नित्यानित्येषु जातयः ।
क्वचित्कार्येष्वभिव्यक्तिमुपयान्ति पुनः पुनः ॥२६॥

kāraṇeṣu padaṁ kr̥tvā nityānityeṣu jātayaḥ |
kvacitkāryeṣvabhivyaktimupayānti punaḥ punaḥ ||26||

निर्वर्त्यमानं यत्कर्म जातिस्तत्रापि साधनम् ।
स्वाश्रयस्याभिनिष्पत्तौ सा क्रियाणां प्रयोजिका ॥२७॥

nirvarttyarmānaṁ yatkarma jātistatrāpi sādhanam |
svāśrayasyābhiniṣpattau sā kriyāṇāṁ prayojikā ||27||

Thus Bhartr̥hari takes *jāti* as an existent real, but with relative reality with respect to the One Supreme, as consistent with Advaita.

Nothing in the world is unique; everything belongs to some type or the other. Bhartr̥hari extolls *jāti* as vital to Creation in the next few *kārikā*s.

There is nothing that ever comes into existence, which does not have a corresponding *jāti*. It is for the very purpose of manifesting itself that all causes all impelled by *jāti*. Taking a foothold in both eternal and non-eternal causes, the universals manifest repeatedly somewhere or the other. This echoes the concept of *pravāhanityatā*, where even though some effects may perish and others be freshly created, the universal that the manifest endures. Even when an object is just about being created, its *jāti* is already at work, propelling the action. Otherwise, how can we say that the potter is making a jar even before the jar has taken shape? Iyer gives the example of a man readying to make a mat with suitable preparations only because he already has the idea of what he wants to make.

The universals are eternal and omnipresent. They are dependent on the corresponding individuals for manifestation. The universal assists the *kāraṇa*s (causes) further for its own manifestation wherever the *kārya* (effect) is produced. There is no entity ever seen that does not manifest its own *jāti,* although no *kārya* is ever eternal. Things are produced in different points in time and they perish but this process of *jāti* impelling the *kāraṇas* to produce *kārya* goes on. When a potter is sitting down to make a pot, how can we say that he is making a pot when it does not exist? How can a non-existent item be used as the object of the verb in the sentence? The answer is that as the *jāti* exists, the pot that is still being fashioned can also be used as the object of the verb. Helārāja says that *jāti* and *vyakti* are not distinctly separate like a cow and a horse; the *jāti* is latent in the pot still being fashioned. Thus the suitable *kāraṇa*s manifest their respective *jāti*s when they take the shape of *kārya.*

विधौ वा प्रतिषेधे वा ब्राह्मणत्वादिसाधनम् ।
व्यक्त्याश्रिताश्रिता जातेः संख्याजातिर्विशेषिका ।।२८।।

vidhau vā pratiṣedhe vā brāhmaṇatvādisādhanam |
vyaktyāśritāśritā jāteḥ saṁkhyājātirviśeṣikā | | 28 | |

In the case of Vedic injunctions which are of the form of command or prohibition, a universal such as *brāhmaṇatva,* is a means or *sādhana* for carrying it out. The universal is qualified by the one belonging to the number of the individual.

The *jāti* is fully present in every *vyakti*. Thus obeying the Vedic injunction once is adequate to fulfil the injunction such as *brāhmaṇam ālabhet*. Even so prohibition such as *brāhmaṇam na hanyāt*, even if obeyed once but disregarded subsequently would constitute violation. Therefore whenever the intent to kill a brāhmaṇa arises, it has to be suppressed is what the Vedic prohibition means.

As regards the number, Bhartṛhari explains, *parāṅgabhūtam sāmānyam yujyate dravyasaṁkhyayā* in *kārikā* 82 further on. The number of the *vibhakti* used with the *dravyapada* is the *saṁkhyā*. The *saṁkhyā-jāti* qualifies the *padārtha-jāti*. Here, since the injunction uses the word in singular, simultaneous execution of the injunction on several individuals is not prescribed. One shall suffice.

यथा जलादिभिर्व्यक्तं मुखमेवाभिधीयते ।
तथा द्रव्यैरभिव्यक्ता जातिरेवाभिधीयते ।।२९।।

yathā jalādibhirvyaktaṁ mukhamevābhidhīyate |
tathā dravyairabhivyaktā jātirevābhidhīyate | |29| |

यथेन्द्रियगतो भेद इन्द्रियग्रहणादृते ।
इन्द्रियार्थेष्वदृष्टोऽपि ज्ञानभेदाय कल्पते ।।३०।।

yathendriyagato bheda indriyagrahaṇādṛte |
indriyārtheṣvadṛṣṭo 'pi jñānabhedāya kalpate | |30| |

तथात्मरूपग्रहणात् केषाञ्चिद् व्यक्तयो विना ।
सामान्यज्ञानभेदानाम् उपयान्ति निमित्तताम् ।।३१।।

tathātmarūpagrahaṇāt keṣāñcid vyaktayo vinā |
sāmānyajñānabhedānām upayānti nimittatām | |31| |

When the universal is never found apart from the individual, how can we say that the import of the word is only in *jāti*? Bhartṛhari gives two examples here to illustrate. Just as the reflection in water (the surface of a pond which acts as a mirror) is still called a "face" without referring to the fact that what is seen is actually only water, in the same way, even the individuals or particulars are denoted by the universal which they denote. Just as we can perceive different objects and their distinctiveness without perceiving the sense organ itself driving the process, in the same way, the particular, without being perceived uniquely by themselves, still serve to enable cognition of what they manifest, viz. the universal.

We only learn about the sense organs or faculties such as eyesight, hearing, etc. but never ever perceive the senses directly. It is only by hearing other sounds, seeing other forms, tasting something or touching an external object that the sense organ functions, making itself known. And one sense organ cannot perceive the object of another sense, i.e. the eyes cannot perccive sound and so on. In a similar manner, in verbal communication, the universal is understood directly, without the *vyakti* or individual being noted. When something is perceived directly, the individual form, *vyakti*, comes to one's notice along with the universal residing in that *vyakti*. In the case of understanding an uttered word, the *padārtha*, import of the word, directly springs to mind and we do not bother with form of the word or the *vyakti* that is its import.

सत्यास्सत्यौ तु यौ भागौ प्रतिभावं व्यवस्थितौ ।
सत्यं यत् तत्र सा जातिरसत्या व्यक्तयः स्मृताः ॥३२॥

satyāssatyau tu yau bhāgau pratibhāvaṁ vyavasthitau |
satyaṁ yat tatra sā jātirasatyā vyaktayaḥ smṛtāḥ | | 32 | |

सम्बन्धिभेदात् सत्तैव भिद्यमाना गवादिषु ।
जातिरित्युच्यते तस्यां सर्वे शब्दा व्यवस्थिताः ॥३३॥

saṁbandhibhedāt sattaiva bhidyamānā gavādiṣu |
jātirityucyate tasyāṁ sarve śabdā vyavasthitāḥ | | 33 | |

That which cannot present itself, how can it manifest through other *dravya*? The answer is that the eye cannot be perceived by itself, but by perception of colour, etc., the visual sense organ is indirectly perceived.

Helārāja:

यथा इन्द्रियगतो भेद अदृष्टोऽपि ज्ञानभेदाय कल्पते ।

yathā indriyagato bheda adṛṣṭo 'pi jñānabhedāya kalpate ।

Though the distinct *indriya* is not cognised, by the cognition of the object through the *indriya*, we can cognise the sense organ. In the same way, difference between *ghaṭatva, paṭatva* cannot be perceived, but through *ghaṭa* and *paṭa* we can understand the difference. *Jāti*s are not capable of presenting themselves.

Every entity has two aspects, one transitory and other enduring. The permanent aspect that endures is the universal or the class concept whereas the impermanent features are the manifestations or particulars, which may undergo change or perish. As Houben writes — From the point of view of the listener, the two views may be explained as follows. If an unspecified thing is to be expressed through one of its features, it is first of all this feature that should be grasped. And this feature should occur in other instances too, otherwise it cannot be recognised as a feature; so it should be a universal feature. So the universal should be grasped first. On the other hand, if a universal feature is made use of, it is only to point to a specific substance to which it is somehow related. So one first understands that there is some substance, next that it is characterised by this or that universal feature. In the *Mahābhāṣya-Dīpikā* of Bhartṛhari (*MBhD*), the problem is nicely explained as follows.

तस्मिन् विशेषशब्द उच्चरिते स तु यथा पानकद्रव्य आस्वादिते गुडादीन् अपोद्धरति इदं अस्ति इदं अस्तीति, एवं विशिष्टाकारायां बुद्धौ प्रवृत्तायां संभविनस्तद्विषयान् अर्थान् अपोद्धरति । अपोद्धारांश्च कश्चित् कार्यप्रतिपत्त्यर्थं एतद्रूपं प्रतिपद्यमानो नागृहीतविशेषणा विशेष्ये बुद्धिरिति एव पूर्वां जातिः प्रतिपद्यते ।[9]

9. Houben, 1995, p. 87.

tasmin viśeṣaśabda uccarite sa tu yathā pānakadravya āsvādite guḍādīn apoddharati idaṁ asti idaṁ astīti, evaṁ viśiṣṭākārāyāṁ buddhau pravr̥ttāyāṁ saṁbhavinastadviṣayān arthān apoddharati । apoddhārāṁśca kaścit kāryapratipattyarthaṁ etadrūpaṁ pratipadyamāno nāgr̥hītaviśeṣaṇā viśeṣye buddhiriti eva pūrvāṁ jātiḥ pratipadyate ।

There is only one Being which is actually real and enduring, called *sattā*. It is by being with different associations that its divisions such as "cow", "horse", etc., are understood. These divisions are termed as different universals, which are conveyed by words employed for the purpose.

Helārāja quotes *Mahābhāṣya, tadeva hi satyam yasminstattvam na vihanyate*. The Advaitins say *satyam jātiḥ*. For instance, when ornaments such as earrings or rings fashioned from gold are melted, they cease to exist as ornaments; what remains is gold, the base material. When we look at the higher level of differentiation, even gold is only incidental — what matters is that it is of *tejas* category of *dravya*. In this way we can keep going to higher set until we reach *parā-prakr̥ti* which is the embodiment of all-pervasive *Brahman*.

It is this *mahāsattā* identical with *Para-Brahman*, that *jāti*. A universal such as "cow" is a manifestation of the Supreme, limited by the specific attributes of *gotva*. *Gotva* is different from *aśvatva* but both are subordinate to *mahāsattā*. Thus all words are governed by their specific limited connotation.

तां प्रातिपदिकार्थं च धात्वर्थं च प्रचक्षते ।
सा नित्या सा महानात्मा तामाहुस्त्वतलादयः ।।३४।।

tāṁ prātipadikārthaṁ ca dhātvarthaṁ ca pracakṣate |
sā nityā sā mahānātmā tāmāhustvatalādayaḥ | |34| |

Bhartr̥hari's philosophy takes a similar view to the Satkāryavāda of Sāṁkhya school as regards cause and effect theory. There is no real diversity in the different objects we see around us but only seeming variety due to different associations. In grammar, the enduring aspect, permanent feature in meaning of words corresponds to the meaning of *prātipadika* or base and verb root or *dhātu*.

In Sāṁkhya also, all words denote Being, also called *mahat* or *buddhi*. The *tvatā* suffixes in Sanskrit indicate the abstract noun forms, standing for "existence". This is referred to here in *kārikā* 34. *Sāmānya* is of two kinds, *para-apara*.[10] *Parasāmānya* is *sattā* which is all-inclusive. *Aparasāmānya* is lower. *Jāti* covers class property of all entities. It is the *avacchedaka* that carves out of everything else the identity of the class mentioned. *Jāti* is the *lakṣaṇa*, the defining property that limits *sattā* which is the universal class property.

The following *kārikā*s hark back to the *Nirukta* where Yāska broadly divides all words as falling in two categories, noun and verb, *nāma* and *ākhyāta*, where the different actions are enumerated as falling into six types.[11]

This has philosophical reflection in the two kinds of *vivartta*s mentioned, *mūrtivivartta*, *kriyāvivartta* which are discussed under *kārikā* 3 of the Brahmakāṇḍa. When a sequence of events in particular is brought about, it is called action. When the sequence ceases, it is called substance, or existent. Universal takes six different forms in different entities, as transformations of being, which is observed only in sequence on account of its powers. Time is not a separate entity, but also a power of *Brahman* which enables events to occur in sequence. Sequence is really not separate from what has sequence. But because actions appear in sequence, it causes seeming divisions in time such as priority and posteriority. If the different activities such as forming are

10. परमपरं द्विविधं सामान्यम् — *Tarkasaṁgraha*

11. षड् भावविकारा भवन्तीति वार्ष्यायणिः — *Ni*

manifest only by the universal's own power, why is it that they are not observed simultaneously?

Helārāja writes that all words ultimately convey the import of *sattā*. It is therefore the underlying reason for any word to be ever used. Different words convey different meanings as their *upādhi*s (basis) is different. We must not confuse the meaning of say, *prakṛti*, base and *pratyaya*, suffix, by wrongly applying the definition to a word such as *gotva*. *Sattā* is differentiated by different *upādhi*s or limiting factors. The *pratipādika* indicates "cow" whereas *vibhakti* suffix indicates the relevant meaning of that situation.

A verb root that denotes action also attains the status of existence. When an activity1 is taking place, the means, *sādhana*, which is executing the action undergoes some vibrations (excitement).

In a sequence, described by a special word, viz. that particular *dhātu*, e.g. *calati*. Activity is of six types *ṣaḍbhāvavikāraḥ*.

कथं न युगपदवभासः क्रमेणेति कथं ? न हि क्रमो नाम कश्चित् क्रियाविशेष इत्याशङ्क्य कालाख्यापि शक्तिर्ब्रह्मण एव ।

kathaṁ na yugapadavabhāsaḥ krameṇeti kathaṁ ? na hi kramo nāma kaścit kriyāviśeṣa ityāśaṅkya kālākhyāpi śaktirbrahmaṇa eva ।

प्राप्तक्रमा विशेषेषु क्रिया सैवाभिधीयते ।
क्रमरूपस्य संहारे तत्सत्त्वमिति कथ्यते ॥३५॥

prāptakramā viśeṣeṣu kriyā saivābhidhīyate ।
kramarūpasya saṁhāre tatsattvamiti kathyate ॥35॥

सैव भावविकारेषु षडवस्थाः प्रपद्यते ।
क्रमेण शक्तिभिः स्वाभिरेवं प्रत्यवभासते ॥३६॥

saiva bhāvavikāreṣu ṣaḍavasthāḥ prapadyate ।
krameṇa śaktibhiḥ svābhirevaṁ pratyavabhāsate ॥36॥

आत्मभूतः क्रमोऽप्यस्या यत्रेदं कालदर्शणम् ।
पौर्वापर्यादिरूपेण प्रविभक्तमिव स्थितम् ।।३७।।

ātmabhūtaḥ kramo 'pyasyā yatredaṁ kāladarśaṇam |
paurvāparyādirūpeṇa pravibhaktamiva sthitam | |37| |

तिरोभावाभ्युपगमे भावानां सैव नास्तिता ।
लब्धक्रमे तिरोभावे नश्यतीति प्रतीयते ।।३८।।

tirobhāvābhyupagame bhāvānāṁ saiva nāstitā |
labdhakrame tirobhāve naśyatīti pratīyate | |38| |

पूर्वस्मात्प्रच्युता धर्मादप्राप्ता चोत्तरं पदम् ।
तदन्तराले भेदानामाश्रयाज्जन्म कथ्यते ।।३९।।

pūrvasmātpracyutā dharmādaprāptā cottaraṁ padam |
tadantarāle bhedānāmāśrayājjanma kathyate | |39| |

Bhartṛhari gives great importance to *kālaśakti* as the one independent power of *Brahman*. When we speak of any entity disappearing or decaying, that is its non-existence. When the dissolution proceeds with sequence, it is observed as perishing.

When an entity does not have its former properties and is yet to attain its next state, in the interim period when it undergoes change, it is said to be born or created.

Helārāja quotes *Ni.* 1.2.9. We say that an entity exists only after it has come into being, or is created. After it is born, *jāyate*, we say that it exists, *asti*. It can undergo changes, *vipariṇamate*. It could increase, *vardhate* or decrease, *apakṣīyate*. Those activities are observed only in sequence, i.e. it takes some time interval for anything to happen. We do not observe instantaneous changes. This is because the power of time is inherent in Creation. It is the power of time, called Sequence that enables all created entities to appear and be known in a certain order of events, *paurvaparya*, or succession. Time is not a separate entity to be listed as a distinct *dravya*. When things recede into nothingness, we say it is non-existent. As the process of decay takes place, it is said to be under destruction. The earlier phase is called decaying *apakṣīyate* and the next phase, *vinaśyati*.

आश्रयः स्वात्ममात्रा वा भावा वा व्यतिरेकिणः ।
स्वशक्तयो वा सत्ताया भेददर्शनहेतवः ।।४०।।

āśrayaḥ svātmamātrā vā bhāvā vā vyatirekiṇaḥ |
svaśaktayo vā sattāyā bhedadarśanahetavaḥ | |40| |

पृथिव्यादिष्वभिव्यक्तौ न संस्थानमपेक्षते ।
अनुच्छिन्नाश्रयाज्जातिरनित्येऽप्याश्रये स्थिता ।।४१।।

pṛthivyādiṣvabhivyaktau na saṁsthānamapekṣate |
anucchinnāśrayājjātiranitye 'pyāśraye sthitā | |41| |

The next few verses continue on a philosophical note on the nature of *jāti* with respect to Creation. Only *sattā* is real having true existence. But in the transactional world, *vyavahāre avidyāpravṛttirūpe*, according to Helārāja we do cognise variety or differences. This multiplicity in Being is due to the substratum or the fictitious parts or its own powers. Iyer writes that just as the same face reflected in water, oil or mirror appears different so also the One Being appears different when manifested by horse, cow or fish. Although the universal is manifested by the particular, the former is not dependent on the latter. Universals such as earth, clay, gold, etc., do not require the shape of the universal to manifest themselves. A handful of earth is as much the same universal as a mountain. And when the substratum which is not eternal is destroyed, the universal is not destroyed. This leads to the question where would all the universals inhere, when, at the time of *pralaya*, all the particulars are in a state of dissolution?

It is established that activity (*kriyā*) and objects (*dravya*) are both only manifestations of *sattā*. There is no other entity outside of *sattā*, i.e. the omnipotent *Brahman*. Even so, in worldly transactions we do perceive myriad variety due to limitations brought about by *avidyā*. Hence the multiplicity of universals in the transactional level is reasonable. Sometimes we imagine difference when there is actually none. For instance, in *hanti ātmānam ātmanā* we do not understand any *hantā* other than *ātmā* (himself). Thus different *jāti*s seem to appear as different, aided by disparity in time, place or sense perception. Blue lotuses appear to be of one hue by day and another by night. A jaundiced eye perceives a white object as yellow (this is a Śāstrā-based example on the belief earlier all over the world).

Universals such as earth, water, fire, etc. do not depend on the configuration or shape of the manifesting individual. We recognise earth in a pile of sand as much as in a jar. Thus the ocean or even a dewdrop is recognised as water. But other categories such as cow, *śāl* tree or palm tree definitely require the detailed structure or shape for their unique identity. Although the *jāti* resides in the object having specific structure, it is by no means destroyed along with the structure when the *vyakti* itself may be destroyed. *Jāti* is enduring; even when some *vyakti*s perish, there will be others present which can carry the universal on.

अनुच्छेद्याश्रयामेके सर्वां जातिं प्रचक्षते ।
न यौगपद्यं प्रलये सर्वस्येति व्यवस्थिताः ॥४२॥

anucchedyāśrayāmeke sarvāṁ jātiṁ pracakṣate |
na yaugapadyaṁ pralaye sarvasyeti vyavasthitāḥ | |42| |

प्रकृतौ प्रविलीनेषु भेदेष्वेकत्वदर्शिनाम् ।
द्रव्यसत्त्वं प्रपद्यन्ते स्वाश्रया एव जातयः ॥४३॥

prkr̥tau pravilīneṣu bhedeṣvekatvadarśinām |
dravyasattvaṁ prapadyante svāśrayā eva jātayaḥ | |43| |

ब्राह्मणादयो भावाः सर्वप्राणिष्ववस्थिताः ।
अभिव्यक्ताः स्वकार्याणां साधका इत्यपि स्मृताः ॥४४॥

brāhmaṇādayo bhāvāḥ sarvaprāṇiṣvavasthitāḥ |
abhivyaktāḥ svakāryāṇāṁ sādhakā ityapi smṛtāḥ || 44 ||

In answer, *kārikā* 42 says that the substratum of all *jāti*s is not destroyed, as, during *pralaya,* not everything is dissolved at the same time. In the case of those schools who uphold Unity of the Cosmos (such as Sāṁkhya where everything is an evolute of *prakṛti*), it is believed that when everything is dissolved into its primordial cause, *prakṛti,* the universals still have their existence, as one with the ultimate substance. Another school holds that every universal, such as *brahmatva* exists in all living beings. When manifest it produces the effects associated with it.

What happens when all the *ādhāra*s, repositories of all the *jāti*s, get destroyed, such as *mahāpralaya*? Some schools like Mīmāṁsā deny *mahāpralaya,* saying that the world continues in an endless cycle.

na kadācidanīdṛśam jagat.

In this view, the *jāti*s are eternal. Another view is that *pralaya* does not happen simultaneously in all the worlds of Creation. Therefore even when one *brahmāṇḍa* is undergoing dissolution, the *jāti*s may still be present in another *brahmāṇḍa* until it is time for them to manifest again.

In the view that all substances merge into the primordial *dravya,* such as that of Sāṁkhya, the *jāti*s inhere in the *dravya.* In the Vaiśeṣika view, the *jāti*s exist without inhering in the individuals during *pralaya.* In the Monistic view, Bhartṛhari says that the various *jāti*s dissolve into their own pure form, merging into *Brahman* like everything else.

Universals such as "Brāhmaṇatva" are present in every living creature, but manifest in specific instances. Whenever they are manifest they become the efficient cause of the action enjoined.

चित्रादिष्वप्यभिव्यक्तिर्जातीनां कैश्चिदिष्यते ।
प्राण्याश्रितास्तु ताः प्राप्तौ निमित्तं पुण्यपापयोः ।।४५।।

citrādiṣvapyabhivyaktirjātīnāṁ kaiścidiṣyate |
prāṇyāśritāstu tāḥ prāptau nimittaṁ puṇyapāpayoḥ | |45| |

When we recognise a picture of a horse and say, "This is a horse", is it the same universal as in a living animal? Some people say that the universal is manifested even by a picture, image, etc. But *puṇya-pāpa*, merit and demerit or the consequences of any action associated with that universal arise only when it concerns actual individuals of that kind, not images.

The universal can be guessed by looking at a drawing or image of stone or clay, for instance. Some people hold that the images also manifest the universals but Bhartṛhari does not agree with this. In any case, the merits or demerits of performing Vedic injunctions apply only to the real living individuals of that universal.

There is a doubt as to how knowledge of universals is passed on after the Great Dissolution. For this, grammar also endorses that the One Omniscient Being passes this knowledge on through seers as the relation between word and meaning is eternal. In the case of Mīmāṁsā, to avoid such situations, *pralaya* is not conceded. As Helārāja quotes, *na kadācidanīdṛśaṁ jagat*. Not all knowledge is through the logically explained *pramāṇa*s open to all human beings as *Bh* points out in the Brahmakāṇda. The knowledge of *yogī*s and seers is due to their perceptions being at a higher level, just as the trained gemologist, with practice can immediately perceive the qualities of a gem that he examines. This perception and cognition is sharper than that of an untrained eye and cannot be logically deduced.

ज्ञानं त्वस्मद्विशिष्टानां तासु सर्वेन्द्रियं विदुः ।
अभ्यासान्मणिरूप्यादिविशेषेष्विव तद्विदाम् ।।४६।।

jñānaṁ tvasmadviśiṣṭānāṁ tāsu sarvendriyaṁ viduḥ |
abhyāsānmaṇirūpyādiviśeṣeṣviva tadvidām | |46| |

जात्युत्पलादिगन्धादौ भेदतत्त्वं यदाश्रितम् ।
तद्भावप्रत्ययैर्लोकेऽनित्यत्वान्नाभिधीयते ।।४७।।

jātyutpalādigandhādau bhedatattvaṁ yadāśritam |
tadbhāvapratyayairloke 'nityatvānnābhidhīyate | |47| |

अस्वशब्दाभिधानास्तु नरसिंहादिजातयः ।
सरूपावयवेवान्या तासु श्रुतिरवस्थिता ।।४८।।

asvaśabdābhidhānāstu narasiṁhādijātayaḥ |
sarūpāvayavevānyā tāsu śrutiravasthitā | |48| |

The question whether every word indicates the corresponding *jāti* or whether there is any degree in import is raised. In the case of words such as *jātigandha, utpalagandha,* etc., the words indicate the general universal of smell, although the fragrance of specific flower as qualifier is understood. The universal of smell being enduring, that is what is indicated, and not the universal of lotus fragrance or jasmine fragrance. The word *narasiṁha* also does not convey its universal. The word *nara* conveys its own universal as does the word *siṁha* and it is with these halves that the mind conjures the universal of Narasiṁha owing to similarity in parts.

In clarifying doubts, Bhartṛhari time and again stresses the superiority of *pratibhā* over logical reasoning. Sharpness itself may be the failing of scientific reasoning as he points out in the Brahmakāṇḍa, Vedic knowledge has come down to us from the seers of yore, who first grasped the truth and passed it on to the following generations. We cannot compare our faculties with that of the *yogī*s or fault their reasoning. Being endowed with superior senses and grasp, it is for us to follow their teaching in order to progress in our understanding.

Narasiṁha as an entity is not obtained by conjoining the parts; it is a unique being like a demon, wherein the parts seem similar to *nara* and *siṁha*. So the universals of *nara* and *siṁha* help us form the idea, but are not part of the universal *narasiṁha* which has its own identity. The two parts of the word are used to convey the ideas of *narasiṁha* as there is no unique word for it.

THE SIGNIFICANCE OF NUMBER

From *kārikā* 49 up to 72, number denoted by the word and its significance is discussed. The discussion is not only in the context of deriving meaning of word or sentence from the interest of language study, but more importantly, the significance in ritual practice. Understanding meaning is not from the viewpoint of grammar alone, but utmost importance is given to the Mīmāṁsā interpretation of Vedic injunctions. Bhartṛhari's viewpoint is in harmony with the accepted interpretation of Vedic injunctions and nowhere does he point out to any differences between Vyākaraṇa and Mīmāṁsā schools as we understand the two today. In the Brahmakāṇḍa he has clearly stated that it is from Vedas alone that *dharma* can be understood. This is further evidence that *VP* was intendeed as a blend of Vyākaraṇa and Mīmāṁsā philosophies.

जात्यवस्थापरिच्छेदे संख्या संख्यात्वमेव वा ।
विप्रकर्षेऽपि संसर्गादुपकाराय कल्पते ।।४९।।

jātyavasthāparicchede saṁkhyā saṁkhyātvameva vā |
viprakarṣe 'pi saṁsargādupakārāya kalpate | |49| |

लक्षणा शब्दसंस्कारे व्यापारः कार्यसिद्धये ।
संख्याकर्मादिशक्तीनां श्रुतिसाम्येऽपि दृश्यते ।।५०।।

lakṣaṇā śabdasaṁskāre vyāpāraḥ kāryasiddhaye |
saṁkhyākarmādiśaktīnāṁ śrutisāmye 'pi dr̥śyate | |50| |

न विना संख्यया कश्चित् सत्त्वभूतोऽर्थ उच्यते ।
अतः सर्वस्य निर्देशे संख्या स्यादविवक्षिता ।।५१।।

na vinā saṁkhyayā kaścit sattvabhūto 'rtha ucyate |
ataḥ sarvasya nirdeśe saṁkhyā syādavivakṣitā | |51| |

एकत्वं वा बहुत्वं वा केषाञ्चिदविवक्षितम् ।
तद्धि जात्यभिधानाय द्वित्वं तु स्याद्विवक्षितम् ।।५२।।

ekatvaṁ vā bahutvaṁ vā keṣāñcidavivakṣitam |
taddhi jātyabhidhānāya dvitvaṁ tu syādvivakṣitam | |52| |

यद्येतौ व्याधितौ स्यातां देयं स्यादिदमौषधम् ।
इत्येवं लक्षणेऽर्थस्य द्वित्वं स्यादविवक्षितम् ।।५३।।

yadyetau vyādhitau syātāṁ deyaṁ syādidamauṣadham |
ityevaṁ lakṣaṇe 'rthasya dvitvaṁ syādavivakṣitam | |53| |

एकादिशब्दवाच्यायाः कर्मण्यङ्गत्वमिष्यते ।
संख्यायाः खनति द्वाभ्यामिति रूपाद्धि साश्रिता ।।५४।।

ekādiśabdavācyāyāḥ karmaṇyaṅgatvamiṣyate |
saṁkhyāyāḥ khanati dvābhyāmiti rūpāddhi sāśritā | |54| |

यजेत पशुनेत्यत्र संस्कारस्यापि संभवे ।
यथा जातिस्तथैकत्वं साधनत्वेन गम्यते ।।५५।।

yajeta paśunetyatra saṁskārasyāpi saṁbhave |
yathā jātistathaikatvaṁ sādhanatvena gamyate | |55| |

The universal is the import of a word. But the word has both base or verb root and suffix in case of *subanta* and *tiṅganta*. The suffix also conveys number such as singular, dual or plural. This information on number is incidental and indirectly helps in conveying the import as both the *jāti* and number are connected. The connection is that they both inhere in the same particular, the number may be directly conveyed, but in Bhartr̥hari's view it is secondary. Further, the number may or may not even be significant, as seen in interpretation of Vedic injunctions. The significance of a suffix denoting number is always decided on other grounds although it has equal place in the grammatical structure, i.e. the utterance or Śruti.

As the suffix is part of the finished form of the word, *suptiṅgantam padam*, no word can be used without its *pratyaya* denoting some number, which is not necessarily significant. Some people feel that the number in singular and plural are not important as they may express generalities, but the dual, being more specific is significant, e.g., "Duck swims" and "Ducks swim". But here Bhartṛhari brilliantly points out that even the dual number need not matter. In the direction, "If these two fall ill, give this medicine", the number is not important. Even if one of them falls ill, the medicine should be given! In the Vedic utterance, "He digs to the accompaniment of two *mantra*s", the number is significant as it is expressed by the stem and not just the suffix.

The singular or plural number that the suffix carries is not the main import, as it is not relevant in cognising *jāti*. But thus information, although remote does aid in grasping the meaning fully as it is connected to the *dravya* in which the *dravya-jāti* or *kriyā-jāti* inheres.

They give the *prātipadika* a refinement fit for use in a sentence, the *vibhakti pratyaya* and number are employed incidentally. Thus the meaning of *karmatva* (in the case of *dvitīya vibhakti*) and other *kāraka* cases are obtained by *lakṣaṇa* as the main import of the sentence is in the action.

In some cases, the number may also be significant, if it is for a purpose. For example, in the Vedic injunction *paśūnā yajeta*, the action enjoined can lead to *saṁskāra*, or resulting benefit of ritual. Hence, the singular number is as significant as the universal *paśutva* in the word *paśūnā*. Here *paśūnā* is the *sādhana* or means to *yajñaphala*; it is to be understood as means qualified by both *paśutva* and *ekatva*.

NOTE: Helārāja and following him, K.A.S. Iyer and Raghunatha Sarma take *saṁskāra* to mean *śabdasaṁskāra* with which I do not agree. Bhartṛhari does not write with the technical rigidity that later grammarians adopt; in that sense he was not a Vaiyākaraṇa alone but clearly had equal facility in Mīmāṁsā. It is my belief that *saṁskāra* here refers to the merit obtained by *yajña*, that is, the *apūrva* in the practical context of ritual. Taking the *kārikā* to refer to linguistic technicalities is a roundabout explanation.

लिङ्गात्तु स्याद् द्वितीयादेस्तदेकत्वं विवक्षितम् ।
एकार्थविषयत्वे च तल्लिङ्गं जातिसंख्ययोः ।।५६।।

liṅgāttu syād dvitīyādestadekatvaṁ vivakṣitam |
ekārthaviṣayatve ca talliṅgaṁ jātisaṁkhyayoḥ | |56| |

अन्यत्राविहितस्यैव स विधिः प्रथमं पशोः ।
क्रियायामङ्गभावश्च तत्त्वेतस्माद् विवक्षितम् ।।५७।।

anyatrāvihitasyaiva sa vidhiḥ prathamaṁ paśoḥ |
kriyāyāmaṅgabhāvaśca tattvetasmād vivakṣitam | |57| |

Unless the number one is significant, the mention of second, third, etc., in other utterances of the same passage would not be meaningful. This indicates also that both the universal and the singular number are meant in the same object, the sacrificial animal. In the sentence, *paśūnā yajeta* the *paśu* is introduced for the first time as *anaṅga* or important part of the sacrifice. Therefore the number is also significant, as it is required to know how many *paśu*s would be required.

A separate word indicating the number is not used (such as *ekena* or *dvābhyaḥ, tribhiḥ*, etc.). Therefore the number that the suffix conveys is significant.

ग्रहास्त्वन्यत्र विहिता भिन्नसंख्याः पृथक् पृथक् ।
प्राजापत्या नवेत्येवमादिभेदसमन्विताः ॥५८॥

grahāstvanyatra vihitā bhinnasaṁkhyāḥ pr̥thak pr̥thak |
prājāpatyā navetyevamādibhedasamanvitāḥ | |58| |

अङ्गत्वेन प्रतीतानां सम्मार्गे त्वङ्गिनां पुनः ।
निर्देशं प्रति या संख्या सा कथं स्याद्विवक्षिता ॥५९॥

aṅgatvena pratītānāṁ sammārge tvaṅgināṁ punaḥ |
nirdeśaṁ prati yā saṅkhyā sā kathaṁ syādvivakṣitā | |59| |

While the singular in *paśūnā* is significant, the number of every item mentioned is not. It depends on the context and whether the particular utterance is introducing the item, whereby the number is also to be noted. For example, in the case of vessels used in ritual sacrifice, different number of vessels are to be used in different rites separately, such as "vessels dedicated to Prajāpati are nine in number." After indicating the number specifically, when subsequently their cleaning is enjoined, how can the number in the later utterance become significant? When it is said *graham sammārṣṭi* i.e., "wipe cup," it means that all the vessels should be wiped, not just one.

नान्यत्र विधिरस्तीति संस्कारो नापि चाङ्गिता ।
हेतुः संख्याऽविवक्षायां यत्नात् सा हि विवक्षिता ॥६०॥

nānyatra vidhirastīti saṁskāro nāpi cāṅgitā |
hetuḥ saṅkhyā 'vivakṣāyāṁ yatnāt sā hi vivakṣitā | |60| |

सम्मार्जने विशेषश्च न ग्रहे कश्चिदाश्रितः ।
विहितास्ते च संस्कार्याः सर्वेषामाश्रयस्ततः ॥६१॥

sammārjane viśeṣaśca na grahe kaścidāśritaḥ |
vihitāste ca saṁskāryāḥ sarvaṣāmāśrayastataḥ | |61| |

The number is significant only when there is a specific effort to do so — otherwise the number is just considered as an incidental feature to give formal structure to words in the sentence. No special discrimination among the vessels being explained, the vessels being mentioned in groups of different number, all have to be taken.

Since the singular is not used with any further adjective, there is not even a criterion to select any one in particular. Therefore all will have to be taken, as the *jāti* mentioned applies to all of them.

प्रत्याश्रयं समाप्तायां जातावेकेन चेत्क्रिया ।
पशुना न प्रकल्पेत तत् स्यादेवं प्रकल्पनम् ॥६२॥

pratyāśrayaṁ samāptāyāṁ jātāvekena cetkriyā |
paśunā na prakalpeta tat syādevaṁ prakalpanam || 62 ||

एकेन च प्रसिद्धायां क्रियायां यदि सम्भवात् ।
पश्वन्तरमुपादेयमुपादानमनर्थकम् ॥६३॥

ekena ca prasiddhāyāṁ kriyāyāṁ yadi sambhavāt |
paśvantaramupādeyamupādānamanarthakam || 63 ||

यथैवाहितगर्भायां गर्भाधानमनर्थकम् ।
तथैकेन प्रसिद्धायां पश्वन्तरमनर्थकम् ॥६४॥

yathaivāhitagarbhāyāṁ garbhādhānamanarthakam |
tathaikena prasiddhāyāṁ paśvantaramanarthakam || 64 ||

In the case of *paśūnā yajeta*, since the universal is present in full in one individual, sacrificing one animal adequately satisfies the injunction. One would think of a second animal only if one were not sufficient. When the condition or requirement is fulfilled, further attempt to perform the same act will not have any benefit. The example given is that while a woman is in the conceived state, it is of no use sowing further seed, as everyone knows. Thus when one animal has sufficed, sacrificing more would be futile.

While it is possible to perform the sacrifice again with a second *paśu*, Śāstra says that it is not advisable to repeat an attempt for a goal already achieved.

तावतार्थस्य सिद्धत्वादेकत्वस्याव्यतिक्रमम् ।
केचिदिच्छन्ति न त्वत्र संख्याङ्गत्वेन गृह्यते ।।६५।।

tāvatārthasya siddhatvādekatvasyāvyatikramam |
kecidicchanti na tvatra saṁkhyāṅgatvena gr̥hyate | |65| |

द्वितीयादिषु यल्लिङ्गमुक्तं न्यायानुवादि तत् ।
न संख्या साधनत्वेन जातिवत्तेन गम्यते ।।६६।।

dvitīyādiṣu yalliṅgamuktaṁ nyāyānuvādi tat |
na saṁkhyā sādhanatvena jātivattena gamyate | |66| |

The following two *kārikās* present some others' views in understanding the singular in the injunction *paśūnā yajeta*. When the injunction can be satisfied by sacrificing one animal, the singular number one is implied, but not significant as an accessory. Number need not have *aṅgatva*. Further mention of "second", "third", etc., are logically understood, by reasoning. The number is not intended as an accessory, only the universal is in this view, number is indirectly understood, which also means that sacrificing more than one *paśu* would not be a violation.

In the first instance, *paśūnā yajeta* is understood with the singular which is incidental. As only the *jātyartha* is significant, a further performance of *yajña* with *paśūbhyām yejeta*, etc. could also be extrapolated.

अन्वयव्यतिरेकाभ्यां संख्याभ्युपगमे सति ।
युक्तं यत्साधनं स्यान्न त्वन्यार्थोपलक्षणम् ।।६७।।

anvayavyatirekābhyāṁ saṁkhyābhyupagame sati |
yuktaṁ yatsādhanaṁ syānna tvanyārthopalakṣaṇam | |67| |

Bhartr̥hari does not agree with this view and clarifies that the singular is seriously meant. When the singular is required in *paśu* by *anvaya vyatireka* to satisfy the injunction, it has to be taken as accessory, or means, *sādhana*.

Iyer's translation: When both the universal and the

number are equal because both are expressed by the same word, both become accessories. Thereby, the word does not lose its capacity to express the accessory.

साधनत्वे पदार्थस्य सामर्थ्यं न प्रहीयते ।
संख्या व्यापारधर्मोऽतस्तेन लिङ्गेन गम्यते ॥६८॥

sādhanatve padārthasya sāmarthyaṁ na prahīyate |
saṁkhyā vyāpāradharmo 'tastena liṅgena gamyate | |68| |

अपूर्वस्य विधेयत्वात् प्राधान्यमवसीयते ।
विहितस्य परार्थत्वाच्छेषभावः प्रतीयते ॥६९॥

apūrvasya vidheyatvāt prādhānyamavasīyate |
vihitasya parārthatvācchеṣabhāvaḥ pratīyate | |69| |

The purpose is the most important thing, to which the selection of means is subordinate. Since *apūrva* is the merit to be achieved by sacrificing *paśu*, the injunction being satisfied by sacrificing one *paśu*, further *paśu*s will not be of any use. If a sacrificer happens to be wealthy and can afford to sacrifice several *paśu*s and performs *yajña* several times, the *yajña* becomes secondary to his capacity, which is not correct. The goal is primary and all else is secondary as it exists only for the former. *Vidheya* is primary whereas *vihita* is secondary.

Whether the number is significant or not being decided by other criteria, the word *paśūnā* is accessory in two ways — in the *jāti* which is its import and in the singular number denoted by the suffix. The word functioning as accessory has suffix functioning as *liṅga*, denoting the number.

Where the *vidheya* is first mentioned, as unknown item is first taught and all aspects are significant; the *vihita* being already known, takes secondary place in subsequent mention.

संमार्गस्य विधेयत्वादन्यत्र विहिते ग्रहे ।
विधिवाक्ये श्रुता संख्या लक्षणायां न बाध्यते ॥७०॥

saṁmārgasya vidheyatvādanyatra vihite grahe |
vidhivākye śrutā saṁkhyā lakṣaṇāyāṁ na bādhyate | |70| |

विधिवाक्यान्तरे संख्या पशोर्नास्तीति विरोधिनी ।
तस्मात् सगुण एवासौ सदैकत्वेन गम्यते ।।७१।।

vidhivākyāntare saṁkhyā paśornāstīti virodhinī |
tasmāt saguṇa evāsau sadaikatvena gamyate | |71| |

In Pūrva-Mīmāṁsā, whatever is enjoined should belong to predicate part of the sentence and not the subject. *Vidheya* is more important than *uddeśya*. Here *grahaṁ* is *uddeśya* and *sammārjana* is *vidheya*. The singular in the subject need not be taken into account. Since the wiping is enjoined and the cups are taught elsewhere, the singular in the injunction *graham sammārṣṭi* does not inhibit the suggestion, *lakṣaṇā*, to take all. But in the case of *paśūnā yajeta*, the *paśu* is not taught elsewhere with a contradictory number. So it is to be understood with its property (*paśutva*) and singular number.

The cups are first mentioned as nine or ten in number in different *yāga*s in the *vidhivākya*. Hence they become known, *vihita*. Moreover they are used in different numbers in rituals that follow, viz. *somayāga*, etc. So it is reasonable that all the cups be wiped, as clean cups would be required. Hence the singular number in *graham sammarṣṭi* does not inhibit all nine to be understood by *lakṣaṇā*.

Since the *yāga* is enjoined with *paśu*s as the *guṇa* (accessory) the *paśu* is also *vidheya* and hence the singular is significant.

THE ISSUE OF SUBSTITUTION

The next section studies the relation of the qualities (*guṇa*s) with the *dravya* and *jāti*, to justify substitution of an *aṅga* that may not be available in ritual, with some other item. If the import of the word is in *jāti* can it allow substitution? If so, what are the criteria for selecting the right substitute? These issues are of great practical importance and represent the main reasons for Mīmāṁsā's rejection of *akhaṇḍavākya* view. Bhartṛhari reconciles all aspects as justifying substitution of any *aṅga* in Vedic ritual. From *kārikā* 72 onwards, some issues other than number are discussed.

निर्ज्ञातद्रव्यसंबन्धे यः कर्मण्युपदिश्यते ।
गुणस्तेनार्थिता तस्य द्रव्येणेव प्रतीयते ।।७२।।

nirjñātadravyasaṁbandhe yaḥ karmaṇyupadiśyate |
guṇastenārthitā tasya dravyeṇeva pratīyate | |72| |

कश्चिदेव गुणो द्रव्ये यथा सामर्थ्यलक्षणः ।
आधारोऽपि गुणस्यैवं प्राप्तः सामर्थ्यलक्षणः ।।७३।।

kaścideva guṇo dravye yathā sāmarthyalakṣaṇaḥ |
ādhāro 'pi guṇasyaivaṁ prāptaḥ sāmarthyalakṣaṇaḥ | |73| |

In the context of Vedic injunction, some action is enjoined. Action can be accomplished only through a substance or particular. But a substance is always a substratum of several qualities.

Thus the qualities are also connected with the action indirectly. So the qualities are also *sādhana* in ritual, by connection with the *dravya* that is directly mentioned as the *aṅga*. The first few *kārikās* look at the issue of substitution from the *dravyavādī* point of view and examine whether substance or quality is to be substituted. Whenever a *dravya* is mentioned its chief quality is also understood, because of invariable association. In the same way, a particular quality is always associated with a substance.

Without *guṇa*, there cannot be *dravya* and without *dravya* there cannot be *guṇa*. Their mutual relation is discussed. First the *vyakti sambandha* or *dravya sambandha* point of view is discussed and then the *jāti kriyā sambandha* point of view in 76. When the *vyakti* related with activity is known, the quality is also expected and can be brought in. If a quality is specifically enjoined with respect to a ritual, for which the *dravya* or *vyakti* is known, then by the very knowledge of *dravya*, that quality is automatically sought. Just as *dravya* must have some *guṇa, guṇa* also needs some *dravya* as locus.

The action enjoined requires a means to carry it out. No activity can take place without a substance as a base to execute it. When the required substance or item for the enjoined *yajña* is known, the suitable qualities that the substance possesses also spring to mind. The substance is immediately connected with the action, and are *antaraṅga*; the qualities, *guṇas*, are one step away and are *bahiraṅga*. Any *guṇa* is not associated with any *dravya* at random; neither can there be any *dravya* without possessing any *guṇas*. The locus of the *guṇas* are according to capacity or suitability, as the *guṇas* cannot exist without *ādhāra* in our experience of the world.

तयोस्तु पृथगर्थित्वे सम्बन्धो यः प्रतीयते ।
न तस्मिन्नुपघातोऽस्ति कल्प्यमन्यत्र चाश्रुतम् ।।७४।।

tayostu pr̥thagarthitve sambandho yaḥ pratīyate |
na tasminnupaghāto 'sti kalpyamanyatra cāśrutam | |74| |

क्रियया योऽभिसम्बन्धः स श्रुतिप्रापितस्तयोः ।
आश्रयाश्रयिणोर्वाक्यान्नियमस्त्ववतिष्ठते ।।७५।।

kriyayā yo 'bhisambandhaḥ sa śrutiprāpitastayoḥ |
āśrayāśrayiṇorvākyānniyamastvavatiṣṭhate | |75| |

Dravya Guṇas are mutually and invariably related. Their association being recalled in the cognition cannot be denied nor can something new be brought in. As Iyer writes, there is no justification in abandoning this connection and connect any of the two with something not mentioned in the sentence. All this about substance and quality is being said from the point of view of artificial abstraction, *apoddhāra*.

Really speaking, the meaning of the individual word continues to be a universal and only appears to be particularised in association with the meanings of other words.

Though *kriyā* is connected with the *dravya*, it is also related to the *guṇa*, as *guṇa* and *dravya* are related. The relation of *dravya* with *kriyā* is *śrutipramāṇa* whereas relation of *guṇa* with *kriyā* is by *vākya-pramāṇa*.

The words denoting *dravya* and the *guṇa* are both connected to the verb by equivalent *kāraka vibhakti*. Although the sentence conveys one undivided meaning, upon analysing the words, we can explain the sentence, *gām abhyāja śuklām* as follows: *gām abhyāja* and *śuklām abhyāja*. Or, *gām abhyāja, śuklām ca*. Here the main clause being *gām abhyāja*, the *dravya* is connected to action directly and the *guṇa* in the next step, at least in the grammatical analysis, even if not in reality.

As Helārāja puts it,

श्रुत्या कारकविभक्त्या क्रियायां संबन्धो द्रव्यगुणयोः समशीर्षकतया प्रतिपादितः वाक्याद् अखण्डप्रतिभोत्पत्तावप्यपोद्धारेण गामभ्याज शुक्लामभ्याज इति पदार्थविभजनात् । एकं हि कर्म वाक्यार्थभूतं क्रियालक्षणम्।

śrutyā kārakavibhaktyā kriyāyāṁ saṁbandho dravyaguṇayoḥ samaśīrṣakatayā pratipāditaḥ vākyād akhaṇḍapratibhotpattāvapyapoddhāreṇa gāmabhyāja śuklāmabhyāja iti padārthavibhajanāt । *ekaṁ hi karma vākyārthabhūtaṁ kriyālakṣaṇam* ।

तत्र द्रव्यगुणाभावे प्रत्येकं स्याद् विकल्पनम् ।
श्रुतिप्राप्तो हि सम्बन्धो बलवान् वाक्यलक्षणात् ।।७६।।

tatra dravyaguṇābhāve pratyekaṁ syād vikalpanam |
śrutiprāpto hi sambandho balavān vākyalakṣaṇāt | |76| |

In the next *kārikā*, Bhartṛhari points out the limitation of this view. In case the prescribed item is not available, there can be substitute available for either *dravya* or *guṇa* in this view, as the relation expressed directly by the verbal element *kriyā sambandhita śruti* is stronger than the relation expressed by *vākya-sāmānādhikaraṇya.* Thus, in the case where a black goat is enjoined in the sacrifice, it can be substituted either by a black sheep or a white goat made of flour. This result is not desired in the interpretation.

The next verse onwards point out the advantage of taking *jāti* as the import of the injunction, whereby, substitution in Vedic ritual is also effected without contradiction.

यदा तु जातिः शक्तिर्वा क्रियां प्रत्युपदिश्यते ।
सामर्थ्यात् सन्निधीयेते तत्र द्रव्यगुणौ तदा ।।७७।।

yadā tu jātiḥ śaktirvā kriyāṁ pratyupadiśyate |
sāmarthyāt sannidhīyete tatra dravyaguṇau tadā | |77| |

Jāti, equivalent to *śakti* is taken as connected with *kriyā*. But *guṇa* and *kriyā* can be connected only through *dravya*. *Jāti* is permanently associated with *dravya* and is therefore nearer, *sannikṛṣṭa*. *Guṇa* is not permanently present in *dravya* as it can change from time to time or is different in different individuals. It is therefore not as close, *viprakṛṣṭa*. When we take *jāti* as connected with *kriyā*, *dravya* also get connected automatically as a matter of course and *guṇa* also comes into the picture. In *dravya*, *jāti* is *sannikṛṣṭa* and *guṇa* is *viprakṛṣṭa*.

जातीनां च गुणानां च तुल्येऽङ्गत्वे क्रियां प्रति ।
गुणाः प्रतिनिधीयन्ते छागादीनां न जातयः ।।७८।।

jātīnāṁ ca guṇānāṁ ca tulye 'ṅgatve kriyāṁ prati |
guṇāḥ pratinidhīyante chāgādīnāṁ na jātayaḥ | |78| |

Kārikā 78 says that the attributes or qualities, *guṇa*s, can be substituted, but the very categories cannot be substituted, even though universal and quality are both accessories of the action.

व्यक्तिशक्तेः समासन्ना जातयो न तथा गुणाः ।
साक्षाद् द्रव्यं क्रियायोगि गुणस्तस्माद् विकल्पते ।।७९।।

vyaktiśakteḥ samāsannā jātayo na tathā guṇāḥ |
sākṣād dravyaṁ kriyāyogi guṇastasmād vikalpate | |79| |

The next verse gives the reason why one takes preference over the other. The *dravya* is directly connected with action while the qualities are indirectly so. That is why the attributes are optional but the very categories are not.

The capacity is what determines the suitability of an item to an activity. The many qualities that the substance possesses may or may not be relevant to the suitability or capacities in the particular context. Thus the suitability is determined primarily by the universal and secondarily by the *guṇa*s. It is the universal that inheres steadily in its individual from the moment it is created up to its perishing; the qualities such as colour, softness, size, etc. may keep changing. Thus *dravya* is directly connected to activity whereas *guṇa* is so indirectly.

साम्येनान्यतराभावे विकल्पः कैश्चिदिष्यते ।
अतद्गुणोऽतश्छागः स्यान्मेषो वा तद्गुणो भवेत् ॥८०॥

sāmyenānyatarābhāve vikalpaḥ kaiścidiṣyate |
atadguṇo 'taśchāgaḥ syānmeṣo vā tadguṇo bhavet | |80| |

Those who follow the thought of Vyāḍi, perhaps, giving precedence to *dravya*, may consider either *dravya* or *guṇa* as optional, due to similarity of being connected to action and also universal as *guṇa* residing in *dravya* by *samavāya*. For the *padavādin*, both have equal standing, in this case substitution can be of either *guṇa* or *dravya*; i.e. a black goat for white sheep. But this position is not desirable.

जातेराश्रितसंख्यायाः प्रवृत्तिरुपलभ्यते ।
संख्याविशेषमुत्सृज्य क्वचित् सैव प्रवर्तते ॥८१॥

jāterāśritasaṁkhyāyāḥ pravṛttirupalabhyate |
saṁkhyāviśeṣamutsṛjya kvacit saiva pravartate | |81| |

After the digression regarding quality, in *kārikā* 81, the earlier discussion on number continues. We see that *jāti* has application in action sometimes taking into account number of particulars and sometimes not taking into account the number.

This is explained in further detail in the next few *kārikās*.

पराङ्गभूतं सामान्यं युज्यते द्रव्यसंख्यया ।
स्वार्थं प्रवर्तमानं तु न संख्यामवलम्बते ।।८२।।

parāṅgabhūtaṁ sāmānyaṁ yujyate dravyasaṁkhyayā |
svārthaṁ pravartamānaṁ tu na saṁkhyāmavalambate | |82| |

The specific conditions under which one or the other case is considered is explained in the following verses. The general principle is given in *kārikā* 82. When the universal is subsidiary to something else which is the main purpose, the number is significant. But when a thing is stated for itself, then the number is not significant as the main purpose is to convey the *jāti*. In Vedic injunction, the predicate is *pradhāna*, the subject being *guṇa* or secondary. So whether the number is significant or not depends on the factual situation.

George Cardona explains the *kārikā* as having two Principles, P1 and P2 in the two lines. P1: A *jāti* (*sāmānyam*) which has the status of being subsidiary to something (*parāṅgabhūtam* is linked (*yujyate*) with the number of the substance (*dravyasaṁkhyā*) in which it inheres. Corollary P2: a *jāti* that has the status of being a principal, hence acting for its own sake (*svārtham pravarttamānam*), on the other hand, does not depend on such a number (*saṁkhyām nāvalambate*).

यजेत पशुनेत्यत्र यज्यार्थायां पशुश्रुतौ ।
कृतार्थैकेन पशुना प्रधानं भवति क्रिया ।।८३।।

yajeta paśunetyatra yajyārthāyāṁ paśuśrutau |
kṛtārthaikena paśunā pradhānaṁ bhavati kriyā | |83| |

यावतां संभवो यस्य स कुर्यात्तावतां यदि ।
आलम्भनं गुणैस्तेन प्रधानं स्यात् प्रयोजितम् ।।८४।।

yāvatāṁ saṁbhavo yasya sa kuryāttāvatāṁ yadi |
ālambhanaṁ guṇaistena pradhānaṁ syāt prayojitam | |84| |

संमृज्यमानतन्त्रे तु ग्रहे यत्र क्रियाश्रुतिः ।
संख्याविशेषग्रहणं नैव तत्राद्रियामहे ॥८५॥

saṁmṛjyamānatantre tu grahe yatra kriyāśrutiḥ |
saṁkhyāviśeṣagrahaṇaṁ naiva tatrādriyāmahe | |85| |

This principle is illustrated in the case of *paśūnā yajeta* and *graham sammārṣṭi*. In the first case, the sacrifice is the main thing and the animal is an accessory to it. By sacrificing one animal, the condition for the *yajña* is satisfied, hence the number one is significant. An unwarranted repetition of action is also a violation. *Paśūnā* conveys *paśutva jāti* with *kriyāṅgatva* as *yajña* is *radhāna*. If one were to sacrifice with as many animals as one can, the arrangements for the entire *yāga* would be decided by the animal each time and this would be a case of the main thing being determined by subordinate items which is not desirable. The subsidiary should not dictate the terms for them, the very property of being the principal would become doubtful. In the case of *grahaṁ sammārṣṭi, graham* is uttered for its own sake, not for *kriyāṅgatva*. The cup is the main thing to be cleaned. Hence number is not significant.

In this juncture of the *yajña*, the cleaning itself is not a significant ritual whereby cleaning one cup would be adequate — the cups are required in a clean condition and hence all of them indicated in the *utpatti vākya*, are intended.

*Kārikā*s 86 to 91 illustrate the principle stated in 82 in rules of grammar.

शिष्यमाणपरे वाक्ये यदेकग्रहणं कृतम् ।
शेषे विशिष्टसंख्येऽपि व्यक्तं तल्लिङ्गदर्शनम् ॥८६॥

śiṣyamāṇapare vākye yadekagrahaṇaṁ kṛtam |
śeṣe viṣiṣṭasaṁkhye 'pi vyaktaṁ talliṅgadarśanam | |86| |

In the *sūtra sarūpāṇām ekaśeṣa ekavibhaktau*, *P* 1.2.64, the word *śeṣaḥ* is in the singular. The *sūtra* teaches that of many words having the same form, only one remains when they are followed by the same case-ending.[12] But the number one is specified by explicitly stating *eka* and not left to the singular case-ending to convey singularity. This shows that as *śeṣa*, what remains, being what is taught, is the main thing and hence its number is not significant. The required number is learnt from the mention of *eka*.

Prof. Cardona's explanation — An inferential mark (*liṅgam*) indicating that P1-P2 apply in grammar: the *sūtra ekaśeṣa ekavibhaktau*. This provides that only one remains (*ekaśeṣaḥ*) under one alternative, *śeṣa* is an object noun (*śiṣyate iti śeṣaḥ*). The term *ekaśeṣaḥ* refers to the *pradhāna* (*śiṣysamāṇapare vākye*) in the utterance where the principal entity referred to is the remainder) and the singular form also occurs. Yet Pāṇini also specifies that one *eka* remains. This is a clear *vyaktam* inferential indicator *liṅgam* that P2, the corollary of P1, holds.

This is a clear (*vyaktam*) inferential indicator (*liṅgam*) that the number on the word *śeṣa* is not significant, justifying the use of the word *eka* in the *sūtra* to specify the number to be taken.

Prakāśa:

प्रधानभूतं सामान्यमाधारगतसंख्याश्रयेण न प्रवर्तत इत्यस्यार्थस्य ज्ञापकं स्फुटम्।

pradhānabhūtaṁ sāmānyamādhāragatasaṁkhyāśrayeṇa na pravartata ityasyārthasya jñāpakaṁ sphuṭam |

12. Iyer, p. 53.

समासप्रत्ययविधौ यथा निपतिता श्रुतिः ।
गुणानां परतन्त्राणां न्यायेनैवोपपद्यते ॥८७॥

samāsapratyayavidhau yathā nipatitā śrutiḥ |
guṇānāṁ paratantrāṇāṁ nyāyenaivopapadyate | |87| |

The following are illustrations of the first principle in 82, viz., that the number in subsidiary items is significant. In *supsupā*, in *samāsa*, the parts are subsidiary to the whole compound word. The compound word as intact is one and the parts are abstractions; parts are only meant to achieve the whole. Hence the singular number in *sup sahasupā* is significant as only one word combines with another at a time and never more. The *samasta* word combines with another at a time and never more. The *samasta* word containing many words is built up one step at a time, as we see in the *vigraha vākya*. In the *sūtra ṅyāp prātipadikāt* the suffixes come after a single word-ending in *ṅī* or *āp* and after a single *prātipadika*, stem. One suffix cannot come after many of them at the same time.

गुणेऽपि नाङ्गीक्रियते प्रधानान्तरसिद्धये ।
संख्या कर्ता तथा कर्मण्यविशिष्टः प्रतीयते ॥८८॥

guṇe 'pi nāṅgīkriyate pradhānāntarasiddhaye |
saṁkhyā kartā tathā karmaṇyaviśiṣṭaḥ pratīyate | |88| |

यस्यान्यस्य प्रसक्तस्य नियमार्था पुनः श्रुतिः ।
निवृत्तौ चरितार्थत्वात् संख्या तत्राविवक्षिता ॥८९॥

yasyānyasya prasaktasya niyamārthā punaḥ śrutiḥ |
nivṛttau caritārthatvāt saṁkhyā tatrāvivakṣitā | |89| |

The general rule is that the number in subsidiary items is significant. But is this sweeping? No, there are exceptions.

Prakāśa:

कमेष एवोत्सर्गः गुणे सन्ख्या विवक्ष्यते इति । नेत्याह ।

kameṣa evotsargaḥ guṇe sankhyā vivakṣyate iti | *netyāha* |

In the *sūtra karturīpsitatamaṁ karma*, the nomenclature *karman* is the primary purpose of the rule whereas *karturīpsitatamaṁ* is the description which is secondary. Hence the singular in *kartur* may be understood to be singular, which should not be done. The object of several agents, or *kartāraḥ* is also denoted as *karman*, e.g. *vānaraḥ vṛkṣaṁ ārohati, vānarāḥ vṛkṣaṁ ārohanti.*

The reason for this seeming deviation from the general principle is further explained in the next *kārikā*. When something which is possible is expressly mentioned in order to exclude other possibilities, there the number is not significant, as its purpose has been served by the removal of other possibilities. Had the *sūtra* been, *īpsitatamaṁ karma*, it would still be applicable that the goal most desired to reach is denoted as *karman*. But the explicit mention of *kartur* serves to eliminate other *vibhakti*s. Hence the main purpose of mentioning *kartur* is other than conveying the meaning of *karttā*. Therefore, the number need not be taken as significant.

सरूपसमुदायात्तु विभक्तिर्या विधीयते ।
एकस्तत्रार्थवान् सिद्धः समुदायस्य वाचकः ॥९०॥

sarūpasamudāyāttu vibhaktiryā vidhīyate |
ekastatrārthavān siddhaḥ samudāyasya vācakaḥ | |90| |

The next two *kārikā*s sum up the discussion on whether a particular number mentioned in the utterance is to be taken as intended or not. The reference is to *sūtra* 1.2.64, *sarūpāṇ āṁekaśeṣa ekavibhaktau* which says that a single word (stem) of several identical stems, is sufficient to denote the whole group in compound word or *samāsa*, e.g., in the case of *aśva* + *aśva* + *au* a single *aśva* remains, representing both. In the case of plural, *aśva* + *aśva* + *aśva* + *jas*, etc., only one remains, representing the whole group. Although the *sūtra* can be interpreted that a single *vibhaktyanta*, suffix is to follow the *samudāya*, its meaning (*vibhaktyartha*) applying to each member of the compound. Helārāja explains that it is because the compounds *aśva aśva* or *aśva aśva aśva*, etc., qualify as *prātipadika* that they merit the attaching of *vibhaktipratyaya*.

The *kārikā* itself states that there is properly (*siddhaḥ* = established) a single meaningful element (*arthavān*) — namely a complex like *aśva-aśva* or *aśva-aśva-aśva* such that a *vibhakti* which (*yā*) is introduced (*vidhīyate*) after a complex of homophonous items (*sarūpasamudāyāt*) and in such a complex (*tatra*) there is indeed established a single meaningful element that signifies (*vācakaḥ* the meaning of the complex (*samudāyasya*), namely the single complex and the single remainder.

Sometimes a stem can be formed by joining several stems in *samāsa*, e.g. Rāmalakṣmaṇau. In this case also, since the *prātipadika* is Rāmalakṣmaṇa, only one *vibhakti pratyaya* is used at the end of the compound.

प्रत्ययस्य प्रधानस्य समासस्यापि वा विधौ ।
सिद्धः संख्याविवक्षायां सर्वथानुग्रहो गुणे ॥९१॥

pratyayasya pradhānasya samāsasyāpi vā vidhau |
siddhaḥ saṁkhyāvivakṣāyāṁ sarvathānugraho guṇe | |91| |

Kārikā 91 says that thus in the rules for bringing in suffixes or *samāsa*s which are of importance, it has been shown that in secondary items, the indication of number is to be taken as significant.

THE NATURE OF JĀTI

From *kārikā* 92 to the end of the *samuddeśa*, the nature of *jāti* is finally discussed, the definitions given in a broad sense rather thn tightly knit with technicalities. *Jāti* is explained for its wn sake and not necessarily with relation to something else, as is the case in discussions in other places.

अभेदरूपं सादृश्यमात्मभूताश्च शक्तयः ।
जातिपर्यायवाचित्वमेषामप्युपवर्ण्यते ॥९२॥

abhedarūpaṁ sādṛśyamātmabhūtāśca śaktayaḥ |
jātiparyāyavācitvameṣāmapyupavarṇyate | |92| |

To have the class concept, we can use *sādṛśya*, similarity which cnsists of perceiving something as not different from any nother individual or the innate power which is the essence of a thing, these are considered as synonymous with *jāti*.

As Helārāja explains,

तदेतदभ्युपगच्छति । अभेदरूपं अव्यतिरिक्त व्यक्तीनां यत्सादृश्यं एकप्रत्यवमर्शजनकं वा व्यतिरिक्तमेव शक्तिलक्षणं सामर्थ्यं तदपि जातिरिति व्यपदिश्यत एव । अन्विताकारज्ञानजनकं हि व्यक्तीनां किञ्चन रूपं सामान्यमिति सर्वपार्षदो न्यायः ।

tadetadabhyupagacchati | *abhedarūpaṁ avyatirictaṁ vyaktīnāṁ yatsādṛśyaṁ ekapratyavamarśajanakaṁ vā vyatiriktameva śakti-lakṣaṇaṁ sāmarthyaṁ tadapi jātiriti vyapadiśyata eva* | *anvitākārajñānajanakaṁ hi vyaktīnāṁ kiñcana rūpaṁ sāmānyamiti sarvapārṣado nyāyaḥ* |

The question arises as to whether the *jāti* is over and above the individuals. Is not the appearance of the individual with its shape, colour, etc. enough? The answer is that *jāti* is distinctly over and above the individual. The way in which different schools of philosophy view this issue depends on their particular ontology and premises, as discussed in chapter 6.

It is by recognising several individuals to be "of the same form", or identical that *jāti* is perceived. *Jāti* is not perceived as a separate entity. So why should we postulate a distinct entity such as univeral, when the concept of similarity may be enough for cognition? Bhartṛhari stresses that this is not the case. Similarity is not sufficient to identify and individual as identical in class. All schools of philosophy recognise a distinct cause, viz. universal as responsible for cognition of an individul as a member of that particular class. Even if we identify the cause by calling it "similarity" or "capacity" it is the same concept by another name. This view is echoed by Kumārila Bhaṭṭa in the Ākṛtivāda of *Ślokavārttika.*

Every cognition has its own direct cause. Otherwise, things would get very confusing and murky. We would barely be able to logically understand different cognitions. By a man having the intention of holding a staff, we do not get the cognition that he is actually holding one, even if the idea of a stick can be conjured (by mentioning the intention, perhaps). If a person simply has a desire, the others do not understand that he has that desire/intention. Therefore, even though there is potentiality for conveying certain ideas, the actual cognition is based on some other specific reason.

दण्डोपादित्सया दण्डं यद्यपि प्रतिपद्यते ।
न तस्मादेव सामर्थ्यात् स दण्डीति प्रतीयते ।।९३।।

daṇḍopāditsayā daṇḍaṁ yadyapi pratipadyate |
na tasmādeva sāmarthyāt sa daṇḍīti pratīyate | |93| |

नेच्छानिमित्तादिच्छावानिति ज्ञानं प्रवर्तते ।
तस्मात् सत्यपि सामर्थ्यं बुद्धिरर्थान्तराश्रया ।।९४।।

necchānimittādicchāvāniti jñānaṁ pravartate |
tasmāt satyapi sāmarthyaṁ buddhirarthāntarāśrayā | |94| |

Iyer writes that we have to postulate a special cause for the similarity of cognition which we have when we look at different individuals of the same class. Resemblance and particular disposition can account for certain things, but not for this, which can be explained only by the universal, which is over and above the individuals.

If we do not have the class concept to identify different

individuals of the same type, how are we to even differentiate from one another? To say that two individuals have similarity of even a high degree is still not enough to understand them. *Jāti* that inheres in both help us understand that they are two individuals, e.g. cows. This is not to be confused between a cow and a horse, which are individuals of two different universals. Each universal is characterised by its own specific attributes, configuration, shape, etc., which are different in the case of cow and horse. That is why a specific, unique *kāraṇa* is required for every *kārya*. A cognition is also a *kārya* which requires an immediate and specific cause, which in this case is served by the universal.

स्वभावोऽव्यपदेश्यो वा सामर्थ्यं वावतिष्ठते ।
सर्वस्यान्ते यतस्तस्माद् व्यवहारो न कल्पते ।।९५।।

svabhāvo 'vyapadeśyo vā sāmarthyaṁ vāvatiṣṭhate |
sarvasyānte yatastasmād vyavahāro na kalpate | |95| |

If we do not have specific and immediate causes for effects, but go to roundabout causes, it would lead to confusion of causes and ultimately to the root cause of the whole cosmos! *Kārikā* 95 says that in such a case, intelligent verbal communication would become futile.

When everything is rendered indeterminate, verbal communication and all other transactions would have no precision. A sentence such as "Bring the cow" or "Dine on rice" has a specific activity as its meaning. Thus the object that is the root cause of this activity has to be understood without ambiguity, without which the activity cannot be carried out. If there is not tightly knit relation between cause and effect, such activities cannot be performed by identifying objects on the basis of similarity. Knowing something as similar to an object is different to understanding it as of the same kind. Two cows are said to be similar; a cow and a *gavaya* are also said to be similar. Clearly *jāti* and *sādṛśya* are two different things.

यदा भेदान् परित्यज्य बुद्ध्यैक इव गृह्यते ।
व्यक्त्यात्मैव तदा तत्र बुद्धिरेका प्रवर्तते ।।९६।।

yadā bhedān parityajya buddhyaika iva gṛhyate ।
vyaktyātmaiva tadā tatra buddhirekā pravartate ।।96।।

भेदरूपैरनुस्यूतं यदैकमिव मन्यते ।
समूहावग्रहा बुद्धिर्बहुभ्यो जायते तदा ।।९७।।

bhedarūpairanusyūtaṁ yadaikamiva manyate ।
samūhāvagrahā buddhirbahubhyo jāyate tadā ।।97।।

Kārikā 96 says that when the differences are ignored and the essence of the individual is perceived as one, then a single conception comes into existence (following Iyer). Helārāja takes the *kārikā* as indicating the Sāṁkhya view which is to see the one primordial cause manifesting in the myriad variety of the world.

सर्वं ह्यैकस्य परिणामो विवर्त इति वा।
sarvaṁ hyaikasya pariṇāmo vivartta iti vā ।

As Iyer writes lucidly,

> We trace back the whole universe to one cause if we find some common feature in everything. That which does not exist in any way cannot come to be. Thus cause and effect are really the same thing. Everything is like everything else and yet not so.

In my view, this *kārikā* can be interpreted purely in terms of *jāti*, without depending on the Satkāryavāda point of view of Sāṁkhya or Advaita. The *kārikā* seems rather to explain how cognition of *jāti* occurs. When a person is familiar with concept of *gotva* after having seen a brown cow, even when he sees a black cow in a new city, he is able to identify it as a "cow", same as the previous, ignoring the differences in colour, size, shape of horns, etc. Then the individual is cognised in terms of its universal. *Kārikās* 96 and 97 go together in my view, and explain how, upon seeing several individuals in succession, the idea of class is grasped which necessarily points to the idea of several individuals in a group. After all, a single member does not constitute a *jāti*, universal.

एकं नित्यमनेकसमवेतं सामान्यम्।
ekaṁ nityamanekasamavetaṁ sāmānyam | — *Tarkasaṁgraha*

When we see a new entity for the first time, we do not cognise *jāti*. It is only upon seeing a second or subsequent individual that the universal is recognised. The *kārikā* says that when several different members are observed as the same, then the concept of a group is formed.

When we see two or more distinct individuals of the same class and ignoring the specific differences, recognise them as one, we perceive the *jāti*. What meets the eye is the individual, but what we perceive is the *jāti*. This is what Mīmāṁsā calls as bhedābheda. Helārāja points out that everything exists at mutiple levels of organisation; the *abheda* is *sāmānya* and the bheda is the individual, *viśeṣa*. Common to the whole cosmos is *mahāsāmānya* which is divided and subdivided into many tiers of *sāmānyas*. Here, the criteria of division are different limiting factors, avacchedakas, according to context. It is by limiting factors or changes, that certain things are said to be transformations, pariṇāmas, of their causes. Everything is *pariṇāma* or *vivartta* of the One Supreme. Thus nothing is truly distinct from any other thing, it is only in cognition at the worldly level.

When we view an animal for the first time, e.g. on an African safari, we see it as a new individual, and observe its attributes such as size, colour, configuration, gait, sounds, etc. When we move on and come across a second individual that may vary in size or shape, while perceiving that it is a different individual, we are still able to recognise it as of the same group. The mind grasps the concept of universal from the fact that there are many members to that group.

सकृत्प्रवृत्तावेकत्वमावृत्तौ सदृशात्मताम् ।
भिन्नात्मिकानां व्यक्तीनां भेदापोहात् प्रपद्यते ।।९८।।

sakṛtpravṛttāvekatvamāvṛttau sadṛśātmatām |
bhinnātmikānāṁ vyaktīnāṁ bhedāpohāt prapadyate | |98| |

In the Mīmāṁsā view, for instance, *jāti-vyakti* are related by *bhedābheda* relation as explained by Kumārila[13] several centuries after Bhartṛhari. Here the word *sakṛtpravṛttau* seems to refer to the same idea. When different individuals are cognised without focusing on the differences, they are understood as one when the focus is on the class concept; when they are understood in turn as distinct, then the similarity is cognised.

When the reasons for perceiving several individuals as distinct (such as variations in size or shape or even location of the entity, e.g. in a row of identical jars) are ignored and they are all perceived as one and the same thing, it is *sāmānya* at work; when they are simultaneously perceived as identical and distinct, as a group, it is the *sādṛśya* that is cognised. While cognising each member of a group as such, the *sāmānya* is cognised. On the other hand, in the care of a cow and a *gavaya*, they are first cognised as two different things and then due to the common features of configuration they are observed to be similar. Thus in the very cognitions, they cause *sāmānya* and *sādṛśya* are different in nature.

अनुप्रवृत्तेति यथा भिन्ना बुद्धिः प्रतीयते ।
अर्थो व्यावृत्तरूपोऽपि तथा तत्त्वेन गृह्यते ।।९९।।

13. *Ākṛtivāda* in *Ślokavārttikā*.

anupravr̥tteti yathā bhinnā buddhiḥ pratīyate |
artho vyāvr̥ttarūpo 'pi tathā tattvena gr̥hyate | |99| |

The next *kārikā* views the issue from the Buddhist position that everything is momentary and distinct — nothing endures beyond a moment but only seems so due to erroneous knowledge on the part of human beings. Just as the cognitions which are actually a series of momentary perceptions appear to be the same due to similarity, so also an object appears to be the same although in reality it is only a flux of momentary particulars. For instance, an object (or even several individual animals) may appear to be the same cow, whereby we cognise cowness in all of them and hence surmise that the object is an enduring entity, which is really not the case as far as the Buddhist view goes. The *kārikā* says that the repeated cognition that it is the same is the apprehension of *jāti*, whereas when we understand something as distinct from the other (e.g. cow is distinct from deer), even then, it is the class concept that enables understanding.

सरूपाणां च सर्वेषां न भेदोपनिपातिनः ।
विद्यन्ते वाचकाः शब्दा नापि भेदोऽवधार्यते ॥१००॥

sarūpāṇāṁ ca sarveṣāṁ na bhedopanipātinaḥ |
vidyante vācakāḥ śabdā nāpi bhedo 'vadhāryate | |100| |

ज्ञानशब्दार्थविषया विशेषा ये व्यवस्थिताः ।
तेषां दुरवधारत्वाज्ज्ञानाद्येकत्वदर्शनम् ॥१०१॥

jñānaśabdārthaviṣayā viśeṣā ye vyavasthitāḥ |
teṣāṁ duravadhāratvājjñānādyekatvadarśanam | |101| |

The next *kārikā* says that there is no ground to deny the existence of *jāti*. Considering two individuals of the same class, we have no words to convey the distinctiveness between them (unless we resort to specific attributes — *guṇas*, etc.), nor do we perceive any tangible difference to say that the class attribute is insufficient to explain it. Although everything is unique and distinct in the world, we are unable to perceive these differences, hence it is difficult to describe these distinctiveness with words and so we perceive them to be identical.

Although every particular thing in the varied world is unique, we do not have words to express that uniqueness nor do we cognise anything uniquely; we operate by generalities and depend on general cognitions, defined by class. As Iyer says, "Words express a certain identity which we see on account of resemblance." Helārāja explains that we operate twofold by *prakhyā* and *upākhyā,* which are cognition and nomenclature respectively. Word meaning is obtained by *saṅketa,* or convention. Convention cannot grasp the unique nature, *svalakṣaṇa,* of an object. Thus we operate only through generalities. In the study of Nyāya, beginners are informed that as we can never truly grasp each and every entity uniquely, it is important to grasp the categories. Since subtle differences in individuals or in uttering words cannot be easily grasped easily, we do not perceive those differences.

ज्ञानेष्वपि यथार्थेषु तथा सर्वेषु जातयः ।
संसर्गदर्शने सन्ति ताश्चार्थस्य प्रसाधिकाः ।।१०२।।

jñāneṣvapi yathārtheṣu tathā sarveṣu jātayaḥ |
saṁsargadarśane santi tāścārthasya prasādhikāḥ | |102| |

But it is more direct to accept the existence of universals than to explain cognition of sameness as due to absence of any criteria indicating otherwise. In the philosophical view that accepts *saṁsarga,* or connections/associations between entities, it is held that there are universals in 14 Ākr̥tivāda in *Ślokavārttikā* cognitions also, just as there are universals in objects.

ज्ञेयस्थमेव सामान्यं ज्ञानानामुपकारकम् ।
न जातु ज्ञेयवज्ज्ञानं पररूपेण रूप्यते ।।१०३।।

jñeyasthameva sāmānyaṁ jñānānāmupakārakam |
na jātu jñeyavajjñānaṁ pararūpeṇa rūpyate | |103| |

Iyer writes that the next *kārikā* gives another view on the same subject. It is only one universal that is in the object, that functions in the cognitions also — there is no need for two distinct universals such as *ghaṭatva* and *ghaṭajñānatva*. Never does it happen that the cognition is illumined by something else external to it as in the case of the object *jñeya*, such as *ghaṭa*. This *kārikā* focuses on the supremacy of cognition or *jñāna* as *svayamprakāśa*. Bhartṛhari emphasises that like light, *śabda*, equal to *Brahman* or *jñāna* is *svayamprakāśa* and *prakāśaka*, self-luminous as well as illuminating other objects.

Just as a knowable entity is never cognised without its universal, so also knowledge never occurs in any form other than as a cognition. Knowledge cannot become the object of another cognition. All forms of cognition, including awarness of some knowledge, have external entities as the object.

यथा ज्योतिः प्रकाशेन नान्येनाभिप्रकाश्यते ।
ज्ञानाकारस्तथान्येन न ज्ञानेनोपगृह्यते ।।१०४।।

yathā jyotiḥ prakāśena nānyenābhiprakāśyate |
jñānākārastathānyena na jñānenopagṛhyate | |104| |

He further clearly states in the next *kārikā* that *jāti* is a direct cause for cognition. Just as light is not illuminated by another light, in the same way, the form of the cognition is not cognised by another cognition. The Vaiśeṣikas accept that the universal in the object is sufficient to give rise to its cognition, but do not accept the self-luminous nature of knowledge. This goes back to the different philosophical standpoint on nature of *ātmā*. In Vaiśeṣika, *ātmā* is *āśraya* of *jñāna* whereas in Advaita, *ātmā* is equated to *jñāna*. Bhartṛhari in the Brahmakāṇḍa clearly equates *ātmā*, *Brahman* and *pratibhā* with *śabdatattva*.

Helārāja —

यथा घटादीनां दीपः प्रकाशकः स्वप्रकाशे दीपान्तरं नोपेक्षते तथार्थस्य प्रकाशकं ज्ञानमात्मप्रकाशनाय प्रकाशान्तरानपेक्षमिति स्वप्रकाशकं सिद्धम् ।

जडवैलक्षण्यं हि प्रकाश्कत्वमिति तस्यापि प्रकाश्यत्वे जडतापत्तिः।

yathā ghaṭādīnāṁ dīpaḥ prakāśakaḥ svaprakāśe dīpāntaraṁ nopekṣate tathārthasya prakāśakaṁ jñānamātmaprakāśanāya prakāśāntarānapekṣamiti svaprakāśakaṁ siddham ।
jaḍavailakṣaṇyaṁ hi prakāśkatvamiti tasyāpi prakāśyatve jaḍatāpattiḥ ।

घटज्ञानमिति ज्ञानं घटज्ञानविलक्षणम् ।
घट इत्यपि यज्ज्ञानं विषयोपनिपाति तत् ॥१०५॥

ghaṭajñānamiti jñānaṁ ghaṭajñānavilakṣaṇam ।
ghaṭa ityapi yajjñānaṁ viṣayopanipāti tat ।।105।।

The next two *kārikā*s explain the difference between a specific objective cognition and other ideas or cognitions. The knowledge of a pot is objective. In Nyāya-Vaiśeṣika terminology, we can say that the pot, an external object, forms the content of the cognition (*ghaṭaviṣayakam jñānaṁ*). In the sentence, *ayaṁ ghaṭaḥ* there is *ghaṭaviṣayakaṁ jñānam* the awareness that one is cognising a pot is a different kind of cognition, as its content is not directly an external object but another knowledge. For instance, the sentence *ghaṭajñānavān aham* or *ahaṁ ghaṭaṁ jānāmi* conveys a more complex idea, wherein one cognition is grasped by another.

Iyer writes that knowledge illuminates something else and is self-luminous, but is never the thing illuminated. This argument is not valid, because knowledge is not self-luminous. It has to be illuminated by another knowledge. The above doubt is answered as follows — The knowledge "this is a knowledge of the jar" is different from the knowledge "this is a jar", because the former is not produced directly by an external object. Knowledge itself does not figure as an object.

The cognition *ayam ghaṭaḥ* has the jar as its content; the cognition *ghaṭam aham jānāmi* or *ghaṭajñānam idam* also has the jar as its object. It is the jar that qualifies both cognitions; one cognition cannot feature as the object of another although it may seem possible in the second case.

> यतो विषयरूपेण ज्ञानरूपं न गृह्यते ।
> अर्थरूपविविक्तं च स्वरूपं नावधार्यते ॥१०६॥
>
> *yato viṣayarūpeṇa jñānarūpaṁ na gṛhyate* |
> *artharūpaviviktaṁ ca svarūpaṁ nāvadhāryate* ||106||

Bhartṛhari goes on further to say that since this difference between a cognition and its content is very difficult to discern, the form of knowledge as distinct from that of the object is not grasped.

Iyer:

> A cognition having the form of another cognition figuring in it as its object does not arise. There can be no cognition which does not have an external object figuring in it. So, in the cognition *ghaṭamahaṁjānāmi* it is the jar which figures as the object, not the knowledge of it.

Thus it is established that *jāti* is at the bottom of all transactions and cognitions of visible and invisible things.

The Dravya Samuddeśa

As Patañjali himself has discussed in the Paspaśāhnika, *nityatva* in *śabda* is considered in both cases of *śabdārtha* being *jāti* and *dravya*. Patañjali has already illustrated how not only *jāti*, but even *dravya* can be considered as *nitya*, eternal.

Bhartṛhari also shows how the reference of the word can also be considered to be in the permanent aspect of the meaning, even when it refers to the specific individual. The word *vyakti* literally means manifestation and is usually synonymous with object, or *dravya*. In addition to this connotation in language study, Bhartṛhari takes a highly philosophical, all-encompassing view on how the entire cosmos is actually permanent as the same common thread runs through all its seeming variety. *Dravya* is taken to mean substance; as the primordial substance that is the basis of everything, it is one and eternal.

We can loosely group the verses of the Dravya Samuddeśa into three sections. *Kārikā*s 1 to 6 explain how word-meaning is *dravya* and eternal. The next section, from *kārikā*s 7 to 10 take a philosophical view of reality as we find around us, where the substratum of everything is eternal. *Kārikā*s 11 to 15 take a philosophical view of *śabdatattva*, echoing the Monistic thread in the Upaniṣads that explain the oneness of *Brahman* despite the apparent variety and contradiction that are actually perceived due to nescience or *avidyā*, *kārikā* 16 relates the issue to *śabda* and *śabdatattva*, in my view. The section ends with an illustration in *kārikā*s 17 and 18 where all our experiences in the world are likened to a dream, again echoing Vedānta. The *Vākyapadīya* clearly illustrates that the Advaita philosophy was a very popular and mature school of thought even in the fifth century CE.

WORD-MEANING IS DRAVYA

The Jāti Samuddeśa dealt at length with Vājapyāyana's school that import of the word was in universal. The Dravya Samuddeśa pays attention to the view of Vyāḍi, that import of the word is in the object. *Kārikā* 1 lists the synonyms of *dravya* in a few schools of thought. There are two kinds of substance, real and expressional, or *pāramārthika* and *sāmvyavahārika*. It is the second which is the meaning of all words, whereas, here, in this chapter, it is the first kind of substance that we are concerned with, therefore the deeply philosophical tone of the chapter. The Monists call it the self (*ātmā*) which appears as different depending on the particular *upādhi*, whereby that particular thing is the meaning of the word. According to the Buddhists, the thing-in-itself, *svalakṣaṇa*, is the real substance. The followers of *śabdādvaita* consider that substance is nothing but the one being which is the essence of a thing. For others, such as Sāṁkhya, the primordial substance, *prakṛti* that is the structure of a thing, *śarīra*, is the substance. For Cārvākas, the four elements, air, water, fire and earth, are the *tattva*, substance. In this way, reality is defined differently by different systems of thought.

आत्मा वस्तु स्वभावश्च शरीरं तत्त्वमित्यपि ।
द्रव्यमित्यस्य पर्यायास्तच्च नित्यमिति स्मृतम् ।।१।।

ātmā vastu svabhāvaśca śarīraṁ tattvamityapi |
dravyamityasya paryāyāstacca nityamiti smṛtam | |1| |

Words refer to countless different meanings, which correspond to a great diversity of objects in the world. But despite having impermanent forms, all the different objects are in fact only one unchanging entity that is manifest in different forms. In the same way, due to unreal, impermanent associations, *upādhi*, different words that seem to have different connotations, actually refer to one absolute truth.

सत्यं वस्तु तदाकारैरसत्यैरवधार्यते ।
असत्योपाधिभिः शब्दैः सत्यमेवाभिधीयते ।।२।।

satyaṁ vastu tadākārairasatyairavadhāryate |
asatyopādhibhiḥ śabdaiḥ satyamevābhidhīyate | |2| |

We often use obviously impermanent features such as a crow sitting on a house rafter to identify it as belonging to Devadatta, when pointed out from afar, although we understand that only the house, which is relatively permanent, is indicated. Or, e.g., gold, which is spoken of using words such as earrings, rings and necklaces, retains its identity in the pure form of gold, even when referred to by other words indicating articles with impermanent forms.

अध्रुवेण निमित्तेन देवदत्तगृहं यथा ।
गृहीतं गृहशब्देन शुद्धमेवाभिधीयते ।।३।।

adhruveṇa nimittena devadattagṛhaṁ yathā |
gṛhītaṁ gṛhaśabdena śuddhamevābhidhīyate | |3| |

सुवर्णादि यथा भिन्नं स्वैराकारैरपायिभिः ।
रुचकाद्यभिधानानां शुद्धमेवैति वाच्यताम् ।।४।।

suvarṇādi yathā bhinnaṁ svairākārairapāyibhiḥ |
rucakādyabhidhānānāṁ śuddhamevaiti vācyatām | |4| |

Even though every word points to the underlying substratum common to all entities, confusion does not arise in actual practice. When a particular word is used, it recalls its own form and hence its import is restricted to the corresponding specific meaning. This is like limiting the view that the eye can scan by looking through a tube.

आकारैश्च व्यवच्छेदात् सार्वार्थ्यमवरुध्यते ।
यथैव चक्षुरादीनां सामर्थ्यं नाडिकादिभिः ।।५।।

ākāraiśca vyavacchedāt sārvārthyamavarudhyate |
yathaiva cakṣurādīnāṁ sāmarthyaṁ nāḍikādibhiḥ | |5| |

The next verse reconciles words indicating qualities, etc., also as having reference to *dravya*. As in the case of *jāti* and *vyakti*, so also with quality and substance there is invariable association. Iyer refers to *upādhi* as *dharma* and writes that since *upādhi* and *upādhimat* are always found together, there is no contradiction.

तेष्वाकारेषु यः शब्दस्तथाभूतेषु वर्तते ।
तत्त्वात्मकत्वात्तेनापि नित्यमेवाभिधीयते ॥६॥

teṣvākāreṣu yaḥ śabdastathābhūteṣu vartate |
tattvātmakatvāttenāpi nityamevābhidhīyate ||6||

DRAVYA IS ETERNAL

The 7th *kārikā* onwards, it is pointed out that there is no philosophical contradiction in seeing unity among diversity. Our tradition teaches that there is no difference between real and unreal. It is not as if everything we see in the world is unreal and there is some reality different from it. Both are the same thing. It is our understanding that helps us discern between the two. The real, at the level of *avidyā*, where it is not fully understood, is called unreal.

न तत्त्वातत्त्वयोर्भेद इति वृद्धेभ्य आगमः ।
अतत्त्वमिति मन्यन्ते तत्त्वमेवाविचारितम् ॥७॥

na tattvātattvayorbheda iti vr̥ddhebhya āgamaḥ |
atattvamiti manyante tattvamevāvicāritam ||7||

The next *kārikā* discusses the factor of sequence in time which is so crucial to the philosophy of Bhartġrhari also discussed in the Brahmakāṇḍa and Jāti Samuddeśa. Here he says that the Ultimate Reality, *Brahman*, appears and is understood to be differentiated whereas actually, it is beyond temporal sequence or distinctions brought about by time. This verse connects the concept of Ultimate Reality parallel to the concept of *śabdatattva* which has the same attributes with relation to time.

विकल्परूपं भजते तत्त्वमेवाविकल्पितम् ।
न चात्र कालभेदोऽस्ति कालभेदश्च गृह्यते ॥८॥

vikalparūpaṁ bhajate tattvamevāvikalpitam |

na cātra kālabhedo 'sti kālabhedaśca gṛhyate | |8| |

Even earlier, Bhartṛhari has explained how the word is taken as one with the meaning, *padārtha*, as the difference is not easily discernible, *duravadhāra*. The same principle is recalled here in explaining how words try to grasp the ultimate reality by grasping portions of it or even apparent, unreal portions. This concept is totally compatible with Bhartṛhari's own view. But Helārāja and Iyer recall the parallel in the Vijñānavādi Buddhist view that consciousness appears to have various external forms which appear as external.

यथा विषयधर्माणां ज्ञानेऽत्यन्तमसंभवः ।
तदात्मेव च तत् सिद्धमत्यन्तमतदात्मकम् ॥९॥

yathā viṣayadharmāṇāṁ jñane 'tyantamasaṁbhavaḥ |
tadātmeva ca tat siddhamatyantamatadātmakam | |9| |

यथा विकाररूपाणां तत्त्वेऽत्यन्तमसम्भवः ।
तदात्मेव च तत्तत्त्वमत्यन्तमतदात्मकम् ॥१०॥

yathā vikārarūpāṇāṁ tattve 'tyantamasambhavaḥ |
tadātmeva ca tattattvamatyantamatadātmakam | |10| |

DRAVYA IS ŚABDATATTVA

The next line clearly equates the Single Underlying Principle of the whole cosmos with the Ultimate Word Principle. When all forms dissolve, what endures is the substratum which is the eternal aspect. It is denoted by the word and is not different from the essence of the word. Just as in the world, all entities dissolve into one *Brahman*, in the same way, all the individual words with myriad form and meaning all merge with the word principle when the differences are ignored.

सत्यमाकृतिसंहारे यदन्ते व्यवतिष्ठते ।
तन्नित्यं शब्दवाच्यं तच्छब्दतत्त्वं न भिद्यते ॥११॥

satyamākṛtisaṁhāre yadante vyavatiṣṭhate |

tannityaṁ śabdavācyaṁ tacchabdatattvaṁ na bhidyate | | 11 | |

Kārikās 12 and 13 echo the Upaniṣad to show the unity in the seeming diversity. *Brahman* is all-encompassing. It is everything. Even contradictory attributes describe the one *Brahman*. This is to show that at different times, in different people's minds *Brahman* can seem different as mentioned. Vedānta also explains this seemingly contradictory explanation as any single epithet being inadequate to describe *Brahman*. All the words that we can use would describe *Brahman* and yet not be sufficient to convey the full meaning. In Bhartṛhari's philosophy, the same attributes describe *śabdatattva*.

न तदस्ति न तन्नास्ति न तदेकं न तत् पृथक् ।
न संसृष्टं विभक्तं वा विकृतं न च नान्यथा ॥१२॥

na tadasti na tannāsti na tadekaṁ na tat pṛthak |
na saṁsṛṣṭaṁ vibhaktaṁ vā vikṛtaṁ na ca nānyathā | | 12 | |

तन्नास्ति विद्यते तच्च तदेकं तत् पृथक् पृथक् ।
संसृष्टं च विभक्तं च विकृतं तत्तदन्यथा ॥१३॥

tannāsti vidyate tacca tadekaṁ tat pṛthak pṛthak |
saṁsṛṣṭaṁ ca vibhaktaṁ ca vikṛtaṁ tattadanyathā | | 13 | |

In the pure undifferentiated state, there is only one *Brahman*. All divisions merge in it. Even the trinity of word, meaning and relation between them, which forms the subject of linguistics, merge into one, formless state. For any transaction, we require some dichotomy. But this is only in the transactional level, *vyāvahārika*, which is provisional. When we understand the unity in the cosmos, the seen, the act of seeing, the seer and the fruit of the seeing, all merge to one level. This line echoes the idea in *VP* I.4 where Bhartġrhari refers to the potency of *Brahman* in all capacities as the *śakti* being that of enjoyer, enjoyed and the very activity of enjoyment, *bhoktṛ bhoktavya bhogarūpeṇa ca saṁsthitaḥ*.

तस्य शब्दार्थसम्बन्धरूपमेकस्य दृश्यते ।
तद् दृश्यं दर्शनं दृष्टा दर्शनं च प्रयोजनम् ॥१४॥

tasya śabdārthasambandharūpamekasya dṛśyate |
tad dṛśyaṁ darśanaṁ dṛṣṭā darśanaṁ ca prayojanam | |14| |

To the doubt as to whether anything remains at all when all divisions disappear, Bhartṛhari asserts that there is a substratum that endures. It would not be right to say that this world springs from nothing. Just as when the shapes are destroyed, or even when the different forms do not matter, all ornaments remain as gold, which is the substance undergoing transformation.

विकारापगमे सत्यं सुवर्णं कुण्डले यथा ।
विकारापगमे सत्यां तथाहुः प्रकृतिं पराम् ॥१५॥

vikārapagame satyaṁ suvarṇaṁ kuṇḍale yathā |
vikārāpagame satyāṁ tathāhuḥ prakṛtiṁ parām | |15| |

That primordial substance is what all words actually convey. The words themselves are fashioned out of it. When they are not different in reality, we still speak of the relation connecting them as they seem to have much variety. This *kārikā* clearly connects the stand on *dravya* with the monistic philosophy of Bhartṛhari, equating it to *Brahman*.

As Houben puts it, "And it is not called Existence (*sattā*) but referred to by another derivative from the root 'as', 'to be', viz., *satya*, 'true' or 'real.'"[14]

There is no contradiction in this *samuddeśa* with the previous. True harmony and unity in thought is able to resolve any seeming disparity in this profound philosophy. When the philosopher is so clear in his monistic view, should calling the Reality as *jāti* or *dravya* lead to any dispute? Bhartṛhari lucidly resolves these dilemmas for the reader.

14. Houben, Section, 3.2.

वाच्या सा सर्वशब्दानां शब्दाश्च न पृथक् ततः ।
अपृथकत्वे च सम्बन्धस्तयोर्नानात्मनोरिव ।।१६।।

vācyā sā sarvaśabdānāṁ śabdāśca na pṛthak tataḥ |
apṛthakatve ca sambandhastayornānātmanoriva | |16| |

The *samuddeśa* ends with an illustration in *kārikās* 17 and 18 showing that equating dichotomy to a unity is not inconsistent with other experiences in life such as dream state, wherein there is nothing outside one's own mind which projects as self, others, animate and inanimate objects. Yet, the total experience in a dream has a variety of situations, feelings and viewpoints, some animate and some inanimate. In the same way we imagine or understand creation, destruction, movement, gradation, etc., in that which is actually eternal and immutable, all-pervasive, never freshly born and devoid of temporal sequence.

आत्मा परः प्रियो द्वेष्यो वक्ता वाच्यं प्रयोजनम् ।
विरुद्धानि यथैकस्य स्वप्ने रूपाणि चेतसः ।।१७।।

ātmā paraḥ priyo dveṣyo vaktā vācyaṁ prayojanam |
viruddhāni yathaikasya svapne rūpāṇi cetasaḥ | |17| |

अजन्मनि तथा नित्ये पौर्वापर्यविवर्जिते ।
तत्त्वे जन्मादिरूपत्वं विरुद्धमुपलभ्यते ।।१८।।

ajanmani tathā nitye paurvāparyavivarjite |
tattve janmādirūpatvaṁ viruddhamupalabhyate | |18| |

The Bhūyo Dravya Samuddeśa

संसर्गरूपात् सम्भूताः संविद्रूपादपोद्धृताः ।
शास्त्रे विभक्ता वाक्यार्थात् प्रकृतिप्रत्ययादिवत् ।।१।।

saṁsargarūpāt sambhūtāḥ saṁvidrūpādapoddhṛtāḥ |
śāstre vibhaktā vākyārthāt prakṛtipratyayādivat | |1| |

निमित्तभूताः साधुत्वे शास्त्रादनुमितात्मकाः ।

केचित् पदार्थां वक्ष्यन्ते संक्षेपेण यथागमम् ॥२॥

nimittabhūtāḥ sādhutve śāstrādanumitātmakāḥ |
kecit padārthā vakṣyante saṁkṣepeṇa yathāgamam | |2| |

वस्तूपलक्षणं यत्र सर्वनाम प्रयुज्यते ।
द्रव्यमित्युच्यते सोऽर्थो भेद्यत्वेन विवक्षितः ॥३॥

vastūpalakṣaṇaṁ yatra sarvanāma prayujyate |
dravyamityucyate so 'rtho bhedyatvena vivakṣitaḥ | |3| |

In the Bhūyo Dravya Samuddeśa or further chapter on substance, the indivisibility of the sentence is once again stressed. In this short section consisting of only three verses after the Sambandha Samuddeśa, the gamut of *dravya* as sole referent of all words is extended to pronouns (*sarvanāma*) Every pronoun refers to some substance; sometimes it may be action or quality, as in the case of cooking (*pacanam*) or redness (*raktatvam*) that is referred to by *tat*, "this". But there is always a substratum, *ādhāra* which is some *dravya*. Every entity is connected to several others inevitably in the cosmos and so every word can be taken to indicate the *dravya* directly or indirectly as explained in the previous section. The word is eternal, the meaning which is *dravya* is eternal and their relation is also eternal. *Śabda, artha, sambandha* are all *nitya* as explained earlier. But a pronoun may connote a different entity each time it is used. It is uttered by different people in different situations to indicate different things. Therefore, how can we say that the word and meaning are *nitya*? To remove this doubt, Bhartṛhari says that the purpose of using a pronoun is to indicate a specific thing, as differentiated from everything else, while still referring to some *dravya*. This is from the philosophical standpoint of the *Vākyapadīya*.

Helārāja studies the Bhūyo Dravya Samuddeśa from the point of view of language alone. The first two verses repeat the standpoint of the *Vākyapadīya* on the indivisibility of the sentence-meaning, the words being interconnected (*saṁsargabhūtāḥ* and abstracted out *samvidrūpād apoddhṛtāḥ*) only in our understanding, as a step towards grasping the full sentence. In reality, there are no isolated words in language. They are only taken out artificially as a provisional means to reach the sentence-meaning, as the words are uttered in sequence and not all at once.

The sentence-meaning is grasped in a flash, at once, just as the taste of *pānaka* is one distinct flavour, although it is brought about by several ingredients mixed in a certain proportion. But the trained tongue can perhaps discern the individual ingredients that are contributing to the resulting taste. The total flavour is the result of all the individual flavours put together and yet not just the sum, having its own identity as the flavour of *pānaka*. Similarly the sentence is one single idea composed of several words.

Language has words of broadly two varieties — words in popular usage, in *loka* and those in specialised branches of learning, or technical jargon.

Prakāśa:

लोकप्रसिद्धा वैशेषिकादिशास्त्रपरिभाषिताश्च ।

lokaprasiddhā vaiśeṣikādiśāstraparibhāṣitāśca ।

The third *kārikā* is explained thoroughly by Helārāja and following him, Iyer, in the context of grammar. Some pronouns denote general things, such as *sarva* while others denote particular things, e.g., *anyatara*, etc. The first kind is what denotes substance. *Dravya* can be said to be that which can be indicated by a pronoun in the conventional sense.

Prakāśa:

इह सर्वनाम्नां द्वयी गतिः । वस्तुमात्राभिधायिनः केचिद् यथा सर्वादयः ।

विशिष्टवस्तुवाचकाश्चन्ये यथान्यतरादयः । तत्र पूर्वैर्द्रव्यं लक्ष्यन्ते । तथा हि इदं तदिति सर्वनामप्रत्यवमर्शयोग्यं द्रव्यम् ।

iha sarvanāmnāṁ dvayī gatiḥ । vastumātrābhidhāyinaḥ kecid yathā sarvādayaḥ । viśiṣṭavastuvācakāścānye yathānyatarādayaḥ । tatra pūrvairdravyaṁ lakṣyante । tathā hi idaṁ taditi sarvanāmapratyavamarśayogyaṁ dravyam ।

Raghunatha Sarma explains that when we use words such as "this" for something nearby and "that" for something afar, the words may be generalities, but they stand for some specific *dravya*.

Ambākartrī:

इदमस्तु सन्निकृष्टमिति तदिति परोक्षे विजानीयात् इति च अमरकोशात् । तथा चप्रत्यक्षपरोक्षाकारभेदः सर्वनागार्थे वस्तुसामान्ये उपलक्षणं न तु विशेषणम् ।
idamastu sannikṛṣṭamiti taditi parokṣe vijānīyāt iti ca amarakośāt । tathā capratyakṣaparokṣākārabhedaḥ sarvanāmārthe vastusāmānye upalakṣaṇaṁ na tu viśeṣaṇam ।

Since there are innumerable *dravya*s and their characteristics endless, all are defined together in general, being impossible to enumerate. Helārāja quotes *Nirukta* as

अद इति यत् प्रतीयते तद् द्रव्यम् ।
ada iti yat pratīyate tad dravyam ।

Yāska's sweeping definition is as follows:

अद इति सत्त्वानामुपदेशः ।
ada iti sattvānāmupadeśaḥ । — *Ni.* 1.1.13.

Durgācārya explains that action is also nothing but existent entity, *sattva* as whatever is connected to the action (the agent or the substratum of the action) is what is referred to, and what is that? That which can be defined by general or specific terms.

Durgācārya's Commentary under *Ni.* 1.1.13:

भावोऽधिकृतः । स च पुनः सत्त्वभूतो नेतरः । यतस्तत्सम्बन्धेनैव नाम्नो

यदवशिष्यत् तदुच्यते । किं पुनष्तत् । सामान्यविशेषवाचित्वम् । तत्र अद इति सत्त्वानामुपदेशः । सामान्यतः इति वाक्यशेषः ।

bhāvo 'dhikṛtaḥ । *sa ca punaḥ sattvabhūto netaraḥ* । *yatastatsambandhenaiva nāmno yadavaśiṣyat taducyate* । *kiṁ punaṣtat* । *sāmānyaviśeṣavācitvam* । *tatra ada iti sattvānāmupadeśaḥ* । *sāmānyataḥ iti vākyaśeṣaḥ* ।

The second point in the definition of *dravya* as expressed by the pronoun is that it can be differentiated. Helārāja explains that class or universal serves as *upādhi* to differentiate one *dravya* from another, or to delimit what is indicated, from everything else. But this distinction need not really be present in the eternal object — it is sufficient to understand the distinction in the mind, *bauddha*.

Prakāśa:

द्वितीयमपि विशेषलक्षणमाह - भेद्यत्वेन विवक्षित इति । सामान्यादिभिः उपाधिभिरवच्छेद्यत्वेन विशेष्यत्वेन वक्तुमभिप्रेतमिति अर्थः । विवक्षितग्रहणेन न वस्त्वर्थस्येदं लक्षणमपि तु शब्दार्थस्येत्याह ।

dvitīyamapi viśeṣalakṣaṇamāha - bhedyatvena vivakṣita iti ।
sāmānyādibhiḥ upādhibhiravacchedyatvena viśeṣyatvena vaktumabhipretamiti arthaḥ ।
vivakṣitagrahaṇena na vastvarthasyedaṁ lakṣaṇamapi tu śabdārthasyetyāha ।

Pronouns refer to things as present or past — when the tense factor is not part of the indication, then the substance alone remains, that is *dravya*. The pronoun can even indicate a universal, if that is the thing to be qualified. Universals include action (*kriyā*) such as *vrajyā*, *paktiḥ*, etc. The same idea is referred to in *kārikā* 34 of the Jāti Samuddeśa where it is said that existence can be referred by *tva* and *tal pratyaya*s.

6

Sāmānya in the Realists Philosophy

THIS chapter addresses the main issues in Nyāya, Mīmāṁsā, the Buddhist objections and the response to it. Raja Ram Dravid discusses the subject thoroughly in his book, *The Problem of Universal in Indian Philosophy.*

The Nyāya Concept of Sāmānya

The Nyāya philosophy is pluralistic and realistic. The world in all its variety exists independent of the cognising mind — there are no different levels of reality, such as provisional reality due to *avidyā*, but only absolute reality. All experience, cognition is founded on something in the external world. Cognition is proof that something exists; the world can be directly cognised, internalised by the process of *pramāṇa*. Our experience tells us that there is plurality among the reals; nothing tells us otherwise. Cognition is of two kinds — we sometimes perceive variety or differences and at other times some unity or sense of sameness. If everything were totally distinct, with nothing in common, the world would go beyond the comprehension of the human intellect. Thus we must be able to understand common features or class concept, in order to make sense of the world. Thus the Nyāya ontology neatly divides all reals into seven *padārtha*s, which are well known.

द्रव्यगुणकर्मसामान्यविशेषसमवायाभावाः सप्त पदार्थाः

dravyaguṇakarmasāmānyaviśeṣasamavāyābhāvāḥ sapta padārthāḥ ।

— *Tarkasaṁgraha*

Thus *sāmānya* is a fundamental entity which is real and distinct existent, distinguishable from the particular in which it inheres. It is impossible for anybody to cognise every entity individually in the world — the solution is to understand by categorisation.[1] Thus the universals unite the innumerable particulars into various classes. Denying the existence of the class would be, according to Nyāya, a denial of the very possibility of all knowledge.[2]

Early definitions of *sāmānya* or *jāti* explain it as the unity which is the cause of identical conception of particular things and had the two divisions of *para-apara*, higher or extensive and lower or non-extensive, which are relative terms. In later times *sāmānya* came to be used synonymously with *jāti* and was given an independent and eternal existence apart from the individual objects.[3]

Gautama gives *jāti* as *samānaprasavātmikā jātiḥ* in *NS* II.ii.70. Praśastapāda defines it as the unity which is the cause of identical cognition of particular things, and which subsists identically and wholly in each of its subjects.

While the universal always assists in identifying an individual, it is not always the cause of perception of similarity. For example, concept such as "cow", "man", "pot", etc. are based on real universals but is not the case

1. सम्विदेव हि भगवती वस्तूपगमे नः शरणम् — *Upaskāra* on *VS* III.ii.26.
2. Dravid, 2001, p. 14.
3. Athalye-Bodas, p. 91.

with "cook", "teacher", "blind man", etc. Thus a more precise definition had to be found. Later Nyāya texts, such as *Muktāvalī* and *Tarkasaṁgraha* define *sāmānya* as one which is eternal and inherent in several individuals. *Ekaṁ nityaṁ anekasamavetam, paramaparaṁ dvividhaṁ sāmānyam.*

The Neo-Naiyāyikas redefine the universal in order to make its conception precise. They define it as that which is eternal and inherent in many individuals. *Nityatve sati anekasamavetam.* Thus the universal is said to have three essential characteristics: (1) eternality, (2) commonness and (3) inherence.

The intimate, eternal relation that connects the universal and particular is *samavāya*. When two things are connected by *samavāya*, it means they are *ayutasiddha* or one never found without the other. The Nyāya philosophy aims at describing the world on scientific terms based on experience. The purpose of categorisation is to enable a comprehensive analysis, without overlap or omission of any entity. Thus, the *samavāya* relation forms an ontologically distinct, real entity enumerated as a *padārtha*. The universal and particular, though invariably connected are considered existentially distinct, as they are cognised as distinct. For example, the universal *gotva* must be distinct from the individual *go* as it is understood as a different concept and designated by a different word.

The individual and particular are opposed in their characteristics. The particulars are many in number, limited in size, non-eternal and subject to changes; the universal is one, omnipresent, eternal and immutable. How can two things so radically different having no common bond, be intimately connected? This is not a problem at all, as even whole and parts are radically different but still related by *samavāya*. The universal is unaffected by the production, change or destruction of the particulars.

The cognition of the universal depends upon the cognition of the particular. Although present everywhere at all times, the universal can be perceived only when there is a particular manifesting it. That is why the word *vyakti* is used. The universal does not have independent perceptibility and can be cognised only in sensible objects. The existence of a thing can be established by *pratyakṣa* or *anumāna* in Nyāya. Thus the *jāti* of such entities as *manas, buddhi, paramāṇu, ātmā* are shown by *anumāna*, as they cannot be directly perceived.

The Nyāya theory of causality which endorses Asatkāryavāda or Ārambhavāda, also supports the existence of universal. Universals are eternal whereas particulars are created and destroyed. But everything coming into existence must have a corresponding unique cause. For a *kārya* to come into being, it must have suitable *kāraṇa*. If the *kārya-kāraṇa* pair is not clearly defined, anything can give rise to anything and this would lead to hopeless confusion. If weaving threads synthesises cloth, it is because threads are suitable raw material to create cloth. Thus, not only thread and cloth are related, but also the universals inhering in thread and cloth. Similarly, the fact that clay is suitable cause for making a jar shows that the potential for jarness is found in clayness. This is opposed to the Sāṁkhya stand that the effect pre-exists in the cause, Satkāryavāda. The substance of Udayana's contention is that specific class natures of things must be admitted to account for the determinate causal relations between them.[4] The Nyāya philosophy holds the highest universal to be Existence, *sattā*, which comprises all entities.

The universal aids cognition in two ways — in

4. Dravid, p. 22.

understanding identity and difference. When we perceive another individual of the same class as the "same", it is due to identity. When we perceive an individual as different, e.g. a horse as distinct from a cow, it is due to difference. When two particulars of the same class are perceived as separate at the *paramāṇu* level, it is due to *vyāvṛtti*, distinctness, which is a feature of *viśeṣa* or particulars.

While the utility of the universal as a means to aid cognition can be clearly illustrated, the problem is in distinguishing it from any feature formulated for this purpose. This leads to the concept of *upādhi*. Not all general characteristics are recognised as universal. The *jāti* is the natural and eternal class essence such as *gotva, raktatva, gamana kriyā*, etc. It is found only in the first three *padārthas*, viz. *dravya, guṇa, karma*. These are considered *akhaṇḍopādhi* or non-analysable features. There are other features, *sakhaṇḍopādhi* which are analysable, such as "loudness", "cook", "tallness", etc., which are qualifying features but not *jātis*. There are six criteria called *jātibādhakas*, which help in logically distinguishing *jāti* from *upādhi*. These are (1) *vyakterabheda*, (2) *tulyatva*, (3) *sāṅkarya*, (4) *anavasthā*, (5) *rūpahāni*, (6) *asaṁbandha*.

The Mīmāṁsā Concept of Jāti

The Mīmāṁsā school also supports the real ontological position accorded to *jāti*, considered synonymous with *ākṛti, sāmānya*.

THE BHĀṬṬA SCHOOL

Kumārila Bhaṭṭa expounds on the universal in the Ākṛtivāda chapter in the *Ślokavārttika* and establishes it without any room for doubt. *Jāti, ākṛti* is that common feature which enables the identical cognition of different individuals as the same. Although *ākṛti* also means configuration, it is not used in that sense because in that case, it would be specific to each particular and not a general characteristic at all. Further, certain classes of things such as air, fire, earth, etc., have no configuration to speak of.[5]

The *jāti* helps in all cognitions — whether in identifying a thing as the same, or as different. The universal and particular are indispensably and mutually linked; the comprehension of one independent of the other makes no sense and is not even possible.

विशेषमात्र इष्टे च न सामान्यमतिर्भवेत् ।
सामान्यमात्रबोधे तु निर्निमित्ता विशेषधीः ॥६॥
अन्योन्यापेक्षिता नित्यं स्यात् सामान्यविशेषयोः ।
विशेषाणां च सामान्यं ते च तस्य भवन्ति हि ॥९॥
निर्विशेषं न सामान्यं भवेच्छशविषाणवत् ।
सामान्यरहितत्वाच्च विशेषास्तद्वदेव हि ॥१०॥

viśeṣamātra iṣṭe ca na sāmānyamatirbhavet ।
sāmānyamātrabodhe tu nirnimittā viśeṣadhī ॥6॥
anyonyāpekṣitā nityaṁ syāt sāmānyaviśeṣayoḥ ।
viśeṣāṇāṁ ca sāmānyaṁ te ca tasya bhavanti hi ॥9॥
nirviśeṣaṁ na sāmānyaṁ bhavechaśaviṣāṇavat ।
sāmānyarahitatvācca viśeṣāstadvadeva hi ॥10॥

It is only when a particular is cognised associated with its class, that its capacity for any purpose is understood. Nothing is cognised purely on a unique basis.

भवेन्निर्विषया बुद्धिर्यदि शक्तिर्न गृह्यते ।
न हि सद्भावमात्रेण विषयः काश्चिदिष्यते ॥१४॥

bhavennirviṣayā buddhiryadi śaktirna gṛhyate ।
na hi sabhāvamātreṇa viṣayaḥ Kaścidiṣyate ॥14॥

As word and meaning are related by an external relation,

5. *Ākṛtivāda*, 3.

they have to be individually eternal. The import of a word is in *jāti*, which is also eternal. Thus the *śakti* is qualified; the particular and the universal are understood together. The *jāti* is distinct from the particular, present everywhere and wholly in each individual.

भिन्ना विशेषशक्तिभ्यः सर्वत्रानुगतापि च ।
प्रत्येकं समवेता च तस्माज्जातिरपीष्यताम् ॥१७॥

bhinnā viśeṣaśaktibhyaḥ sarvatrānugatāpi ca ।
pratyekaṁ samavetā ca tasmājjātirapīṣyatām ॥27॥

We can call it by any name, but without *jāti*, we cannot have any qualified cognition.

तेनात्मधर्मो भेदानामात्मधीविषयोऽस्ति नः ।
सामान्यं आकृतिर्जातिः शक्तिर्वा सोऽभिधीयताग् ॥१८॥
ननु भिन्नेऽपि सत्तादौ सामान्यमिति जायते ।
बुद्धिर्विनापि सामान्यादन्यस्मात् सा कथं भवेत् ॥१९॥

tenātmadharmo bhedānāmātmadhīviṣayo 'sti naḥ ।
sāmānyaṁ ākr̥tirjātiḥ śaktirvā so 'bhidhīyatam ॥18॥
nanu bhinne 'pi sattādau sāmānyamiti jāyate ।
buddhirvināpi sāmānyādanyasmāt sā kathaṁ bhaveta ॥19॥

Without *sāmānya* we would not be able to understand the world using inference or verbal knowledge, as *anumāna* and *śabdapramāṇa* rely on *sāmānya*. Since these facts are obvious in our daily experience, there is no need to logically postulate and prove what is self-evident.

अनिष्यमाणे सामान्ये वृत्तिः शब्दानुमानयोः ।
नैव स्यात् न हि सम्बन्धो भेदैरानन्त्यतो भवेत् ॥३९॥

aniṣyamāṇe sāmānye vr̥ttiḥ śabdānumānayoḥ ।
naiva syāt na hi sambandho bhedairānantyato bhaveta ॥39॥

Similarity is not enough to explain the cognition of particulars as the same; we do not say that two cows are similar, but that they are the same. What is achieved by a different terminology, *sārūpya* instead of *sāmānya*?

सामान्याषानपोद्धृत्य पदं सर्वं प्रवर्तते ।
समस्तवस्त्वपेक्षां च पदार्तानाम् अपोद्धृतिम् ।।६४।।

sāmānyāṣānapoddhṛtya padaṁ sarvaṁ pravartate |
samastavastvapekṣāṁ ca padārtānām apoddhṛtim ||64||

It is frequently asked whether the universal resides partially or wholly in each individual and whether the *jāti* is present in all particulars at once, *vyāsajya vṛtti* as whole in parts, or whether it is completely contained in a single particular — *pratyekam paryāptam*. Kumārila says that this question is unnecessary, as it is clear that the universal exists wholly in each particular. When we cognise individuals in their class nature, they are apprehended as identical and when we cognise the universal in its individual instances, they are apprehended as different.

The point where the Bhāṭṭas depart from Nyāya is the relation of *jāti* with *vyakti*. Kumārila does not accept the *samavāya* relation, but says that *jāti* and *vyakti* are related by *tādātmya* or *bhedābheda* relation, which is identity-in-difference. Pārthasārathi Miśra criticises the Nyāya view and says that our cognition of an individual is in the form of "This is cow", not "This has cowness in it" we cognise *gauḥ*, not the *āśraya* of *gotva*. Also, our cognition of the individual as cow, does not eliminate awareness of individual differences.

It is much better to take the stand that the universal is both identical with and different from the individual. When we say that this is a cow, the differences and unity between "this" and "cow" is expressed. An objection to this view can be that the same thing cannot be eternal and non-eternal, common and uncommon. The answer is that this is not the case where the same thing is represented differently.

> The universal as identical with the individual is non-eternal, and the individual as identical with the universal is eternal. There will be a contradiction if eternality and non-eternality were asserted in the same character. The universal as universal is eternal, and the particular as particular is non-eternal. So there is no contradiction.[6]

Since *guṇa-guṇī* are also related by *tādātmya* relation, Bhāṭṭa school does not require *samavāya* relation. *Bhedābheda* can be illustrated with the example of a green mango. There is no difference *abheda*, between the fruit and its colour; but when it ripens to a golden yellow, we see that the same *guṇī* has a different *guṇa*. Then the difference, *bheda*, becomes apparent.

THE PRĀBHĀKARA VIEW OF UNIVERSALS

The Prābhākara theory of Universals is very close to that of Nyāya. Universals are existent reals, eternal, immutable and different from the individual. *Jāti-upādhi* distinction is also accepted. The *jāti* is recognised due to the repetition of the same form in our experience. Śālikanātha writes[7] in the *Prakaraṇapañcikā* (93-94):

> (i) यच्च पिण्डेभ्य: जाते: अभिन्नत्वम् उभयरूपत्वञ्च दूषितं तदस्माकं सहायकमेव आचरितम् । कोहि नाम सचेतन: पदार्थान्तरप्रत्यभिज्ञाम् अभेदाश्रयेण साधयेत् । को वा परस्परविरोधिनी द्वे रूपे एकस्य प्रतिजानीते । भेदवाद: पुन: अस्माकमपि सम्मत एव।

> (ii) न च तत्र इह प्रत्ययापत्ति: दोष: । प्रतीत्य हि आधारं आधेयं च संबन्धं प्रतीयात्। सर्वं च रूपं रूपिग्रह्णमन्तरेण न प्रतीयते । अत: समानेन्द्रियग्राह्यतया जातिरपि व्यक्तिप्रत्ययानुप्रवेशिनीति न इह प्रत्ययसंभव: ।

> (i) *yacca piṇḍebhyaḥ jāteḥ abhinnatvam ubhayarūpatvañca dūṣitaṁ tadasmākaṁ sahāyakameva ācaritam* | *kohi nāma*

6. Dravid, p. 53.

7. *Prakaraṇapañcikā: Jātinirṇaya.*

sacetanaḥ padārthāntarapratyabhiñām abhedāśrayeṇa sādhayet | *ko vā parasparavirodhinī dve rūpe ekasya pratijānīte* | *bhedavādaḥ punaḥ asmākamapi sammata eva* |

(ii) *na ca tatra iha pratyayāpattiḥ doṣaḥ* | *pratītya hi ādhāraṁ ādheyaṁ ca saṁbandhaṁ pratīyāt* | *sarvaṁ ca rūpaṁ rūpigrahaṇmantareṇa na pratīyate* | *ataḥ samānendriyagrāhyatayā jātirapi vyaktipratyayānupraveśinīti na iha pratyayasambhavaḥ* |

The difference lies in the Prābhākara school holding the *samavāya* relation between *jāti* and *vyakti* as non-eternal. The Nyāya holds *samavāya* as eternal, as anything non-eternal is *kārya*, which means that it must have three kinds of causes, inherent, non-inherent and efficient. But how can we ascribe any inherent *kāraṇa* to inherence itself? Thus *samavāya* in *nyāya* is accorded a separate ontological status and is considered eternal.

The Prābhākara Mīmāṁsakas, however, consider *samavāya* to be of two kinds, eternal and non-eternal. The *samavāya* between eternal things, such as *ākāśa* and its magnitude, *mahattva* is eternal whereas that between a universal and a particular is non-eternal. According to the Prābhākara, the destruction of the *samavāya* following the destruction of the individual is the cause of the non-perception of the individual, while according to the Nyāya, the destruction of the individual alone is the cause of the said non-perception.[8] When a *ghaṭa* is destroyed, although *ghaṭatva* is eternal, how can their relation be said to continue to exist? A relation having a non-eternal relatum cannot be called eternal. If the relation were actually existing, the *ghaṭa* should still be perceived even after it has broken into shards.

From the *Nyāyasiddhi* (92):

8. Dravid, p. 55.

(i) समवायं च न वयं काश्यपीया इव नित्यमङ्गीकुर्मः ।

(पप) समवायं च वैशेषिकादय इव न वयं नित्यमुपयेमः । समवायः आकाशमहत्त्वयोः नित्यः अनित्ययोः अवयवावयविनोः अनित्यः । अनित्ययोः अन्यतरोत्पत्तिकारणादुत्पद्यते। तस्मात् प्रतिसम्बन्धि समवायो भिन्नः । सम्बन्ध रूपत्वात् संयोगवत् ।

(i) *samavāyaṁ ca na vayaṁ kāśyapīyā iva nityamaṅgīkurmaḥ* ।
(ii) *samavāyaṁ ca vaiśeṣikādaya iva na vayaṁ nityamupayemaḥ* । *samavāyaḥ ākāśamahattvayoḥ nityaḥ anityayoḥ avayavāvayavinoḥ anityaḥ* । *anityayoḥ anyatarotpattikāraṇādutpadyate* । *tasmāt pratisambandhi samavāyo bhinnaḥ* । *sambandha rūpatvāt saṁyogavat* ।

Śālikanātha writes that when the particular is destroyed, the universal does not migrate elsewhere, wait anywhere nor is it destroyed, as it exists in some other *ādhāra* or locus. The *samavāya* between the universal and particular has withdrawn; hence the imperceptibility. Since the universal can inhere only in the particular, it does not hover anywhere; but it cannot be said to cease to exist as it can be recognised in other particulars. Only if it cannot be found anywhere can we say that it is destroyed.

विनष्टायामपि व्यक्तौ न जातिः अन्यत्र याति, न च तत्र अवतिष्ठते न विनश्यति । केवलम् तद्व्यक्तिसमवायः तस्याः निवर्तते । तेन तस्यानुपलम्भनम् । तथापि न याति निष्क्रियत्वात् नावातिष्ठते व्यक्तिमात्राश्रयत्वात् तदभावे अवस्थानासम्भवात् न च विनश्यति पिण्डान्तरे प्रत्यभिज्ञायमानत्वात् । विनाशो नाम आत्यन्तिकोऽनुपलम्भः इत्यमृतकलायां वक्ष्यते । अतो न सङ्कटं किञ्चित् ।

vinaṣṭāyāmapi vyaktau na jātiḥ anyatra yāti, na ca tatra avatiṣṭhate na vinaśyati । *kevalam tadvyaktisamvāyaḥ tasyāḥ nivartate* । *tena tasyānupalambhanam* । *tathāpi na yāti niṣkriyatvāt nāvātiṣṭhate vyaktimātrāśrayatvāt tadabhāve avasthānāsambhavāt na ca vinaśyati piṇḍāntare pratyabhijñāyamānatvāt* । *vināśo nāma ātyantiko 'nupalambhaḥ ityamṛtakalāyāṁ vakṣyate* | *ato na saṅkaṭaṁ kiñcit* | —*Pr.Pa.* 93

Prabhākara's school does not admit *sattā jāti* as the highest universal as do the Naiyāyikas. Just as other *padārtha*s such as *sāmānya, viśeṣa* and *samavāya* are accorded status of existent by *svarūpasatva* property which is not a *jāti*, the *dravya guṇa karma* group can also be given existent status by *svarūpasatva*. It is interesting that Śālikanātha distinguishes *brāhmaṇatva* as an *upādhi* brought about by a certain parentage rather than a *jāti*.

The Criticism of the Buddhists

The Buddhists severely criticise the Realists stand on the universal. Jayanta, Kumārila, Śālikanātha, Pārthasārathi Miśra, Udayana, Vācaspati and other important writers devote large sections of their works to discuss and refute the Buddhist position on *jāti*. The Buddhists hold the universal as a mental construct, a fiction. Diṅnāga first established the concept of *apoha*, negation and criticised *jāti* in *Pramāṇavārttikam*. Even the import of a word is *anyāpoha*, negation of everything other than what is mentioned. Kumārila Bhaṭṭa challenged this concept so thoroughly in the *Ślokavārttika* that later Buddhist writers, notably Śāntarakṣita in *Tattvasaṁgraha* were compelled to modify their theory to answer Kumārila's charges. Śāntarakṣita's revisions are addressed in the writings of Jayanta Bhaṭṭa and Vācaspati Miśra, whose arguments were so strong and sound, that Ratnakīrti later defended his views to establish the theory in *Apohasiddhi*.

In this view, the import of a word is a subjective idea, hypostatised as an objective reality. When we hold negation as the import of a word, negation is not directly denoted but understood by implication. A word arouses a conceptual image of the reality. The image has a distinctive identity of its own which is felt and distinctiveness of an identity means negation of what it is not.[9]

In the Buddhist view everything in the world is a momentary particular, *svalakṣaṇa,* identical to itself and lasting no more than a moment. The reality as we see it, is a series or flux of momentary particulars and appears to be constant only due to similarity of each *svalakṣaṇa* with the previous. The other kind of object is the *sāmānya lakṣaṇa,* which corresponds to the universal. The particular has causal efficiency while the universal does not. The cognition of the universal does not depend on its real existence, but only on the working of the mind. The universal thus has only empirical reality, *samvṛttisat* and imaginary existence, *kalpanāmātra-vyavahāra.*

The universal, according to the Buddhists, is not an object of perception, but only conception.[10] Dharmakīrti recognises the universal as *jñānākāra* but does not accord it real status as an external thing. But as an idea, it is not a universal in the same sense of an enduring entity; all ideas are mental states which are particulars.

According to the Buddhist explanation of perception, each cognition is distinct and unique, momentary, caused by the corresponding momentary particular. How can a series of such cognitions lead to an identical conception, such as "this is cow"? To this the Buddhist replies with an illustration. Just as different medicines, having different properties can still show the same causal efficiency in being

9. Gaurinath Sastri Preface to *Nyāyamañjarī,* vol. II.

10. Dravid, 2001, p. 62.

able to cure a particular malady, different particulars having nothing in common can still give rise to an identical cognition, as Śāntarakṣita explains.

The particular is only an indirect cause of the cognition of universal, i.e. general cognition, the direct cause being recollection of the conventional name. Śāntarakṣita says that upon cognising the particular, the conventional name is recollected due to similarity in the cognition and this is sufficient to recognise the general concept; there is no need to postulate the *sāmānya*. Dharmakīrti also writes that in apprehension of a particular as "the same" the cognition is determined by the particulars themselves.

याप्यभेदानुगा बुद्धिः काचिद्वस्तुद्वयेक्षणे, सङ्केतेन विना सार्थप्रत्यासत्तिनिबन्धना ।

yāpyabhedānugā buddhiḥ kācidvastudvayekṣaṇe, saṅketena vinā sārthapratyāsattinibandhanā ।

Śāntarakṣita has a powerful argument in the concept of *upādhi* which Nyāya and Mīmāṁsā accept. He says that if concepts such as "cook", "teacher", "negation", "universal" can operate as class concepts without being real universals, why cannot all general conceptions including *jāti*s operate the same way? Why should some universals, such as *gotva, ghaṭatva, paṭatva, naratva* be accorded real status and *upādhi*s are not accorded ontological reality?

The Buddhists find many loopholes and practical absurdities in the Realist's definition of *sāmānya*.

Dharmakīrti asks whether the universal, which is said to be everywhere, is contained in its own particulars or is it ubiquitous? Why is it not perceived everywhere? In the case of being present only in its particulars, how does a newborn thing acquire the universal? The universal, being eternal cannot be created with the thing, neither can it move, so it cannot migrate into it. Even if it does, would it not deprive its former locus of its class-essence? The universal cannot exist partially in its prior and partially in the current locus. This is described in Dharmakīrti's *Pramāṇavārttikam*, also quoted by Jayanta Bhaṭṭa.

> न याति, न च तत्रासीदस्ति पश्चान्न चांशवत्,
> जहाति पूर्वं नाधारमहो व्यसनसन्ततिः ।
>
> *na yāti, na ca tatrāsīdasti paścānna cāṁśavat,*
> *jahāti pūrvaṁ nādhāramaho vyasanasantatiḥ* ।
>
> — *PV* III.151

An eternal entity cannot be a cause for anything. The Buddhists accept only two relations, identity and causality, neither of which can exist between universal and particular. Hence, the Buddhist concludes that the universal is a non-entity. Dharmakīrti says that there is nothing universal in the external world nor in the mental world.

The Response of the Realist Schools

THE BUDDHIST OBJECTIONS CLARIFIED

The Realists hold that experience clearly indicates that the general characteristics we cognise in different individuals help clarify them and differentiate from other categories. Each particular cannot be apprehended individually with no connection to the rest of the world! Language and verbal communication is based on experience, the conventional nomenclature of things is based on their categorisation. The Buddhist view that class-notions are based on similar causal efficiency is not true. But different causal efficiencies cannot be considered similar unless there is some common nature. Cows give birth only to cows. Commonness cannot be attributed to similar functions alone, such as the nature of giving milk, as buffalo and goat would also then be designated as "cow". Or, when a cow stops giving milk, can we say that it is no more a cow?

Were we to wait for every particular thing to be individually cognised, progress would be slow indeed! Jayanta points out that if we were not to admit universls, we cannot explain inference. The Realists reject the Buddhist stand that particulars by their own nature produce general cognition. The general nature of the particulars has to be accepted. The physical shape of the particular is not a common property, but as individual as the particulars themselves. If it is regarded as a common property, as even similarity may be, why, then it is only a different name for *sāmānya*.

The reason the *sāmānya* is not perceived everywhere is that it manifests only where there is a medium, viz., its own particulars. When a particular is born, it is born with its own *sāmānya* inherent in it along with its individuality; there is no question of transference or migration of the class category. Just as the new entity is created from its material cause, *samavāyī kāraṇa*, it is created possessing its own *jāti*.

Pārthasārathi Miśra explains in the *Śāstradīpikā* that the Buddhist contention that the universal being eternal does not produce incessant cognition and therefore non-existent, is futile. No doubt causal efficiency can belong only to an existent. But there is no reason why an existent should be constantly causing some effect to happen all the time, neither is it necessary that every existent should produce its cognition all the time. There may be many things which are not known yet. Also, certain things may require auxiliary causes for their causal efficiency to operate. A dry seed in a granary will not sprout, but requires the presence of soil, water, etc., for it to sprout.

THE APOHAVĀDA OF KUMĀRILA BHAṬṬA

Kumārila shows that the concept of *apoha* is logically and practically untenable, in the Apohavāda in *Ślokavārttika*. He shows that the concept of negation presupposes the universal. Those who say that *anyāpoha* is the meaning of a word, are actually using the very *samavāya* that they wish to deny. *Abhāva* is also considered as a *bhāva padārtha*, as the *pratiyogī* of the *abhāva* is a *padārtha* on which the cognition is based. We never state the absence of a non-existent thing, but only of existent entities.

अगोनिवृत्तिः सामान्यं वाच्यं यैः परिकल्पितम् ।
गोत्वं वस्त्वेव तैरुक्तमगोऽपोहगिरा स्फुटम ।।१।।
भावान्तरमभावो हि पुरस्तात् प्रतिपादितः ।
तत्राश्वादिनिवृत्त्यमात्मा भावः क इति कथ्यताम् ।।२।।

agonivr̥ttiḥ sāmānyaṁ vācyaṁ yaiḥ parikalpitam I
gotvaṁ vastveva tairuktamago 'pohagirā sphuṭam II1II
bhāvāntaramabhāvo hi purastāt pratipāditaḥ I
tatrā śvādinivr̥ttyamātmā bhāvaḥ ka iti kathyatām II2II

Since all *pratyakṣa* according to the Buddhist is *nirvikalpaka*, how can *avastu* be cognised? When they denounce the existence of *sāmānya* as a positive entity, how can they use it as a negative entity to explain *apoha*? For instance, in *agovyāvr̥tti*, when *go* is not understood, how can *ago* be comprehended? The Buddhist replies that words are used in negation or *apoha* in normal language also in instances such as *abrāhmaṇa* or *aghaṭa* in *nañ samāsa* compound words. Kumārila analyses the issue brilliantly, the main points being as follows. *Abrāhmaṇa* refers to a person of any of the three *varṇa*s other than a brāhmaṇa. The *nañ samāsa* has several meanings, only one of which is negation. We do not use *abrāhmaṇa* to describe a jar or a stone, but only a person. Hence, the word assumes the next higher universal of *naratva*, although it is true that *brāhmaṇatva* is denied. In the same way, *aghaṭa* refers to something other than a jar, so it assumes *pārthivatva*. When asked if a particular person is in a room and it happens to be empty, the reply *na kaścidasti* need not mean that there is not even any furniture in the room, but only that there are no people in it. *Aghaṭa* cannot convey *ghaṭatva* but it does convey *pārthivatva*.

अनित्यत्वं विनाशाख्यक्रियासामान्यमुच्यते ।
अब्राह्मणत्वं किन्तु स्याद् भिन्नेषु क्षत्रियादिषु ।।१३।।
पुरुषत्वं चतुःसंस्थम् विशेषेषु च नास्तिधीः ।
सामाअन्यप्रत्ययश्चैषु प्रत्येकमुपयुज्यते ।।१४।।
पुरुषत्वं नञा चैतद् ब्राह्मणेभ्यो निवर्तितम् ।
चातुर्वर्ण्यप्रसक्तं सद् गम्यतेऽर्थादिभिर्यथा ।।१८।।

anityatvaṁ vināśākhyakriyāsāmānyamucyate ।
abrāhmaṇatvaṁ kintu syād bhinneṣu kṣatriyādiṣu ।।3।।
puruṣatvaṁ catuḥsaṁstham viśeṣeṣu ca nāstidhīḥ ।
sāmāanyapratyayaścaiṣu pratyekamupayujyate ।।14।।
puruṣatvaṁ nañā caitad brāhmaṇebhyo nivartitam ।
cāturvarṇyaprasaktaṁ sad gamyate 'rthādibhiryathā ।।18।।

The prefix *nañ* used as negation with verb alone indicates absence. Used with other words such as *dravya, guṇa* it refers to some positive entity.

पार्थिवत्वादिसामान्यम् एवमेवाघटादिषु ।
घटत्वादिविनिर्मुक्तं विषयः सम्प्रतीयते ।।२३।।
असाधारणभावाच्च नञा शब्दो विशेषितः ।
तावन्मात्रेण रहिते सामान्ये व्यवतिष्ठते ।।२४।।

pārthivatvādisāmānyam evamevāghaṭādiṣu ।
ghaṭatvādivinirmuktaṁ viṣayaḥ sampratīyate ।।23।।
asādhāraṇabhāvācca nañā śabdo viśeṣitaḥ ।
tāvanmātreṇa rahite sāmānye vyavatiṣṭhate ।।24।।

The *nañ samāsa* can convey some other meaning which is not

even connected to what is denied. For example, in the dictum that a *brahmacārī* should not view the rising sun, this may not be possible at times. So, the dictum is understood in a positive sense such as the decision or intention, *saṅkalpa*, not to view the early morning sun.

क्वचिद् विनापि सादृश्यात् साहचर्यादिहेतुका ।
नञ्युक्तशब्दवृत्तिः स्याद् यथा वक्ष्यत्यणीक्षणे ॥३१॥
ईक्षणव्यतिरिक्ता हि क्रिया तत्राप्यपेक्षिता ।
प्रत्यासत्तेर्न सङ्कल्पमतिक्रम्य प्रतीयते ॥३२॥

kvacid vināpi sādṛśyāt sāhacaryādihetukā ।
nañyuktaśabdavṛttiḥ syād yathā vakṣyatyaṇīkṣaṇe ॥31॥
īkṣaṇavyatiriktā hi kriyā tatrāpyapekṣitā ।
pratyāsatterna saṅkalpamatikramya pratīyate ॥32॥

Kārikā 40 clearly mentions *vākyārtha* as a *jāti* understood with the aid of *pratibhā*. Just as a sentence-meaning is cognised even without the objects mentioned in the Buddhist conceives of reality as a flux of self-identical particulars. All the *svalakṣaṇa*s are separate but not different in fundamental nature. There is no way to distinguish one cognition from another. When words that convey *sāmānya, viśeṣa* all become the same, where is the ground for *apoha*? If reality and therefore cognition is of the form A..A..A..A..A..A......etc., where there is no B; A cannot be the *apoha* of itself.

बुद्ध्यन्तराद् व्यवच्छेदो न च बुद्धेः प्रतीयते ।
स्वरूपोत्पादमात्राच्च नान्यमंशम् बिभर्ति सा ॥४१॥
भिन्नसामान्यवचना विशेषवचनाश्च ये ।
सर्वे भवेयुः पर्याया यद्यपोहस्य वाच्यता ॥४२॥

buddhyantarād vyavacchedo na ca buddheḥ pratīyate ।
svarūpotpādamātrācca nānyamaṁśam bibharti sā ॥41॥
bhinnasāmānyavacanā viśeṣavacanāśca ye ।
sarve bhaveyuḥ paryāyā yadyapohasya vācyatā ॥42॥

Kumārila asks what new purpose is served if the concept of *apoha* leads to the *sāmānya* itself.

ननु भेदादपोहानां प्रसङ्गोऽयं न युज्यते ।
सामान्यापोह क्लृप्तया चेद् वस्तुमात्रे समं तव ।।४३।।

nanu bhedādapohānāṁ prasaṅgo 'yaṁ na yujyate ।
sāmānyāpoha kḷptayā ced vastumātre samaṁ tava ।।43।।

Going by the *apoha* theory, cow has *hastyāpoha*, as cow is not elephant. Cow also has *aśvāpoha* as cow is not horse. How can two contradictory features be understood in the same thing?

गौश्च हस्त्याद्यपोहेन नाश्वरूपाद् विशेष्यते ।
करोति तदपोहं चेदैकरूप्यं विरुध्यते ।।५५।।

gauśca hastyādyapohena nāśvarūpād viśeṣyate ।
karoti tadapohaṁ cedaikarūpyaṁ virudhyate ।।55।।

In the same way, *aśvāpoha* exists in lion, etc. The cow, *go* is also not a horse, *aśvāpoha*. Hence, by *apoha* doctrine, the lion is a cow! If it is given that $A = B$ and $C = B$, then it follows that $A = C$.

सर्वशब्देषु चैकैकम् अपोह्यमतिरिच्यते ।
तरासाधारणत्वेन तन्मात्रापोह्यता भवेत् ।।५६।।
ततोऽश्वापोहरूपत्वात् सिंहादिः सर्व एव ते ।
तन्निमित्तमगोऽपोहं बिभ्रदुच्यते गौरिति ।।५७।।

sarvaśabdeṣu caikaikam apohyamatiricyate।
tarāsādhāraṇatvena tanmātrāpohyatā bhavet।।56।।
tato 'śvāpoharūpatvāt siṁhādiḥ sarva eva te।
tannimittamago 'pohaṁ bibhraducyate gauriti।।57।।

How can the opposite of an entity be negated? The opposite of existent entity being negated implies the existent itself. The negation of absence leads to some positive entity, *bhāva* itself. A double negation is an affirmation.

कथम् वाऽवस्त्वपोह्येत नाभावो भावमृच्छति ।
अपोह्यमाने चाभावे भाव एवावशिष्यते ।।६४।।

katham vā 'vastvapohyeta nābhāvo bhāvamṛcchati ।
apohyamāne cābhāne bhāva evāvaśiṣyate ।।64।।

Kumārila's concepts are clear in the mind's eye with mathematical precision. Thus he gave a spirited, invincible defence of the universal against the Buddhist notions of *śūnya* and *apoha* such that later Buddhist writers had to modify their theory as it could not face the onslaught of Kumārila's attack, although they were the first ones to point out its limitations and mock the concept.

Conclusion

Vāk

SINCE early Vedic Age, the study of language has been recognised as very important to understanding the working of the mind. *Vāk* has been venerated alongside *Brahman* as the Creator of the world and its knowledge. The divisions of *Vāk* or speech among different levels of life forms and in the different levels of the recesses of the mind have been discussed in Vedic literature. The spoken language in manifest form is considered only a part of the speech process. Bhartṛhari is the first writer to mention the different levels of *vāk* as *paśyantī*, *madhyamā* and *vaikharī*. The *parā* level corresponds to *śabdatattva*, the supreme level equated to *Brahman* in Bhartṛhari's monistic philosophy. Bhartṛhari is known as the Śabdabrahmavādī in tradition.

Śābdabodha

Knowledge that can be had from direct experience and inference, *pratyakṣa – anumāna* is very limited, as it is restricted to what we directly come in contact with. It is through verbal knowledge that the horizon of human beings expands enormously. Verbal knowledge or *śabda pramāṇa* is a vital means to knowledge. *Śābdabodha* is analysed in great detail in all schools of Indian philosophy. The Vedas are held as sacred and reliable authority on *dharma* by the six orthodox systems of Indian philosophy. Perception and inference and even logic has limited reliability in understanding the truth about *Brahman*, or *dharma*, which can only be understood from the Vedas. As Bhartṛhari says, only the Vedas can inform us about *dharma* as what one clever man shows as valid by logic can be shown to be quite different by *sattva* a logician more clever.[1] Thus Veda is vital as a means to knowledge.

Nature of Sound

The different philosophical schools have different standpoints on issues of cosmology, which invariably influence the ontology. Some schools such as Nyāya are pluralistic in outlook and endorse Ārambhavāda, Asatkāryavāda in which effects are created from their cause. Others such as Sāṁkhya and Advaita are *pariṇāmavādīs*, endorsing Satkāryavāda, where the effect pre-exists in the cause. Thus even *śabda* is *nitya*, eternal, or *anitya, kārya*, according to their different ontologies. The word *śabda* has three significant meanings — sound, verbal testimony and word or language. Nyāya, Mīmāṁsā and Vyākaraṇa often have differing views on these issues.

Mīmāṁsā holds Veda as *pramāṇa* and *apauruṣeya*. *Śabda* therefore has independent ontological status, it is eternal, immutable and *varṇa-rūpa*. *Śabda* is defined as nothing more than a string of *varṇa*s having audibility. Mīmāṁsā does not admit *jāti* in *śabda* and denounces *sphoṭa*. Relation of word and meaning is natural and of the nature of *pratyāyya-pratyāyaka*. *Padārtha* of words in a sentence gives rise to *vākyārtha*, by *abhihitānvaya* process in Bhāṭṭa and *anvitābhidhāna* in Prābhākara schools. The Nyāya holds *śabda* as a quality, *guṇa* of *ākāśa*, space. It is *kārya, anitya* and has *jāti*. Verbal

---

1. यत्नेनानुमितोऽप्यर्थः कुशलैरनुमातृभिः ।
अभियक्ततरैरन्यैः अन्यथैवोपपाद्यते । — *VP* I.34

knowledge is by *saṅketa* or *śakti* which connects word and meaning.

Careful study of *Śābara-Bhāṣya*, *Śikṣā*, *Nyāya-Sūtra*, *Praśastapāda-Bhāṣya* and *Vākyapadīya* show many interesting passages on the physical nature of sound, its production and transmission. The Nyāya-Vaiśeṣika view of sound travelling in a wave series like ripples in water is well known and widely accepted in Śāstra. The Mīmāṁsā view was that sound, *dhvani* was transformation in air particles, travelling in a series of compressions and rarefactions, *pracaya-apacaya*. *Dhvani* is the changing, ephemeral feature that manifests the eternal *śabda*. While the propagation of sound (*dhvani*), by *śabdaja* series is generally accepted by all, the *saṁyoga-vibhāga* pair has different significance in different Śāstras.

In the Vaiśeṣika school, it is the impact and tearing asunder of sound-producing bodies. In the Mīmāṁsā school it refers to the conjunction and disjunction or compressions and rarefactions of air particles. In Śikṣā and Vyākaraṇa they refer to the contact and separation of various parts of the mouth used for articulation such as throat, tongue, lips, palate, etc.

Linguistic Philosophy of Bhartṛhari

Vyākaraṇa considers word, meaning and their relation as *nitya*. In Bhartṛhari's view, *śabda* is a manifestation of *Brahman*. He establishes that *śabda* is *nitya* as the word in the mind, in the form of *sphoṭa*, which relies on the concept of *jāti* in *śabda*. The main thrust of the Brahmakāṇḍa is in establishing *jāti* in *śabda* and *sphoṭa*, which are two sides of the same coin. Since uttered language is manifest with the temporal sequence invariably imposed on it, the process of *śābdabodha* cannot be explained without *sphoṭa*. *Śleṣa*, *pun*, *maunī ślika*, *upāṁśu kathana*, *vākyārtha* and the different levels of *vāk* are best explained by the concept of *sphoṭa*. Both *sphoṭa* and *dhvani* are aspects, *aṁśa* of *Brahman*, or *śabdatattva*.

The sentence-meaning is more than a string of words or syllables. *Vākyārtha* cannot be mechanically conveyed by the syllables, but is a creative process in the mind called *pratibhā*. *Dhvani*, which manifests the *śabda* is of two kinds, *prākr̥ta* and *vaikr̥ta*. The former directly manifests the *sphoṭa* while the latter is responsible for the transmission of the sound to the hearer and the enduring perception of the *sphoṭa* during the interval of utterance and audibility. The *sphoṭa* has no divisions in time such as *hrasva dīrgha pluta*, but that of the *prākr̥ta dhvani* is imposed on it; the speed of utterance is an attribute of the *vaikr̥ta dhvanis*.

Bhartr̥hari's philosophy conforms to the Mīmāṁsā stand on Vedas being *svataḥ pramāṇa*, reliable authority on *dharma*. Whereas Mīmāṁsā advocates a realistic and pluralistic ontology, with *Puruṣa-Śabda* both being *nitya*, Bhartr̥hari solves this dichotomy by combining *śabda* in Consciousness. In his Monistic view, *śabda*, *ātmā* and *jagat* are one, appearing as different due to different capacities or powers (*śakti*). In the Oneness and eternality of *śabda* being in unison with *ātmā*, *sphoṭa* is the logical means by which *śabda* is present in the mind, not in the external world.

THE DEVELOPMENT OF SPHOṬA

From the permanent acoustic pattern of Patañjali to the *śabdatattva* of Nāgeśa and eight divisions with varying relative validity discussed by Kauṇḍa Bhaṭṭa, the concept of *sphoṭa* has undergone much evolution. Mīmāṁsā and Nyāya denounce it as an unnecessary fiction. Although they are all agreed on the process of *śābdabodha* to a good extent, they solve the problem of temporal sequence in language differently. They object to the enunciation of a new entity such as *sphoṭa,* saying that *saṁskāra* is sufficient to convey meaning. Kumārila demolishes the concept according to Mīmāṁsā tenets in the Sphoṭavāda. Maṇḍana is the only Mīmāṁsaka to admit *sphoṭa* and showed that Kumārila's charges were actually misplaced and that *sphoṭa* is compatible concept in *śābdabodha*. Jayanta Bhaṭṭa refutes it totally in the *Nyāyamañjarī* using *pratyakṣa* and *anumāna* as *pramāṇa*. The later grammarians, notably Nāgeśa, were influenced by the Tantra and Pratyabhijñā schools of philosophy in their elaboration of *sphoṭa*.

Vākyapadīya

VP is a voluminous, fascinating work written by Bhartṛhari in the fifth century CE in a style similar that of *Ślokavārttikā* of Kumārila Bhaṭṭa, which is fluid, melodious and almost like spoken language. Technical points are spread over the verses and have to be carefully gleaned. While Kumārila is challenging and assertive to counter the criticism of the Buddhists, displaying great wit and acumen, Bhartṛhari's style is affirmative and softer. He accomodates averybody's views, showing great temperance of spirit and maturity. He is intolerant of the sole issue of absolute reality of *pada-padārtha*. He repeatedly explains that *apoddhāra* is provisional and only a practical abstraction; the parts should always be understood with regard to the whole and never confused as an end in themselves. The true *śabda* is the *akhaṇḍa vākya* whose meaning, *vākyārtha,* is a divisionless unity.

Bhartṛhari's Conception of Jāti

Bhartṛhari's philosophy is Absolute Monism as opposed to the pluralism of the Realists. There is only one common thread running through all creation, living and non-living, as also in *śabda*, whether implicit as *sphoṭa* or explicit as the external sounds. *Śabdatattva* and *Brahman* are One. While this unity is understood by *vidyā*, in the transactional world, cognised by *avidyā*, everything is understood with provisional, relative, reality. The concept of *apoddhāra* being fictional divisions as an aid to understanding the whole is relevant in Bhartṛhari's linguistics as well as general philosophy.

Although Bhartṛhari discusses *jāti* in many *kārikā*s in the Brahmakāṇḍa and Vākyakāṇḍa in the context of linguistics, he enunciates it completely in all aspects in the Jāti Samuddeśa which is philosophical to a good extent. He straightaway states that *apoddhāra* being a fictional division to aid understanding, words are divided into different categories in different ways. Some people hold that the import of the word is in *jāti* while others hold that it is in *dravya*. This debate in the Jāti and Dravya Samuddeśas is unlike the discussions in *Mahābhāṣya* where the debate is between universal and individual being meaning of the word. *Dravya* here refers to substance and does not seem to refer to the particular. In the discussion on number, individuals or particulars are indicated, but the word *dravya* is never used in that sense.

As explained in the Brahmakāṇḍa 66, 67, 68, and Jāti Samuddeśa 6, every word first conveys its own form before conveying its meaning or import. Thus all words primarily convey *jāti*. First the *śabda-jāti* is conveyed after which the *artha-jāti* is conveyed, due to their *vācya-vācaka* relation. While the Vaiśeṣikas deny universal in universal, Vyākaraṇa has no problem in admitting that there is a universal in *jāti śabda* also, just as there is in every other word. In the case of polysemic words, we can say that the *śabda-jāti* is the same, but the *artha-jāti* is different, with suitable aids to ascertain the purport.

The grammarian is concerned with the usage of words in language, not the ontology of any particluar school. After all, the language is common to all philosophies and should be able to convey everybody's views. Thus Bhartṛhari shows an accomodating attitude on a wide range of issues. The word functions by conveying *bauddhārtha*, the idea in the mind, no matter what the situation outside. That is how we are able to understand words such as *kinnara*, *svarga*, etc., and use them with case endings to convey meaning. As the saying goes,

प्रयोगशरणाः वैयाकरणाः, प्रतीतिशरणाश्च दार्शनिकाः ।

prayogaśaraṇāḥ vaiyākaraṇāḥ, pratītiśaraṇāśca dārśanikāḥ ।

The *jāti* is what enables cognition, while recognising something as the same, or as distinct from other entities. Everything is interconnected in this world-nothing can be cognised in isolation. All our understanding, impressions and experiences are interconnected with innumerable things. Thus our entire make-up in the transactional level of *avidyā* is in relation to some other factor. Only when the Absolute is reached, in the state of *vidyā*, is there Oneness where there is no second entity or relativity. The *jāti* can be said to be that recognisable feature that runs in common in all the entities. The separate individuals can be considered as the *dravya*s. *Bh* clearly states the reality of the *jāti* yet he seems to accept that it is an idea, a concept. This is again clarified by his philosophical stand that whatever is real in the *vivartta* level may not be true in the *saṁvartta* level.

Bhartṛhari is in agreement with the enunciation of *jāti* in all the well-known schools of philosophy — early Nyāya-Vaiśeṣika, Mīmāṁsā, Sāṁkhya and Advaita. He has no ontological disputes with anybody and is not at all troubled by the *vyasana santati* that Jayanta Bhaṭṭa quotes! For Bhartṛhari, *jāti* is real and existent. In the *vyāvahārika* level, it is manifold and in the supreme level, it is *sattā*. When asked what happens to the universals at the time of Dissolution, he tersely states that not all particulars perish simultaneously and also that the universals inhere latently in the Primordial Substance. At one place, he even agrees with the view that universal is a mental concept that aids cognition. Bhartṛhari does not distinguish between *jāti* and *upādhi*; his view is that the unity in the world appears as diverse due to *upādhi*, therefore even *jāti* can be likened to *upādhi*. What Bhartṛhari emphasises is that *jāti* is real because in cognition, creation and communication, its causal efficiency is undisputed.

Every entity has two aspects, real and unreal. The real aspect is *jāti* while the unreal ones are the individuals as they come and go. All entities, belonging to different universals as understood commonly in the world, are only different aspects of the one true universal, *sattā*. *Sattā* is the highest universal, encompassing all of creation.

Bhartṛhari's philosophy does not present the illusory projection of the world that is well known in later Advaita Vedānta. The world is a real projection of *Brahman*; verbal communication is a real manifestation of the same supreme principle whose essence is *śabda*. In fact, we cannot even have any unique cognitions where we can truly grasp the particular — we have no words to convey specific attributes, but only operate with general ideas.

Bhartṛhari clearly says that there is no separate real other than the world which we call unreal. The difference is only in the comprehension; when the unity is understood in true light by *vidyā* it is real whereas all else is unreal. In the *vyāvahārika* world, every event must have a specific and direct cause to avoid chaos. Thus *jāti* is a direct cause for all cognition, for our sytematic grasp of the well-ordered world around us. With great poetic beauty Bhartṛhari exalts *jāti* as the creator of the world. *Jāti* impells all activity in the world, setting foot in the causes, only to manifest itself! Nothing is ever formed, which does not have a corresponding *jāti*. Only *Brahman* is *eka*, with a sole, unique identity. It is only knowledge, like light, *prakāśa* that can shine on its own, without any interconnection required with anything else. No entity other than *Brahman* is ever unique.

When *jāti* is manifest with sequence in time it is called activity. This corresponds to the *kriyāvivartta* whereas material objects correspond to *mūrti vivartta*.

In the *Vākyapadīya*, *jāti-dravya* both merge, conceptually and philosophically. In the Jāti Samuddeśa, Bhartṛhari says that some universals such as clay, gold, etc., do not require configuration for their manifestation. In Dravya Samuddeśa, these are the same *dravya*s called substances, which form the enduring material that the world is made up of. Verse 16 of Dravya Samuddeśa clearly explains that all words convey the primordial substance and are also fashioned from it; although there is no difference in reality we still speak of the connections between them. Thus Bhartṛhari uses both features, *jāti* and *dravya* to describe the One Reality. As *jāti*, universal, all creation is *sattā*, existence. *Brahman* is manifest in myriad ways and described in myriad ways. All words convey the *jāti* which in its all-encompassing form corresponds to *sattā*. As *dravya*, all of creation is understood in its primordial substance. From this are formed the existents, *sattva*. When we say that *Brahman* appears in the great variety of *jāti*s that we perceive, it is *vivartta*. When we say that all creation is fashioned out of one *dravya* it is *pariṇāma*. Thus Bhartṛhari combines both the views harmoniously in his Monistic philosophy.

Bibliography

Bhartṛhari, *Vākyapadīya of Bhartṛhari — Brahmakāṇḍa, with Commentary of Pt. Vamadeva Acharya*, Varanasi: Chaukhamba Krishnadas Academy, 2000.

Bhartṛhari, *Vākyapadīya of Bhartṛhari — Brahmakāṇḍa, with Vṛtti and Ambākartrī of Pt. Raghunath Sarma*, Sampoornanand Sanskrit University, Varanasi, 1990.

Bhartṛhari, *Vākyapadīya*, vol. 3, *Padakāṇḍa with Helārāja's Prakāśa Commentary and Pt. Raghunatha Sarma's Ambākartrī*, Varanasi: Sampurnanand Sanskrit University, 1991.

Bhatia, Kanta, *Bhartṛhari kā Vākyapadīya Puṇyarāja kī Dṛṣṭi Meiṁ*, Delhi: Bharatiya Vidya Prakashan, 1992.

Bhaṭṭa, Jayanta, *Nyāyamañjarī of Jayanta Bhaṭṭa*, vol. I, Varanasi: Sampurnanand Sanskrit University.

Bhaṭṭa, Kumārila, *Mīmāṁsāślokavārttika with Nyāya Ratnākara of Pārthasārathi Miśra*, Varanasi: Ratna Publications, 1993.

Chaturvedi, Mithilesh, *The Vṛtti Samuddeśa of Vākyapadīya: A Study*, Delhi: Shivalik Prakashan, 2001.

Dahiya, Yajnaveer, *Saṁskṛta Bhāṣā Darśanam*, Delhi: Bharatiya Vidya Prakashan, 2001.

Devasthali, G.V., *Mimamsa: The Ancient Indian Science of Sentence Interpretation*, Delhi: Sri Satguru Publications, 2nd edn. 1991.

Dravid, Raja Ram, *The Problem of Universals in Indian Philosophy*, Delhi: Motilal Banarsidass, 2nd edn. 2001.

Dvivedi, Kalikaprasad, *Śabdasvarūpatacchaktivicārāḥ*, Varanasi: Sampurnanand Sanskrit University, 1979.

Houben, Jan E.M., *The Sambandha Samuddeśa and Bhartṛhari's Philosophy of Language*, Edbert Forsten, The Netherlands, 1995.

Jayanta Bhaṭṭa, *Nyāyamañjarī of Jayanta Bhaṭṭa*, vol. II, Varanasi: Sampurnanand Sanskrit University.

Jhalakikar, M.M. Bhimacarya, *Nyāyakośa: A Dictionary of Technical Terms of Indian Philosophy*, Pune: BORI, 1996.

Joshi, S.D. tr. & ed., *The Sphoṭa Nirṇaya of Kauṇḍa Bhaṭṭa*, Pune: University of Poona, 1967.

Kantawala, S.G., ed., *A Dictionary of Sanskrit Grammar*, Baroda: Oriental Institute, 1986.

Krishna, Matilal Bimal, *The Word and the World*, Delhi: Oxford University Press, 1990.

Mishra, Parthasarathi, *Śāstradīpikā*, ed. Krishnadas Swami, Swami Ramtirth Mission, Dehra Dun, 1996.

Mishra, Ram Narayan, *Sphoṭamīmāṁsā*, Varanasi: Sampurnanand Sanskrit University, 1991.

Mookerjee, Satkari, *The Buddhist Philosophy of Universal Flux*, Calcutta: University of Calcutta, 1975.

Nāgeśa, *Vyākaraṇa Siddhānta Parama Laghumañjuṣā of Nāgeśa*, Varanasi: Chaukhambha Surbharati Prakashan, 3rd edn., 2001.

Pandeya, Ramajna, *Vyākaraṇa Darśana Pratimā*, Varanasi: Sampurnanand Sanskrit University, 1979.

Pandurangi, K.T, ed., *Śabdataraṅgiṇī of V. Subramania Sastri*, Bangalore: Dvaita Vedanta Studies and Research Foundation, 2006.

Pandurangi, K.T., ed., *Pūrvamīmaṁsā from an Interdisciplinary Point of View*, New Delhi: PHISPS, 2006.

Pandurangi, K.T., tr. & ed., *The Prakaraṇapañcikā of Śālikanātha*, New Delhi: Indian Council for Philosophical Research, and D.K. Printworld, 2011.

Patnaik, Tandra, *Śabda*, New Delhi: D.K. Printworld, 1994.

Pillai, Raghavan, tr., *The Vākyapadīya: Critical Text of Cantos I and II with Translation, Summary and Notes*, Delhi: Motilal Banarsidass, 1971.

Pingle, Pratibha M., *The Concept of Vac in Vedic Literature*, Delhi: Sri Satguru Publications, 2005.

Raja, K. Kunjunni, *Indian Theories of Meaning*, Chennai: The Adyar Library and Research Centre, 2nd edn., 1969.

Rath, Gayatri, *Linguistic Philosophy in Vākyapadīya*, Delhi: Bharatiya Vidya Prakashan, 2000.

Sarma, Peri Sarvesvara, *Kalāsamuddeśa of Vākyapadīya*, Delhi: MLBD, 1972.

Sarma, Syamsundar, *Kumarilabhaṭṭa Mīmāṁsā Ślokavārttika Bṛhad Hindi Bhāṣyasahit*, Varanasi: Bharatiya Vidya Sansthan, 2002.

Sarma, Umashankar, ed., *Mīmaṁsādarśanam with Śābara Bhāṣya, Tarkapada*, Varanasi: Chowkhamba Surbharati Prakashan, 1981.

Sarup, Laksman, ed., *Nirukta of Yāska*, Delhi: MLBD.

Sastri, Charudev, ed., *Vyakāraṇa Mahābhāṣya of Patañjali*, Delhi: MLBD, 1968.

Sastri, Gaurinath, *A Study in the Dialectics of Sphoṭa*, Dehli: MLBD, 1980.

Sastri, Gaurinath, *Philosophy of Bhartṛhari*, Varanasi: Bharatiya Vidya Prakashan, 1991.

Sastri, Gaurinath, *Philosophy of Word and Meaning*, Calcutta: Sanskrit College, 1959.

Sastry, M.H., ed., *The Vākyapadīya of Bhartṛhari Brahmakāṇḍa with Commentary Hariharaputtriyam*, Eng. tr. K.K. Hariharan and V.K. Moosathu, Thiruvanantapuram: Sree Ramadasa Ashramam, 2001.

Sastry, Naganatha, tr., *Kāvyālaṁkāra of Bhāmaha*, Delhi: MLBD, 1970.

Scharf, Peter M., *The Denotation of Generic Terms in Ancient Indian Philosophy: Grammar, Nyāya and Mimāṁsā*, Philadelphia: American Philosophical Association, 1996.

Seal, Brajendranath, *The Positive Sciences of the Ancient Hindus*, Delhi: MLBD,

Sharma, Ranganatha, *Vākyapadīya Brahmakāṇḍa* (*Kannada*), Heggodu: Akshara Publications, 1995.

Sharma, Ranganatha, *Vākyapadīya Kālasamuddeśa* (*Kannada*), Heggodu: Akshara Publications, 1995.

Subramania Iyer, K.A., *Bhartṛhari*, Poona: Deccan College.

Subramania Iyer, K.A., ed., *Vākyapadīya Kāṇḍa I with Vṛtti and Paddhati*, Poona: Deccan College, 1966.

Subramania Iyer, K.A., ed., *Vākyapadīya of Bhartṛhari Kāṇḍa II with Ṭīkā and Vṛtti*, Delhi: MLBD, 1983.

Subramania Iyer, K.A., tr. & ed., *Sphoṭa Siddhi of Maṇḍana Miśra,* Poona: Deccan College, 1966.

Subramania Iyer, K.A., tr., *The Vākyapadīya of Bhartṛhari,* Chapter III, pt. I, Poona: Deccan College, 1971.

Subramania Iyer, K.A., tr., *The Vākyapadīya of Bhartṛhari, with the Vṛtti,* Chapter I, Poona: Deccan College, 1965.

Tatacarya, Ramanuja, *Śabdabodhamīmāṁsā,* New Delhi: Rashtriya Sanskrit Sansthan, 2005.

The Cultural History of India, vol. I, Calcutta: Ramakrishna Mission, 1982.

Tripathi, Ramdev, *Bhāṣā Vijñan kī Bhāratīya Paramparā aur Pāṇini,* Patna: Bihar Rashtrabhasha Parishad, 1977.

Vattanky, S.J. John, *Nyāya Philosophy of Language,* Delhi: Sri Satguru Publications, 1995.

Index